...nating account of how a brave man's loyal sons discovered that a
...e design flaw had doomed him and his crew. Touching and eloquent."

—JOHN KOSTER, *author of* Operation Snow: How a
Soviet Mole in FDR's White House Triggered Pearl Harbor

...spenseful...a chilling conclusion."

—PUBLISHERS WEEKLY

FATAL DIVE

FATAL DIVE

SOLVING THE
WORLD WAR II MYSTERY
OF THE USS *GRUNION*

PETER F. STEVENS

REGNERY
HISTORY

Library of Congress Cataloging-in-Publication data

Stevens, Peter F.
  Fatal dive / by Peter F. Stevens.
     pages cm
  ISBN 978-1-59698-767-8
1. Grunion (Submarine) 2. World War, 1939-1945—Naval
operations—Submarine. 3. World War, 1939-1945—Naval operations,
American. 4. Underwater exploration—Alaska—Kiska Island Region.
5. Kiska Island Region (Alaska)—Antiquities. I. Title.
  D783.5.G78S74 2012
  940.54'51--dc23
                                        2012011559

Published in the United States by
Regnery Publishing, Inc.
One Massachusetts Avenue NW
Washington, DC 20001
www.Regnery.com

Manufactured in the United States of America
10 9 8 7 6 5 4 3 2 1
Books are available in quantity for promotional or premium use. Write
to Director of Special Sales, Regnery Publishing, Inc., One Massachusetts
Avenue NW, Washington, DC 20001, for information on discounts and
terms, or call (202) 216-0600.

Distributed to the trade by
Perseus Distribution
387 Park Avenue South
New York, NY 10016

*This book is dedicated to Lieutenant Commander Jim Abele,
the sixty-nine other men aboard the submarine USS Grunion—
heroes all—and their families. Also, to Jim's remarkable wife, Catherine, and
three sons Bruce, Brad, and John who went searching against all odds for
their father, his sub, his crew, and answers.*

Table of Contents

The Crew of the USS *Grunion* ix

Prologue xiii

Chapter One
"We've Got a Target" 1

Chapter Two
An Unconventional Course 7

Chapter Three
The Submariner 17

Chapter Four
"Into the Thick of Things" 27

Chapter Five
Battle Stations 39

Chapter Six
The Enemy Awaiting Them 49

Chapter Seven
A Mysterious Message 57

Chapter Eight
"As We Waited for the End" 63

Chapter Nine
"Missing and Presumed Lost" 73

Chapter Ten
Making Do with Less 83

Chapter Eleven
A Chart, a Clue, and a Chance Meeting 91

Chapter Twelve
Logistics of a Long Shot 99

Chapter Thirteen
"We Haven't Seen the Worst of It Yet" 105

Chapter Fourteen
"That Looks Like a Sub" 115

Chapter Fifteen
"Don't Let Your Desire for This to Be the Right Target Fool You" . . . 127

Chapter Sixteen
By Land, Sea, and Air 135

Chapter Seventeen
"There She Is" 143

Chapter Eighteen
Lost and Found—Again 147

Chapter Nineteen
From Bow to Stern 153

Chapter Twenty
"They Wanted to Be Found" 165

Epilogue
There One Moment, Gone the Next 169

Appendix 175

Acknowledgements 233

Notes 237

Selected Bibliography 245

Index 249

THE CREW OF THE USS *GRUNION*

July 30, 1942
On Eternal Patrol

———◄►◄►———

Abele, Mannert L., *Lieutenant Commander, Commanding Officer*
Alexander, Frank E., *Signalman Third Class*
Allen, Daniel E., *Signalman Third Class*
Arvan, Herbert J., *Mess Attendant Second Class*
Banes, Paul E., *Chief Motor Machinist's Mate*
Bedard, Leo J. I., *Chief Motor Machinist's Mate*
Blinston, Wesley H., *Radioman Third Class*
Bonadies, Nicholas R., *Fireman Second Class*
Boo, Robert F., *Electrician's Mate Third Class*
Bouvia, Chester L., *Machinist's Mate First Class*
Caldwell, George E., *Chief Electrician's Mate, Warrant Officer*
Carroll, Richard H., *Seaman Second Class*
Clift, John S., *Torpedoman's Mate Second Class*
Collins, Michael F., *Fireman Second Class*
Cooksey, Lee D., *Motor Machinist's Mate First Class*
Cullinane, Daniel, *Chief Motor Machinist's Mate*

Cuthbertson, William H., Jr., *Ensign*

Deaton, Lawrence D., *Seaman Second Class*

DeStoop, Albert E., *Chief Torpedoman's Mate*

Devaney, William P., Jr., *Seaman Second Class*

Dighton, Samuel R., Jr., *Lieutenant Junior Grade*

Doell, Louis H., Jr., *Radioman Second Class*

Franck, Leon H., *Seaman First Class*

Graham, Merritt D., *Chief Torpedoman's Mate, Chief of the Boat*

Hall, Kenneth E., *Seaman Second Class*

Hellensmith, Ernest G., *Electrician's Mate Third Class*

Henderson, Hollice B., *Motor Machinist's Mate Second Class*

Hutchinson, Charles R., *Torpedoman's Mate Third Class*

Kennedy, Sylvester J., Jr., *Motor Machinist's Mate Second Class*

Knowles, Edward E., Jr., *Seaman Second Class*

Kockler, Lawrence R., *Torpedoman's Mate First Class*

Kornahrens, William G., *Lieutenant, Communications Officer*

Ledford, Moore J., *Chief Yeoman*

Lehman, Woodrow W., *Electrician's Mate First Class*

Loe, Sidney A., *Motor Machinist's Mate Second Class*

Lunsford, Samuel E., Jr., *Electrician's Mate Second Class*

Lyon, James W., *Fireman First Class*

Martin, Carson R., *Chief Motor Machinist's Mate*

Martin, Thomas E., *Electrician's Mate First Class*

Mathison, Ryder, *Electrician's Mate First Class*

McCutcheon, Richard G., *Torpedoman's Mate Third Class*

McMahon, John M., *Lieutenant, Engineering and Diving Officer*

Miller, Ernest C., *Fireman Second Class*

Myers, David O., *Fireman First Class*

Nave, Frank T., *Motor Machinist's Mate Second Class*

Newcomb, Arthur G., *Radioman First Class*

Nobles, John W., *Motor Machinist's Mate First Class*

Pancoast, John E., *Motor Machinist's Mate Second Class*

Parziale, Carmine A., *Torpedoman's Mate Third Class*

Paul, Cornelius, Jr., *Mess Attendant Second Class*

Pickel, Bernard J., *Seaman First Class*

Post, Arnold C., *Seaman Second Class*

Randall, William H., *Radioman Second Class*
Ryan, Loyal, Jr., *Seaman Second Class*
Sanders, Howard A., *Motor Machinist's Mate First Class*
Schumann, Elmer T., *Chief Quartermaster*
Sullivan, Paul P., *Pharmacist's Mate First Class*
Surofchek, Steven, *Ship's Cook First Class*
Swartwood, David N., *Seaman Second Class*
Templeton, Samuel A., *Gunner's Mate First Class*
Thomas, Millener W., *Lieutenant, Executive Officer*
Traviss, Byron A., *Seaman Second Class*
Ullmann, Albert, *Seaman First Class*
Van Woggelum, Marshall F., *Fireman Third Class*
Walter, Melvin H., *Fireman Third Class*
Webster, Raymond E., *Electrician's Mate Second Class*
Welch, Donald F., *Fire Controlman Second Class*
Wells, John H., *Torpedoman's Mate Second Class*
Wilson, John E., Jr., *Ship's Cook Third Class*
Youngman, Ralph J., *Fireman Second Class*

PROLOGUE

———◆———

At just about 3:30 on the sunny afternoon of September 30, 1942, at home in Newton, Massachusetts, Kay Abele received a Western Union telegram. She read the message, went to the front door, and called her sons—twelve-year-old Bruce, nine-year-old Brad, and five-year-old John—in from the street in front of the house where they were tossing a football.

As the boys stood in the sunlight streaming through a window into the living room, she read them the telegram. Their father, the commander of the submarine USS *Grunion*, was "missing following action in the performance of his duty and in the service of his country." It was the message dreaded by every American whose beloved husband, father, or son was engaged in the fight with Nazi Germany and Imperial Japan.

And across America, sixty-nine other families received the same
heart-rending notice. Lieutenant Commander Jim Abele and his
entire crew were missing in action. That was all. No answers about
the fate of the submarine's captain or his men would surface for
more than six decades. The *Grunion* had simply vanished.

CHAPTER ONE

"WE'VE GOT A TARGET"

————◆————

John Abele (pronounced EY-bool-ee) glanced at his watch: 11:31 p.m., August 22, 2007. He was in the wheelhouse of a 165-foot-long commercial fishing boat 1,300 miles west of Anchorage, Alaska. He and the others aboard the *Aquila* knew they did not have much time. A massive low-pressure system, bringing hundred-mile-per-hour winds and monster waves, was moving in.

Tethered by a steel cable to the *Aquila* was the Max Rover, the very same kind of Remotely Operated Vehicle (ROV) already celebrated for having found two famous wrecks, the *Titanic* and the *Bismarck*. Now it was more than 3,000 feet below, in the dark, icy depths of the Bering Sea, five miles off the Aleutian Island of Kiska. Five men were crammed in the *Aquila's* wheelhouse, peering into three glowing video monitors, hoping against hope that the Rover would find its target before the storm hit.

1

Kale Garcia, the *Aquila*'s forty-three-year-old skipper, had fished the Bering for black cod and king crab since he was eighteen. Though the sea had gone suddenly and strangely calm, he knew that an Aleutian storm could bring waves capable of splitting 3-inch-thick steel. A sturdy commercial fishing boat could be lifted fifty feet by swells rising one after another—the dense anchor chain pulling taut with a metallic shriek each time. He knew well those stomach-churning seconds when the *Aquila* sat poised atop a huge swell's crest.

Then, as the crew clung to steel rails and supports in the wheelhouse, the chart room, or the cramped berths fore and aft, the ship's thick steel prow would dip at nearly a ninety-degree angle and plunge into the trough—then slam against the surface of the sea. As every inch of the *Aquila* shuddered, several feet of her bow would vanish beneath the surface.

Then the ship's bow would snap back upward and above the Bering Sea. The anchor chain holding the ship would right herself for the next swell in the "Aleutian roller coaster."[1]

Over his decades in the Bering, Garcia had seen these "roller coasters" unnerve even veteran crabbers and codders. Garcia himself would never have set out from Kiska at night under normal circumstances, not even for the short five-mile trip to the ship's present position. The harbor might as well be 500 miles away if the wind and waves were to roar in without warning. The *Aquila*'s mission, however, was not an ordinary voyage for Garcia. This was no fishing trip.

The *Aquila* was on a mission—a mission Garcia viewed as, at best, highly quixotic. The Bering Sea veteran didn't believe that John Abele had the proverbial chance in hell of finding what he and his brothers, Bruce and Brad, were seeking.

The Abele brothers were engaged in a decades-long quest to solve one of World War II's last and most baffling mysteries: the fate of the submarine USS *Grunion*. She had disappeared without a trace somewhere off Kiska on July 30, 1942.

The mission was personal for the brothers. They had last seen their father, thirty-eight-year-old Lieutenant Commander Mannert "Jim" Abele, at Sunday lunch at the New London, Connecticut, Naval Officers' Club in May 1942. For sixty-five years, all the Navy would tell his widow, Catherine "Kay" Abele, and her boys was that Jim Abele and his sixty-nine crewmen were missing and presumed lost.

It was an official line that Kay and her sons questioned all their lives. Now, John, Bruce, and Brad were united in an ambitious and highly dangerous attempt to achieve their mother's last wish: find Jim and his submarine.

Their search had led them to the Aleutians for a second summer straight. Kiska, some 1,500 miles from the Alaskan mainland, was and is a forbidding site—treeless and fogbound, guarded by a looming active volcano. Magnitude 9 earthquakes constantly rock the island, stirring up what Garcia told the brothers were "the worst, most horrible waves on earth." After John Abele saw Kiska for the first time, he told his wife, Mary, "It's *Lord of the Rings* meets *Nanook of the North*, the edge of the earth."

Garcia had reasons besides deadly weather to regard the Abeles' mission with skepticism. *National Geographic* had backed out of the expedition at the last minute—after asking to send a writer and a photographer aboard the *Aquila*—because Robert Ballard, the world-renowned oceanographer and explorer who had found the *Titanic*, doubted the *Grunion* could be found. Even if the submarine had not broken apart on volcanic outcrops on her way to the bottom, Ballard had little confidence that a successful search in the Bering's rough currents was possible, whether by sonar or submersible.

Other experts agreed that the submarine was lost forever. David Gallo, an oceanographer and Ballard protégé who had joined John

Abele aboard the *Aquila*, confessed that his colleagues at the Woods Hole Oceanographic Institute rated the chances of finding the sub at "zero." The *Aquila*'s crew placed bets on how long it would take the Abeles to give up their search.

So U.S. Navy officials, a legion of scientists and seamen, and the world's preeminent shipwreck hunter had all told the Abeles repeatedly that no one would ever find the *Grunion*. The submarine was a tiny target in a vast and untamable sea.

But John and his brothers had sedulously pursued every possible clue—from long-forgotten Japanese naval records to a sonar scan hit that Ballard had dismissed as merely "an underwater volcanic mass or a surface ship."

And finally they were about to find out whether their long quest was in vain. The sudden calm of the Bering Sea had allowed them to complete their run to the spot where they believed the *Grunion* lay—just a few miles off Kiska. But the ocean floor there was 3,000 feet below the surface. And the storm approaching from the west meant they didn't have much time. At 9 p.m., Garcia cut the engines. After taking depth soundings and computer mapping the sea bottom, the team decided to send down the ROV. At 10:20 p.m., with a deafening rasp of the winch, the crew lowered the Max Rover, a steel vehicle the size of a minivan, into the Bering.

The vehicle's thin steel tether-line lay slack for the moment. Joe Caba, a deep-sea search veteran, piloted the ROV from the *Aquila*'s wheelhouse. He hit a switch on the remote control, and the Rover's powerful directional propellers thrashed to life, kicking up spurts of seawater. At another prompt from Caba—one of the best ROV operators in the business—the Max Rover splashed away from the *Aquila* "like an enormous yellow puppy." Several hundred yards from the ship, the ROV slipped under the surface.

For nearly a half hour, the group in the wheelhouse peered at camera images of startled black cod and basketball-sized orange jellyfish. As the ROV reached a depth of 3,100 feet, a volcanic slope slowly appeared.

John Abele drew a sharp breath. Two long parallel tracks etched into the gray soil bed pointed toward the ocean bottom.

Caba said, "Let's see where they lead…"

At 3,200 feet, the vehicle reached the ocean floor and continued to follow the tracks.

"We've got a target," Caba said, "out at 045 degrees and about 60 meters."

An object slowly materialized from the gloom. At first, it looked like a brownish-gray mass of kelp. Then, as the Rover's phosphorus-white beacons knifed through the murky depths of the Bering Sea, the ghostly contours of a submarine took shape.

A sizable chunk of the bow was missing, exposing the forward torpedo room and bunk beds, whose only inhabitants now were shimmering amber starfish. Exposed pipes framed the conning tower. Radio antennae stuck up like spikes. Old hydraulic hoses snaked across the steel hull.

"There she is," Abele said in a near whisper.

The Max Rover slid to the wreck's port side, the cameras revealing spots where the hull had buckled and cracked along weld seams. But most of the sub was remarkably intact.

Halfway across the globe, in his Newton, Massachusetts, living room, John Abele's oldest brother Bruce sat transfixed in front of the computer screen, tears welling as the images from the Max Rover streamed up from the sea bottom. They were images of his father's sub, the first glimpses of the USS *Grunion* in sixty-five years.

Navigator Richard Graham stared at the images, looking intently for the propeller guards that would prove the wreck was, in fact, the *Grunion*—prove it even to the U.S. Navy.

But as Caba started to navigate the Rover toward the sub's stern, the *Aquila* lurched to port as a large foaming wave hit the vessel.

"Damn it!" muttered Caba. "We've lost her!"

After sixty-five years, the Bering Sea was not ready to give up the *Grunion* or her secrets—not yet.

CHAPTER TWO

AN UNCONVENTIONAL COURSE

O n July 11, 1903, in the shipbuilding city of Quincy, Massachusetts, Dr. Francis Abele and his wife, Lou, welcomed the birth of their second child. They christened him Mannert Lincoln Abele, but as a small boy, Mannert decided that he preferred to be called "Jim." The name stuck so tightly that, years later, even his own sons called him Jim, never father or dad—not even when he donned his Navy dress-whites and gold-braided, black-visored officer's cap, the very picture of a commander. But Jim Abele wasn't a conventional guy; he charted his own course.

Jim's parents had met when his father, busy establishing his veterinary practice in Quincy, placed a newspaper ad in hopes of renting a room: "A young veterinarian desires board and lodging with stable facilities. F. Abele, Faxon House."[1] Dr. Abele's ad caught the eye of Mrs. Frank Hall, who clipped it out of the paper and strode across Spear Street to a two-storey clapboarded house with a barn, originally built in 1818.

Mrs. Hall knocked and handed the clipping to Mrs. Addie Tupper when she answered the door. Addie was a widow whose husband, Trescott Tupper, had built up a successful tannery leather business only to see it destroyed—as he lay bed-ridden with cancer—by a partner who "played the ponies." That left his wife, their two daughters (Lou and Laura) and three sons (Fred, George, and Russell) with a large home and little cash. They were barely scraping by on what Lou and Fred made working at a local surveying office (Fred as an apprentice).

In blunt Yankee fashion, Mrs. Hall pointed out that the Tuppers needed more income—Addie should talk to the young veterinarian. Addie listened, but was concerned that "a horse doctor was no better than a blacksmith or even a sailor." With two attractive daughters in the house, she refused to take in any boarder of questionable character or background. Mrs. Hall prodded—surely it would do Addie no harm just to talk with Dr. Abele.

Despite her misgivings, Addie decided to reply to Francis Abele's ad. The young man who needed a room turned out to be well-dressed, polite, serious, and genial; to her approval, he had been a teacher for several years after his graduation from Bridgewater (Massachusetts) Normal School and had then gone on to college to study veterinary medicine. She deemed teaching a respectable occupation and was delighted that he had a degree. No one in her own family had graduated from college (though her daughter Lou was a graduate of the prestigious Thayer Academy in neighboring Braintree). She offered him the room in the barn and meals with the family, comfortable that he was a respectable gentleman and certain that his board would help her pay the mounting bills.

Francis Abele became such a part of the family that he started taking Lou and Laura with him on his calls to outlying farms where he tended to livestock, dogs, cats—and in one case a bear. While Laura was pretty and vivacious, Jim was increasingly drawn to Lou, a tall young woman who was closer to his age and equally serious and mature. Lou was interested Frank, too. But when he proposed she balked, saying she could not quit her job and marry him because her family depended on her salary.

Frank assured Lou that he would continue to pay Addie board and lodging—now for his wife as well as himself—and help with the household expenses. So Lou accepted Frank's proposal, and the couple arranged to rent a two-room "suite" from Addie, with the barn serving as Frank's veterinary office. The Abeles and the Tuppers had to live frugally, but as Frank's practice grew so did his ability to provide for his extended family. He eventually paid his mother-in-law a thousand dollars in cash—more than double the average annual wage at the time—to buy the house, the barn, and the lot. It turned out to be a shrewd investment.

Frank and Lou welcomed their first child in 1901. They named him Trescott Tupper Abele, after Lou's father. A little over two years later, in 1903, Mannert Lincoln Abele was born—"Jim."

Trescott, nicknamed "Tet," recalled that he and Jim grew up in "a happy home"—which just happened to be across the street from the granite church containing the crypt where President John Adams, his wife Abigail, and their son President John Quincy Adams are buried. There was history in Quincy, and plenty of diversity too, with all the new immigrants. Jim learned quickly how to hold his own with rough-and-tumble boys, and as his brother recalled, Jim "was…a happy, friendly, handsome extrovert, popular, a natural leader," and a natural athlete.

Their parents never argued in front of the boys. Both mother and father seemed always to defer to the other, and Frank Abele never spanked his children except for willful disobedience. He expected the boys listen to what he said and act accordingly.

The constant stream of locals' ailing cats, dogs, and other animals provided Frank Abele with a solid practice and steady income for the family. He replaced the old coal stove with a new gas one, put in electricity to replace the house's antiquated gas lamps, and had a modern inside bathroom installed in place of the outhouse. While most of his neighbors were still clattering around Quincy's crowded streets with horses and buggies, Dr. Abele bought a jaunty new car.

The boys played baseball (or three-o-cat, a form of baseball with three bases and six players) and were dare-devil sledders and bicycle riders. Sometimes they would square off with boxing gloves in the Spear Street barn. Other times they engaged in wild snowball fights with a gang of Italian boys from an adjoining neighborhood. Whether hurling snowballs or baseballs, Jim's arm was always an asset. He had a lively fastball and a sharp-breaking "outdrop" or curveball. He knew better, however, than to incur his father's anger by taking part in rock fights between rival neighborhood bands; stone-throwing was one thing Frank Abele would not tolerate.

Jim was so popular with schoolmates that the boys from Presidents' Hill, where the mansions of Quincy's wealthiest families had panoramic views of the Atlantic, asked him to join their ranks. He chose to stick with his own "Spear Street Gang."

The lure and romance of what might lie beyond the waters of Quincy Bay had hit Jim by the time he turned nine. He wrote a letter to an officer aboard the USS *Chester*, the U.S. Navy's first light cruiser, which was stationed at the Boston Navy Yard. The officer replied to Jim on September 19, 1911:

My dear Mannert,

Your letter came this morning and I think you are a very brave boy to want to go to Africa. I should like very much to take you and my boy…what a fine time you two could have! But, Mannert, Uncle Sam does not permit me to take boys, much as I want to take them. Some day when you are older, I hope you will have the opportunity of seeing Africa and other parts of the world. You ask your Uncle Arthur to tell you of what he sees in Africa. When we come back to Boston, you visit the ship and I will answer all the questions you want to ask about the Arabs and Turks.… Good-bye my brave and bright boy. I am sorry that we cannot take you, but Uncle Sam must be obeyed.

The Uncle Arthur mentioned in the letter was Dr. Abele's brother, Lieutenant Commander Clarence Arthur Abele, who in a short span of years had become a U.S. Navy legend. He had graduated from the Naval Academy in just three years. On April 25, 1898, Congress had declared war on Spain, and in June of what should have been his senior year, Abele was posted as a gunnery officer aboard the armored cruiser USS *Brooklyn*, flagship of Commodore Winfield Scott Schley's "Flying Squadron" and Rear Admiral William T. Sampson's North Atlantic Squadron, preparing for combat against the Spanish fleet in Santiago Harbor.

The Spanish fleet—four armored cruisers, and two torpedo boats under the command of Admiral Pascual Cervera—made a run for open waters on July 3, 1898. In a furious battle, the American warships turned five of the Spanish vessels into flaming wrecks and ran the sixth, the state-of-the-art armored cruiser *Colon*, aground. Aboard the *Brooklyn*, which was the first ship fired upon, young

Ensign Abele commanded his 5-inch guns in a deadly hour-long duel with the Spanish flagship, the armored cruiser *Infante Maria Theresa*, and the cruiser *Vizcaya*. Both Spanish vessels were ablaze. Cervera's entire squadron was lost, with 323 killed, 151 wounded, and 70 officers—including the admiral—and 1,500 enlisted men taken prisoner. Only one American, a yeoman aboard the *Brooklyn*, was killed.

In 1901 Ensign Abele took the helm of his first command, the new torpedo boat USS *Barney* at the Naval Torpedo Station in Newport, Rhode Island. By January 1903 he was assigned as a gunnery officer aboard the battleship USS *Massachusetts*, and when an 8-inch gun exploded in the forward turret during target practice off San Juan, Puerto Rico, and threatened to set off stacked shells and charges, Arthur reacted quickly and coolly. He flooded the turret to prevent the other loaded cannon from exploding and setting off the magazine just below the two guns. He was cited for his bravery and "splendid discipline."

Young Jim had an understandable case of hero worship for Arthur. It seemed Jim was determined to go Navy from five years old, when Arthur had given him a sailor suit. By high school he displayed many of the attributes one might look for in a young naval officer. He was not the student his brother was, but Jim was intelligent, popular, and a fine athlete, especially on the soccer field. He liked science and was mechanically minded, able to understand complex machinery instinctively. And especially after the death of their father in 1917, his Uncle Arthur was his inspiration. Arthur Abele, a captain now, had been awarded the Navy Cross during World War I "for distinguished service...as commanding officer of the USS *Maui* engaged in the important, exacting, and hazardous duty of transporting and escorting troops and supplies to European ports through waters infested with enemy submarines and mines."

Young Jim wanted to apply to Annapolis, but the pragmatic, no-nonsense captain admonished his nephew that he needed better grades to meet the Naval Academy's lofty academic requirements. There might be another way, Arthur advised—a long shot, but possible: if Jim enlisted in the Navy, studied on his own, and took the fleet-wide exam, a high score could earn him a place at Annapolis.

Seventeen-year-old Jim Abele signed his enlistment papers at the Boston Navy Yard on August 20, 1920, after completing just three years at Quincy High School. Following basic training, the new seaman shipped out aboard the USS *Utah*, a 21,825-ton battleship, or "dreadnought," which bristled with ten 12-inch cannons mounted two apiece in five turrets. Jim joined a crew of 941 men and 60 officers commanded by Captain William Benson. Part of the Atlantic Squadron, the *Utah* anchored in numerous European ports and off Constantinople. Jim Abele's boyhood dreams of visiting famous, exotic ports was coming true, but his most earnest hope was to rise from the ranks of the "swabbies" and become an officer. That meant long off-duty hours studying for the fleet-wide Annapolis entrance exam. If he needed an additional incentive, he got it from the sight of Naval Academy midshipmen scrambling around the battleship's deck during their summer tours of training duty. In the 1920s, only the top two applicants from the Atlantic Fleet and the top two from the Pacific Fleet were offered slots at the Academy each year.

Jim took the exam in 1921 and did well in every section except the spelling portion, which sank him. He resolved to study even harder, and on the 1922 test achieved a winning score. He received the news that he was accepted as a plebe for the Annapolis Class of 1926 as the *Utah* rode anchor off Constantinople. Jim was soon aboard another vessel bound for Hampton Roads, Virginia, in time for the traditional "plebe summer" at the picturesque Maryland campus nestled along Chesapeake Bay. Prospective freshmen, midshipmen fourth class, were drilled in the traditions of the Naval Service and the Naval Academy, in basic military skills, and in the high standards and obligations inherent in service as a midshipman and naval officer. On Jim's first day of plebe summer, he and his fellow newcomers were escorted to their small rooms in Bancroft Hall and told they would need to be mentally, morally, and physically tough if they wanted to succeed at the Academy and in the Navy.

At first Jim struggled with the endless physical and mental challenges of life at Annapolis. He was so miserable during his plebe summer that he wanted to quit. Upperclassmen were hard on all the plebes, but they singled out those who had come to Annapolis through fleet-wide appointments for especially rough ritual hazing. The majority of the midshipmen at the Academy had been at the top of their high school class and been accepted for admission on the strength of their academic record—upon formal nominations from their congressmen and senators. They derided the handful of plebes who got to Annapolis by way of the fleet-wide exams as interlopers who had used a "back-door" route and had to prove themselves worthy of their "betters." Of course plebes who had actually served aboard a ship loathed many of the conventional midshipmen as children of privilege whose families had pulled strings for them.

Captain Arthur Abele knew his nephew measured up, and he insisted that Jim stick it out. Jim repaid his uncle's confidence by proving himself in the classroom and on the varsity soccer pitch as a ball-hawking center-forward for all four years. Jim had a memento of his uncle ever present at Annapolis—the *Reina Mercedes*, one of the Spanish cruisers Arthur Abele had dueled at the Battle of Santiago, was anchored in the bay. The captured warship, which had been refurbished by the U.S. Navy, was used by the midshipmen as both a barracks and a brig throughout Jim's years at Annapolis.

Despite being one of a handful of midshipmen selected for naval aviation training on account of their exceptional hand-eye coordination and the ability to think quickly under extreme pressure, Jim declined that career path. He had joined the Navy to serve at sea, and he requested that he be allowed to do so. His request was granted.

Jim Abele graduated with the Annapolis class of 1926 and was assigned as an ensign to the battleship USS *Colorado*. One of his first assignments was to coach the *Colorado*'s soccer squad against the teams of other warships at bases from New York to Portsmouth, Great Britain, and Sydney, Australia. His teams excelled.

An officer was expected to marry and raise a family, and after his graduation from the Academy, Jim began courting a smart, attractive, and accomplished music teacher named Catherine "Kay" Eaton, a distant cousin who had boarded at his family house in Quincy with her sister, Frances, for a time after Jim's father died.

Kay had been born and raised in the rural Massachusetts town of Middleboro, a classic Yankee hamlet with cranberry bogs, farmland hacked from dense woods, and one of the region's oldest Congregationalist churches. An accomplished musician, she had taught violin in both Quincy and Lowell, Massachusetts, before continuing her studies at the Eastman School of Music in Rochester, New York.

Kay had no shortage of suitors, and Jim Abele knew it. He also knew that not all women were well suited to Navy life, but he sensed that because of her practical personality, Kay might be.

In the spring of 1927, Jim was hospitalized for minor surgery. While convalescing, he pursued Kay and won her hand. They were married on June 8, 1927, in a small outdoor ceremony at the home of her sister, Frances, in Brookline, Massachusetts. Shortly afterwards Jim was ordered to report back to the *Colorado*, which was stationed with the Pacific Fleet at Pearl Harbor. The newlyweds headed immediately for Hawaii, where Kay adjusted well to her new life, making friends easily with the other officers' wives and teaching piano and violin to augment the couple's income.

CHAPTER THREE

THE SUBMARINER

While stationed at Pearl Harbor, Jim became fascinated by submarines. Known lovingly as "pig boats" to the "submariners" (pronounced "submar-EEN-ers," not "sub-MAHR-iners"), the underwater service of the era attracted the Navy's more adventurous and colorful sailors. To the surface Navy, the submarines had another name—"iron coffins," and with good reason. Once a submarine slipped beneath the surface, there was no such thing as a routine dive.

A submarine skipper needed equal measures of nerve, coolness in a crisis—crises were inevitable in a pig boat—and the ability to command tough, fractious men crammed into quarters so tight that only a captain who commanded utter trust and respect could maintain shipboard discipline. On virtually every level, the submarine fleet posed more challenges for officers than any other branch of the Navy. Jim Abele wanted in on those challenges.

In the fall of 1928, he applied to the submarine officers' school in New London, Connecticut, and was accepted. The five-month course started in mid-January 1929. While the training proved arduous, and the washout rate for prospective submarine officers was high, Jim thrived both in the classroom and on the training sub. Four times a month he and the other candidates went out on training subs for two-day deep-water tests. The presence of sub-tenders, surface ships equipped with salvage equipment and deep-sea dive teams, testified to the ever-present risk of training accidents from rookie mistakes.

Jim completed his training in June 1929 and was assigned as an engineering officer to the submarine *S-23*, which was soon slated to depart the Portsmouth Naval Base in New Hampshire and join the Pacific Fleet in Pearl Harbor. As he began his new career, he also looked forward to another role: first-time father. Kay was pregnant, and they decided she would stay in Boston with her sister and then join Jim in Hawaii after she delivered their child. For the next few months, Jim and Kay wrote to each other frequently. Kay gave birth on October 14, 1929, to a boy they named Bruce. Several weeks later, mother and child arrived in Pearl Harbor.

Jim and Kay loved the submarine service's close-knit informality. Submarine officers' wives were often on a first-name basis with seamen's wives, something unheard of in the surface Navy. Jim and the other submariners, along with naval aviators, comprised the "brown-shoe Navy," so called because they chose to wear brown shoes, rather than the traditional black, with their khaki uniforms. Tweaking naval nomenclature, submarine personnel referred to their vessels as "boats" instead of "ships," the surface Navy's term for *all* vessels (in much the same manner, naval pilots called the front of their carriers "the pointy end" rather than the traditional "bow").

In Honolulu, Kay taught music at the Kamehameha School and also played violin in the local symphony. The busy couple's household expanded on January 25, 1933, when Kay gave birth to a second son, Bradford, who was quickly dubbed "Brad."

Jim was a clever, troubleshooting officer—even when the initial result might be a chewing out from his commander. While running engineering tests aboard the S-23 in 1932, Jim discovered a wiring problem that created a severe lack of compression in cylinders within the diesel engine. As a drop in compression could prevent a submerged sub from generating enough power to resurface, it was a potentially fatal issue. Jim and a crewman working with him changed the sub's wiring to fix the problem and increase the boat's speed and power. When Jim told his skipper, Jim was ordered to keep his mouth shut and "put it back the way you found it or you'll be court-martialed." Later Jim was to receive a special commendation for his action by the Bureau of Navigation in Washington, D.C.

In early January 1933 Jim was transferred to another sub, the S-21, but requested shore duty, perhaps to spend more time with his growing family. Three months later he received orders to report to the Navy's Bureau of Navigation in Washington, D.C.

For nearly the next four years, Jim manned a desk. He and Kay maintained an active social life. As pleasant as these years were, Jim inevitably longed to get back to sea, and in May 1936 he was assigned to the submarine USS R-11 in New London, Connecticut. In February 1937, Jim and Kay's third son, John, was born, and Jim was given command of his own submarine, the USS R-13. Designed for coastal and harbor defense, with diesel-electric engines, the submarine was a little more than 186 feet long and had a top speed of 13.5 knots (15.5 miles per hour) on the surface and 10.5 knots

(12.1 miles per hour) submerged. The *R-13* carried a crew of only one other officer and twenty-seven men. She was armed with four 21-inch torpedo tubes and a .50 caliber machine gun mounted on the foredeck. She wasn't young; she had been built at Fore River Shipyard, just about a mile from Jim's boyhood home, and launched in 1919. But Jim could take her down to a depth of 200 feet, and by year's end his superiors awarded the skipper and his sub the Navy's highest operational award—"E" for "excellence in all regards."

While bringing the *R-13* back to the New London submarine base on August 26, 1938, after a routine patrol, Jim was inspecting "some trouble in the circuit-breaker interlocks" when he noticed a bolt was missing. Suspecting that it was lodged in the adjusting mechanism at the bottom of the breaker, he picked up a heavy Navy flashlight and guided the beam warily around the breaker because of the danger from a short. He was alone in the battery room.

There was an explosive blinding white flash followed by waves of thick smoke. A ship's cook, G. K. Hauber, rushed into the aft battery room to find his skipper severely burned on his face, hands, thighs, and scrotum. The boat's junior officer and several other crewmen raced to Jim's side and administered first aid. An emergency radio message was sent to the base. As pain pulsated through Jim, the *R-13* raced into New London Harbor, stopping alongside the destroyer USS *Tattnall* to pick up a chief pharmacist's mate, perhaps to administer morphine to sedate the skipper.

As the *R-13* hurried up the Thames River to the submarine base, one of the crewman's wives spotted the sub and suspected something was wrong. The moment the *R-13* docked, Jim was strapped on a stretcher and maneuvered vertically through the tubular main hatch—just twenty-eight inches in diameter and the only way out. An ambulance rushed him to the New London Naval Hospital, where he remained for a month. He carried scars from the accident for the rest of his life.

The Submarine Division-Navy launched the required investigation to determine whether Jim had been negligent in any way and had endangered his command. If so, his career could be jeopardized. Jim, unable to rise from his hospital bed, testified that he had "no recollection of touching anything...[and] was careful in his handling of the [flash]light."

To Jim's relief, his division superiors quickly determined that "Lieutenant Commander Abele was injured in the line of duty and not as the result of his own misconduct. Since the circumstances of the accident are clear, no further investigation will be held."

The report went further: "Lieutenant Abele is considered the ablest Commanding Officer in the Division. He is well balanced, thorough, conscientious, and hard working. It is believed that this accident cannot be ascribed to carelessness nor lack of knowledge."[1]

Jim's reputation remained intact. There was no guarantee, however, that he could ever return to a submarine. Even after being discharged from the hospital, he faced at least several months' recovery at home. Bedridden for the first six weeks, Jim lay beneath a tent because the mere touch of covers on his burns caused agony. Kay bathed him, fed him until he could hold utensils again, and administered his pain medications and salves for his burns. Although in constant pain and unable to move much, Jim nonetheless remained stoic in front of his sons, and Brad Abele later recalled that even though his father was incapacitated those months after the accident, he remained a commanding presence and completely involved in the family's daily life.

Eventually, Jim felt fit enough to take an administrative job at the base. If there was any serious consolation in his injury, it was that he got to spend so much time with his sons—teaching them to carve wood, tie nautical knots, pitch a tent in the backyard. He enjoyed watching his sons toss a baseball and football, but his burns prevented him from joining in. With a soccer ball, it was a different matter, the boys seeing firsthand the deft coordination and reflexes that had made Jim a standout center-forward at the Naval Academy. Though the Great Depression still battered the nation, and reduced naval salaries forced Jim and Kay to cut corners, the family lacked for nothing essential; and New London, with the sea, a river, woods, and ball fields, was a great place for the boys. It was also a great place for Jim, who kept himself busy despite his physical limitations. Bruce Abele remembers his father as a fine carpenter and craftsman. When Jim was not on duty, it seemed that what he loved to do most was to work around the house or in his workshop area. He never enjoyed relaxing in the traditional sense, but "would soon have to get up and start creating something."

In 1939, Jim requested a transfer to either Harvard or Yale as the head instructor of the Navy ROTC program. He needed more time to recover before he could think about returning to the rigors of submarine duty, and both universities were close to his and Kay's relatives, offering his boys the chance to bond with their family in New England. In July 1939 Jim was given the post of engineering teacher and head instructor of the naval ROTC program at Harvard. The family moved into a house in nearby Brookline.

At Harvard, Jim quickly became a popular teacher, regarded as informative and informal. He also encouraged some of his students, including Endicott "Chub" Peabody, who was an All-American grid-iron great at Harvard and went on to become governor of Massa-chusetts, to choose service in the "brown shoe" Navy.

Jim's teaching career, however, was short-lived. With war raging in Europe, Admiral Chester Nimitz, the Navy's commander, began to prepare for America's inevitable entry into the conflagration. Most military men knew that the United States could not stay on the sidelines against Hitler and Imperial Japan. Nimitz ordered that all personnel with submarine experience be transferred back to sea duty.

So after one year at Harvard, Jim received orders to take command of the USS *S-31* in Philadelphia and ready her through sea trials for war. His new sub, launched in December 1918, stretched 219 feet from bow to stern, with a beam of 21 feet and a 42-man crew. She was armed with four 533mm torpedo tubes and a 102mm deck gun and had a top speed of 14 knots on the surface and 11 knots submerged. She had been decommissioned on December 7, 1937, and berthed at League Island, off Philadelphia, but was returned to service on September 18, 1940. Jim's job was to make her seaworthy again and train a crew of mostly raw recruits.

Once Jim had the *S-31* overhauled to the point she could head out to sea, he was ordered to join the submarine division at New London; Kay and the three boys remained behind, as Bruce and Brad were already halfway through their school year in Brookline and Jim expected to be at sea with his new sub for most of the next nine months.

Orders came in December 1940, when the *S-31*, her fellow S-boats in New London, and a tender and rescue vessel headed down the Thames and into the Atlantic, bound for practice exercises in deep waters and for patrol duty off the Panama Canal. Jim wrote to Kay that among the Axis powers, "the Japs are the only ones who have ships using the canal."[2] American newspapers were running frequent stories about unidentified periscopes breaking the surface on both sides of the Panama Canal.

Heavy seas plagued the submarines as they sailed from Cape Hatteras to Florida on their way to Key West. Pressure weighed on all the subs' officers and crews, as Admiral William Edwards, commander of Submarine Division 44, and other brass were on hand to critique every move. Jim wrote, however, that the "crew is really beginning to whip into shape," and he proudly mentioned that a fellow officer had heard Admiral Edwards remark, "Abele knows how to get things done."

Buffeted by gusts and waves, the S-22, sailing in formation close to Jim's boat, "went aground hard and fast on a coral reef." Jim kept the S-31 moving south. The tender stayed behind to try to free the trapped S-22 when the weather abated. "She [S-22] is still there," Jim wrote. "Admiral Edwards must be about fit to be tied."[3]

On Christmas Day, the S-31 battled "stormy currents and shoals" in the Caribbean. Jim wrote to Kay that night, describing in his characteristically unruffled way a close encounter with disaster in a blinding Caribbean squall. The S-31 had been running on the surface when one of the lookouts spotted a massive shape emerging from the torrential rain and bearing down on the sub at some 18 knots per hour. Every man on the S-31's bridge stared at the huge, oncoming prow and billowing smokestacks of one of the world's largest passenger liners, the SS America. The liner had cleared the sub by a mere seventy-five yards. Jim wrote, "I would not like it to have been closer."[4]

As Jim guided the S-31 into waters off Panama, lookouts on the sub's bridges peered through binoculars for the slightest hint of tiny washes that might be kicked up by unidentified periscopes. Jim trained his men hard with deck-gun and dive-and-surface drills and non-fire "torpedo runs." He commented, "The crew handled things well, as did the officers considering what training they have had."[5]

Every officer and crewmember in U.S. Navy vessels patrolling in and around the Canal felt he was on a near war-footing. Jim never lost his calm, cool demeanor, but it was tested suddenly off Panama when the S-31 was running on the surface on January 22, 1941. A "tremendous and sudden wallop" rocked the submarine from bow to stern. His first thought was that a torpedo had slammed into the boat. Then he spotted a dying whale vanishing into the waters near the sub. To Jim's relief, the *S-31* suffered only a few dents.

About a week later, on January 28, 1941, Jim took the *S-31* down on her deepest dive yet. Above the submarine, the tender USS *Mallard* waited, as usual on practice dives, with rescue lines and a team of deep-water divers ready just in case.

Fathom by fathom the *S-31* descended, Jim coolly peering at gauges and listening for any telltale sounds of trouble. He took her down to 209 feet and leveled her off. That evening, he wrote to Kay that the boat had sprung "a few minor leaks, and the relief valve popped when we tried to pump with the high-pressure pump. But in general the dive was very successful."[6]

. To Jim's experienced eyes and ears, the popped valve and leaks were minor. Those in the crew making their first voyage and first deep dive had sweaty palms, dry throats, and racing hearts that might have been worse if not for their skipper's unruffled demeanor and crisp orders. He was a man in complete command of himself and his submarine.

Jim was awakened the next morning at 4:30 by an urgent call from the conning tower that "there were four commanding officers on deck with a [launch] alongside and that I was to go with them to the *Mallard* immediately in any uniform.... I slipped khakis over my pajamas and was off."

All of the division's submarine skippers and several destroyer captains had been summoned aboard the *Mallard* by Admiral Edwards. He tersely informed his officers "that a destroyer was returning to its anchorage when all of a sudden the men on the bridge discovered the periscope of a submarine dead ahead about 200 yards. Upon checking up they found that none of our submarines had been diving at the time or were even near the spot." Edwards ordered them all to rush back to their boats and search for the suspicious sub. Jim clambered from the launch and onto the *S-31*. He ordered his crew to battle stations and directed the sub to where the periscope had been spotted. At one point, a lookout thought he had sighted it, "but it was too far away to be sure, and he was the only one who saw it."[7] The search went on for days, but that was the closest any boat got to what Jim was convinced was an elusive Japanese submarine.

The *S-31* patrolled off the Panama Canal Zone through the spring of 1941 before being ordered back to New London for training exercises. Then, in November, Jim was ordered to take the submarine to Philadelphia for a complete overhaul to prepare it for war, and he was given a new command.[8]

Admiral Nimitz named Jim skipper of the Navy's newest submarine, the USS *Grunion*, a state-of-the-art Fleet Boat still in the final stages of construction at the Electric Boat Company in Groton, Connecticut. She would cost $6 million, the most the Navy had ever spent on a submarine. The assignment was a choice one, an honor Jim had earned through his ability to think quickly and clearly in a crisis, to command his crews' respect and admiration, and, in Admiral Edwards' words, "to get things done."

CHAPTER FOUR

"INTO THE THICK OF THINGS"

———— ✦ ————

Jim and Kay Abele and their sons were gathered together around the living room radio on December 7, 1941, when they heard the stunning news that the Japanese had attacked Pearl Harbor. Later that day, the boys watched from the front windows as a black car from the base pulled into the driveway and their father, in scarf and dark blue greatcoat, got into the vehicle. Bruce would never forget how grim his father looked as the car drove away.

The USS *Grunion* was launched at Groton, Connecticut, on December 22, 1941, the three Abele boys standing proudly with Jim in the conning tower as the sub slid down the steel ways at the Electric Boat Company and splashed into the Thames River. For the next four months, Jim spent many days and nights at the sub base readying the *Grunion* for war.

A Gato-class sub with a new type of all-welded steel hull, the *Grunion* stretched 312 feet; and her speed of 20.25 knots on the surface (8.75 knots submerged) made her the fastest sub in the fleet. The Navy officially commissioned her on April 11, 1942, and ordered Lieutenant Commander Abele to provision her, commence surface and submerged training exercises "in preparation for action,"[1] and berth her at the New London Submarine Base.

On April 13, the training sub *S-48*, attempting to moor at a Groton Pier where the *Grunion* was temporarily docked, struck the *Grunion*'s stern on the starboard side. Although Jim put her through dive tests and found no damage, a problem in such a complex mechanism may not have shown up immediately.

On April 27, 1942, the *Grunion* slipped into the Newport, Rhode Island, Torpedo Station for three days of crucial training with the Navy's new, top-secret MK 14 "Exploder" torpedo. The weapon featured a revolutionary magnetic detonator that was supposed to explode automatically when the MK 14 passed just below a ship's keel—to shatter the target's "steel spine" and sink her quickly. The MK 14 also had an "impact detonator" that was supposed to explode upon contact with any part of the target's hull.

All of the torpedoes were manufactured in Newport, and because they were new, still in short supply, and prohibitively expensive at $10,000 per torpedo, the Navy ordered that for target drills the MK 14's warhead be filled with water. When the torpedo ran out of fuel, a valve opened and ejected the water—making the weapon float, so that it was easy to retrieve.

What Jim and other skippers who had yet to go out on wartime patrol did not know was that the MK 14 had four major flaws: It tended to run about ten feet deeper than set. The magnetic exploder often failed to detonate. The warhead chronically failed to explode even when it made a direct hit on a target's hull. And most ominously, the MK 14 sometimes passed under or past the target and made a "circular" run, coming back in a large circle to strike the firing sub. While the Navy was aware of the first three problems, the fourth, a circular run, had not fully materialized. It soon would.

Even before Jim and his crew conducted their first target trials with the MK 14 and its dummy warhead, skippers were reporting that the torpedo had huge technical problems. On December 24, 1941, Commander Tyrell Dwight Jacobs of the USS *Sargo* fired a total of eight torpedoes at two Japanese ships in the South Pacific with no results and became very frustrated; when two additional merchantmen came in view, he took extra pains to get it right, pursuing for fifty-seven minutes and making certain the TDC (Torpedo Data Computer, a very early computer) bearings matched perfectly before firing two torpedoes at each ship at only 1,000 yards. All of the MK 14s missed.

A few days after deciding that the torpedoes were running too deep, when Jacobs had devised settings to correct the problem, he encountered a ponderous tanker. His approach was meticulous. He fired one torpedo from only 1,200 yards, but it hissed underneath and past the target. Frustrated and furious, Jacobs radioed superiors and questioned the MK 14's effectiveness on an open radio circuit. The sub fleet's admirals were nearly apoplectic that a skipper on patrol was criticizing the weapon on a wave-length that the Japanese might be able to decipher; they were furious that he had broken radio silence strictures to vent his dismay that he had fired thirteen MK 14s in six attacks and all of them had malfunctioned. Fellow submariner Clay Blair notes in *Silent Victory* that "there was hell to pay" for Jacobs' actions from his supporters.[2]

At about the same time in December 1941, Lieutenant Commander Pete Ferrall attacked several Japanese ships off Indochina and scored only one hit with eight MK 14s. He, too, understood he was supposed to keep his mouth shut. Several American subs going after Nazi shipping experienced similar woes with the torpedo.

Jim had heard rumors about the MK 14 through the sub fleet's grapevine, and there was something else—something that became evident in the waters off Newport—that unnerved every submariner about to head out on patrol with the torpedo. While the MK 14's fast 45-knot speed and 4,500-yard range pleased the skippers, the vapor trail that the steam-powered weapon left on the surface allowed the enemy to spot the torpedoes more easily and threatened the subs by providing a trail right back to the subs themselves. Unless the torpedoes hit their mark and took a ship down quickly, "shooting fast and getting down faster"[3] was the maxim for Jim and his fellow skippers. The MK 14 was a nerve-wracking weapon, potentially lethal to the men who used it.

But skippers had yet to face the worst potential problem with the MK 14: the possibility of a circular run. If a torpedo passed under its target without detonating and swung around and headed straight back to its point of origin—the submarine—it would be going 45 knots. Submerged, the sub could move at only 8.75 knots. The nightmare scenario of an MK 14 taking down an American submarine had not yet become a reality, but it was just a matter of time. With war raging in both the Atlantic and the Pacific, and with submarines one of the few offensive weapons available to the United States in the grim months after Pearl Harbor, the Navy would send its underwater fleet out with the MK 14, despite its defects—defects so dangerous that both Britain and Germany had already pulled their own versions of the magnetic-detonator torpedo out of service as Jim Abele and his crew practiced with the weapon at Newport.

On May 7, 1942, Jim put the *Grunion* through its toughest diving test, taking her down 315 feet to see if her steel plates could withstand the crushing pressure at that depth. With each fathom beyond

200 feet, Jim stared at the depth-pressure gauge, ready to take her back up at the first hint of metallic groans and squeals, the pop of rivets, or the hiss of seawater surging through a sudden leak. The *Grunion* passed its "Deep Submergence Test" easily. She was ready for her first wartime mission.

Only one man on the *Grunion* had ever seen combat. Chief master machinist's mate Danny Cullinane, a "sailor's sailor," was born in County Cork, Ireland, in 1895. He was what the Irish called a "tourist baby," as his parents were American citizens visiting the Emerald Isle. He was raised in Maine and was in Boston in August 1914 when World War I erupted. A tough, gregarious, and charismatic nineteen-year-old, he could easily have settled down in Boston, but his desire for adventure drove him in another direction.

Danny got on an England-bound freighter and enlisted in the British cavalry as soon as the ship docked. Until 1916 he fought in the Horse Brigade, on the Western Front. Under murky circumstances that he never revealed, "there was action inaugurated to return him to the United States,"[4] and Cullinane was honorably discharged late that year and returned to Boston.

With America's entry into the conflict in April 1917, Cullinane, who was working as a teamster, enlisted in the Twenty-third Marine Regiment of the American Expeditionary Force (AEF), and was soon headed back to the horrors of the Western Front. Although his unit was assigned to the Second U.S. Army Division, Cullinane averred, "I was *always* a Marine." Wounded three times and nearly killed by a German mustard-gas attack, Cullinane fought in several of the war's bloodiest battles, including Chateau Thierry. A newspaperman described him as "a real fighting man. Five foot eleven inches tall, he packed 175 pounds onto his rugged frame. His hair was dark brown and the blue eyes which were deep beneath bushy brows were at the same time kindly and firm."[5]

After recovering from his wounds at a Boston hospital, Danny Cullinane was discharged from the U.S. Army on August 13, 1919. Eight days after his discharge, he strode into the nearby Charlestown Naval Yard and enlisted for a two-year hitch in the Navy. He re-upped in 1921 and requested a transfer to the submarine fleet, the most dangerous branch of the U.S. Navy. He had found his calling. On May 20, 1921, he was assigned to the *R-8* for four years.

Cullinane served in the Navy for sixteen years, becoming a master machinist's mate. Officers and seamen alike depended upon Cullinane's calm demeanor in emergencies, his resourcefulness, and his good-natured toughness. In 1932 he married; he and his bride, Genevieve, would have three children—John, Lois, and Norma.

In 1934 Cullinane found himself in the Naval Hospital in Portsmouth, suffering from chronic bronchitis. He was transferred to the submarine USS *R-4*, but—feeling that he had served long enough at sea and hoping to land a shipyard job—he applied for and was granted reassignment to Sub Fleet Naval Reserve. Shortly afterward he was released from active duty and soon found work at the Electric Boat Company, in Groton, Connecticut, as a master mechanic and foreman—his intimate knowledge of submarines making him an invaluable employee. Cullinane was employed there, working on the construction of the USS *Grunion*, when the Japanese struck Pearl Harbor on December 7, 1941.

Sitting by as his country went to war again was simply not in Danny Cullinane's make-up. Despite his family's objections he re-enlisted on April 11, 1942, the day the *Grunion* was launched; and his request to serve aboard the sub he had helped build was granted. Long before he was assigned to the *Grunion*, Danny Cullinane knew Jim's reputation as a skilled, fair skipper, cool under pressure. Jim Abele now had "the best submariner in the Navy aboard the *Grunion*."[6] The war-hardened Cullinane could help prepare "first-timers" aboard the sub for combat. A former colleague said of him, "He was probably the most widely known sailor in the Navy…he'd had many experiences. He was a real 'pig boat' man, all right."[7]

Submariners wanted to serve on Jim Abele's boat. A waiting list took shape as soon as word went out that he had been given command of the state-of-the-art *Grunion*. Nineteen-year-old torpedoman's mate third class Carmine Anthony Parziale, a gifted trumpeter who dreamed of playing professionally after the war, was thrilled to be assigned to the *Grunion*. Carmine was born in Weedville, Pennsylvania, on April 11, 1921, to farmer and coal miner Ralph Parziale and his wife Louise Cimenari. His father died three years later from black lung disease, leaving Carmine's mother with the farm and nine children. Though local authorities expressed qualms that the widow could both run a farm and raise so many children alone, Louise Parziale was determined that no one would break up her family. With her sons and daughters pitching in, Louise held it all together somehow, keeping the crops viable, tending cows and chickens, and selling vegetables and home-made cheeses. A resourceful woman, she even saved enough money to invest in rental properties, despite the Great Depression.

While times were hard, Weedville was a small town where everyone knew each other and tended to look out for each other, a town where no one locked their doors. Carmine grew up hunting and fishing—both pursuits more a necessity than a sport for struggling Depression families—and playing baseball when he could. A personable youth who enjoyed teasing his mother and eight siblings, the self-taught trumpet player organized his own small orchestra, "The Merry Makers," who played regularly in local night spots.

In his teens, Carmine, eager to escape the prospect of a hardscrabble life in the local coal shafts and to see something of the world beyond Weedville, decided to join the Navy and then try for a career as a professional musician. When he graduated from Weedville High School in June 1940 at age nineteen, he enlisted at the Navy Recruiting Station in Pittsburgh, Pennsylvania, for a six-year stint and was transferred to the Navy Training Station, in Newport, Rhode Island, for recruit training. Upon its completion in August, he was assigned to the submarine USS *Barracuda* (SS-163) at the Navy Yard in Portsmouth, New Hampshire. Carmine was assigned in December 1941 to Torpedo School at the Naval Torpedo Station Newport, Rhode Island, where his prowess with his trumpet earned him a spot in the U.S. Naval band. He performed with his fellow musicians for President Franklin D. Roosevelt.

His request to serve on the *Grunion* granted in April 1942, Carmine, a torpedoman's mate third class, joined the crew of the submarine for her commissioning on April 11, 1942—his twenty-first birthday.

On a surprise furlough home that spring of 1942, Carmine told his sister Faye how excited he was to be heading out aboard a brand new submarine on his first wartime patrol and how thrilled he was to be serving under Lieutenant Commander Abele. To a friend, though, Carmine confided something else—"he just knew that this would be his last time home." To a cousin, the young torpedoman said, "I probably won't be back."[8]

Knowing that the *Grunion*'s departure for war was imminent in the spring of 1942, Carmine sent his prized trumpet home to his brother.

One of Carmine Parziale's new shipmates, twenty-five-year-old motor machinist's mate Sylvester J. Kennedy, "Sy" or "Ken" to his friends, had recently become engaged to a stunning young woman named Evelyn Switzer. Born on February 11, 1917, in Flushing, Long Island, New York, he grew up with a deep love of the ocean. His classmate and best friend, Andy Juettner, described Sy as "kind and generous, a very down to earth type of guy." Sy was the best man at Andy's wedding and the godfather of Andy's firstborn son and wanted the same for himself and Evelyn, but "because his parents didn't approve of this engagement, the couple thought it would be best to wait until the war was over so that his parents could get to know her better."

After his graduation from the Hemphill Diesel School, in Manhattan, where he became a skilled diesel machinist, Sy worked in and around New York City for a time, but he had something else in mind for the future. He enlisted in the Naval Reserve on August 19, 1941, at the Naval recruiting station in New York City. Because of his education and experience, he was rated fireman first class and was immediately assigned to active duty at the Newport Naval Training Station and then finished submarine training at New London on March 9, 1942. Assigned to the *Grunion*, he joined the crew for the submarine's commissioning on April 11, 1942. The little time Sy had on furlough that spring he spent with Evelyn, who was working in Manhattan. On June 1, 1942, he was appointed motor machinist's mate second class. Sy assured his fiancée that she need not worry about him because "I'm on Jim Abele's boat."[9] Many of the *Grunion*'s officers and crewmen thought that Sy and Evy looked like a pair of movie stars.

Among the officers commanding Sylvester, Parziale, Cullinane, and the rest of the *Grunion*'s crew was twenty-six-year-old Lieutenant William Gregory "Billie" Kornahrens, a U.S. Naval Academy graduate, Class of 1939. Kornahrens was born in Brooklyn, New York, in February 1916, and grew up in Auburn, Maine, a gifted student and athlete. He began his post-Annapolis career aboard the light cruiser USS *Trenton*.

Like Jim Abele, Billie Kornahrens had seen a lot of the world in the "black-shoe" surface Navy. While the *Trenton* was stationed in

Lisbon Harbor in Portugal in 1940, the ambitious young officer met Trudie Tripp, who had recently arrived there as secretary to Herbert Pell, the American ambassador to Portugal. By the time she returned to the United States in late March 1941, she and Billie had fallen in love and planned to get married. Billie was also headed back across the Atlantic because he had been accepted for submarine officer training. He completed the grueling course at the submarine base in New London, Connecticut, in June, 1941, and was assigned to the USS *O-6* (*SS-67*). On November 16, 1941, he and Trudie were married.

Kornahrens was delighted when his request to serve under Jim Abele as the *Grunion*'s communications officer was granted early in 1942. Trudie Kornahrens and Kay Abele soon became good friends. Trudie learned she was pregnant in April, and Billie was relieved to know that Kay, his senior officer's wife, would look after his wife when the sub headed out to war.

For twenty-three-year-old Jack Pancoast, a motor machinist's mate second class on the *Grunion*, there was no similar sense of relief that he had someone to watch out for his wife and newborn son. A Pennsylvania native, he had served aboard the submarine USS *S-41* in the Philippines from June 1939 to September 1942, and in Manila he had married a gorgeous young Filipina named Julia Zulueta. She gave birth to John (Jack), Jr., in June 1940. On September 19, 1941, Pancoast received orders to report to submarine school in New London. He planned to send for Julia and young Jack as soon as he knew where his next posting would be.

The attack on Pearl Harbor and the massive Japanese invasion of the Philippines in late December 1941 stranded Julia and her son in Manila, and Pancoast was consumed with worry about what would happen to a Filipina with a blond, blue-eyed American child once Manila fell, as it did in January 1942. Assigned to the *Grunion* that spring, all he could do was hope that Julia and their boy might somehow elude the Japanese.

Twenty-four-year-old Cornelius Paul, assigned to the sub as Jim Abele's steward, was an African-American who had joined the Navy to get away from the Jim Crow racism of his hometown, Birmingham, Alabama. In the Navy he had encountered rank prejudice from officers and seamen alike aboard the battleship *Texas* and requested a transfer in January 1942 from the Navy to the Army so that he could serve in the Colored Division. His petition was denied on the grounds that "it has not been the practice of the [Navy] to approve requests for discharge for enlisted service in another branch of the armed forces."[10]

But the Navy did remove him from the *Texas* and reassign him—first to the submarine *Growler* and then, on April 11, to the *Grunion*. Disconsolate, Paul went AWOL from the sub on April 21. He was apprehended roughly two weeks later, brought back to New London in handcuffs, and turned over to Jim Abele. Jim's options ranged from throwing Paul into the brig to await a full-blown court martial and jail sentence to busting him in rank but still allowing him to serve. Jim chose the latter, in keeping with the tough but flexible attitude of the submarine fleet's brown-shoe officers—compared to the harsher tone of the black-shoe surface Navy. Paul was to remain aboard the *Grunion*, but with the knowledge that if he tried to bolt again, or broke any shipboard rules, his skipper would not be so lenient.

As for the commander who had given the frustrated African-American mess mate a break, Jim Abele was not in the image of the rakish Hollywood submarine skipper, later personified by Clark Gable and Burt Lancaster in the classic World War II film *Run Silent, Run Deep*. The thirty-eight-year-old Abele stood five feet ten inches and weighed only 140 pounds, and because of his prominent nose and receding hairline, Kay teased that he should never have his photo taken without his officer's cap on and should always be photographed from the front—never in profile.

What inspired his men's confidence was Lieutenant Commander Abele's proven track record, his unquestioned physical toughness—despite his slight build—and his unruffled demeanor. He rarely raised his voice, rarely if ever cursed, and was always cool in a crisis. His blood pressure ran a calm 110 over 62.

On the sun-splashed afternoon of May 24, Jim and Kay treated their sons to Sunday lunch at the New London, Connecticut, Naval Officers Club. Nothing seemed out of the ordinary that Sunday, even though America had been at war since the Japanese attack on Pearl Harbor some six months ago. As always on weekends, the dining room was set up with white-linen tablecloths, buffed silverware, and glistening china from the Far East. Brad Abele later remembered that the family sat by a window overlooking the Thames River, where the boys could see their father's submarine in its pen.

Around 4 p.m. that Sunday, Jim walked his family to their second-hand blue Chevy sedan and told them that he had to remain at the base for a few more hours to do some "important work"[11] on the *Grunion*.

The telephone jangled that night at the Abeles' home. Kay picked up and heard a sobbing Doris Welch—wife of *Grunion* crewman Donald Welch—on the other end. She had just seen the *Grunion* heading down the Thames and out to sea. Kay calmed Doris down, hung up the phone, and then got Bruce, Brad, and John ready for bed. She decided to wait until morning to tell the boys that their father would be gone for a long time.

As the Grunion slipped into Long Island Sound, a long, dangerous voyage lay ahead. Fleet Command had ordered Jim Abele to take his sub to Pearl Harbor.

CHAPTER FIVE

BATTLE STATIONS

———◆◆◆———

When Kay explained to the boys that their father had been ordered out to sea, they assumed the *Grunion* would return in a few months—though Bruce and Brad were old enough to know that Jim was headed "into the thick of things."[1] The next day Kay received a handwritten note from Jim, the missive dated May 24, 1942. Jim wrote,

> My dear Kay,
>   Just a note to say we are on our way. Sorry I couldn't give you more definite information…
>   Love to you and the boys, Jim[2]

Traveling down the Atlantic Coast into the Caribbean, Jim and his crew got their first taste of the real-life cat-and-mouse game of a sub on wartime patrol. German U-boats prowled the waters off America's eastern and southern coasts. Running on the surface, Jim and his crew in the conning tower were constantly alert for any hint of a Nazi sub, as well as for heavily armed German freighters making the dangerous run to and from the resource-rich nations of Latin America. Below decks, the *Grunion*'s sonar operators listened for any "pings" that could indicate another sub or any Nazi vessel.

The *Grunion* briefly stalked and pursued several suspicious freighters on May 25 and 26, but they eluded the sub by disappearing into fogbanks. Jim's orders to proceed to Pearl Harbor "with all possible haste"[3] stopped him from giving longer chase.

At 12:30 a.m. on May 27, 1942, Cornelius Paul awakened Jim Abele to tell him that a suspicious ship had been sighted some 7,000 yards off the *Grunion*'s port bow. Jim ordered "general quarters" and climbed the steel ladder leading up a narrow passageway from the control room to the conning tower. The distant vessel appeared to be making a run away from the *Grunion* on a zigzag course, a typical maneuver to evade submarines. Jim was convinced the potential target was a Nazi tender for refueling U-boats; he gave the order to load the forward torpedo tubes. Jim closed the distance between the sub and the surface ship to 2,000 yards. Then he ordered the conning tower cleared and took the *Grunion* down to periscope depth. The suspicious vessel, however, had disappeared by the time the #1 periscope was raised. Jim broke off the chase, radioed fleet command with his report, and returned on course for Pearl Harbor.

The *Grunion* reached the Caribbean on May 29, running on the surface by night, submerged by day because of reports of U-boats in the area—one of which had just torpedoed and sunk the U.S. Army transport ship (USAT) *Jack*. At 1:55 p.m. on May 31, rough seas roiled above the sub as Jim took her to periscope depth. He could barely discern anything except towering green waves and was about to give the "down scope" order when he spotted something bobbing in the distance off the *Grunion*'s starboard bow. His cap turned backwards, he pressed his eyes tight against the scope. A lifeboat's prow appeared for an instant above a wave, then dipped out of sight.

Jim had to decide quickly. He had been ordered to take the *Grunion* to Pearl Harbor without exposing her to "undue risk."[4] Surfacing in a storm in waters where a U-boat was operating constituted extreme risk. Jim decided to take his chances and gave the order to "take her up" and "turn hard starboard."[5]

The *Grunion* broke the surface and pushed hard against the waves, her diesel engines straining. On the conning-tower bridge, Jim, protected against the wind and water by his one-piece oilskin "weather suit," peered through his binoculars and spied the lifeboat—so overloaded with men that the craft's gunwales barely broke the surface.

For nearly an hour, the *Grunion* churned toward the lifeboat. As the sub lurched within fifty yards of it, the painted words "USAT *Jack*" appeared for an instant on the lifeboat's prow. Then the nearly flooded craft dipped lower in the water. The shouting men in the lifeboat did not have much time. If the waves swamped the craft, the survivors of the torpedoed *Jack* had no chance.

Jim created a backwash with the diesel engines to slow the sub down as it came within thirty feet of the lifeboat, and Danny Cullinane strapped a life vest on, tied one end of a grappling hook's 50-foot rope line to the *Grunion*'s deck gun, and heaved the hook into the heavy winds at the lifeboat. The hook splashed some ten feet short.

Cullinane pulled the rope back and hurled it a second time. Again it came up short. Reeling the hook back to the sub, he wrapped the hooked end to his wrist and jumped into the water. He turned onto his back and slowly kicked his way to the lifeboat. He then braced himself on the heaving gunwale. One of the survivors unwrapped the hook and fastened it to the slot of an oarlock. Several pairs of arms dragged Cullinane into the boat.

Grunion crewmen began to swivel the deck gun, using it as a makeshift winch to haul the floundering lifeboat foot by torturous foot to the sub. To pull the lifeboat just thirty feet in the huge waves took nearly an hour. Meanwhile, Jim and Lieutenant Billie Kornahrens tensely scanned the surface for any hint of a periscope or a torpedo wake. In the control room, the sonar operator listened for any approaching "pings."

As the *Grunion*'s sailors hauled sixteen exhausted, dehydrated men from the lifeboat and guided them below, Jim was startled to see the familiar face of childhood friend and first cousin George F. Drew. The skipper rushed from the tower to greet Drew, the first engineer of the *Jack*. Drew told him that he and the other men in the lifeboat had been adrift for nearly three days and that thirteen other crewmen had clambered onto two life rafts as the transport sank. Once Jim made sure the survivors were safely inside the sub, he took the *Grunion* to periscope depth and changed course to reach the site where the U-boat had dispatched the *Jack*. He found nothing but debris and called off the search after two hours. At midnight he brought the sub about and resumed course for the Panama Canal.

The *Grunion* dropped off its unexpected passengers at the Naval base at Coco Solo, Panama, in early June, then proceeded through the canal en route to Pearl Harbor. Jim drilled the crew hard, practicing every variation of dive, preparing his men for the emotional and physical hell of Japanese depth-charge attacks, loading and unloading the torpedo tubes fore and aft, and staging mock surface attacks.

On June 20, 1942, the *Grunion* sailed into Pearl Harbor. The charred, twisted wreckage of Battleship Row and the dense oil slick clotting the turquoise waters testified to the carnage of December 7, 1941.

Jim guided the *Grunion* to Berth 10 in the Pacific Fleet's submarine pen, eager to speak with several friends and skippers who had already returned from their first patrol against the Japanese, and to dash off a telegram to Kay and the boys telling them how much he missed them.

The *Grunion*'s first patrol was to unfold at a trying time for the Navy. In his book *Goodbye Darkness: A Memoir of the Pacific War*, Marine veteran William Manchester wrote,

> Ever since Pearl Harbor, the Japanese forces had been on a string of unbroken victories and had by that time gained control over not only an enormous sea area but also over a land area larger than that acquired by Nazi forces at the height of their successes. The record of conquest was phenomenal. Within days after the attack on Pearl Harbor, Japan had swallowed up Guam, Indochina and Thailand; she had sunk the only major allied warships west of Midway—the British leviathans *Prince of Wales* and *Repulse*. By Christmas she had taken Wake and Hong Kong. Within two months she had occupied Manila, Singapore and Malaya; in February at Java Sea she sank 10 allied ships; in March the Allies lost Java and Burma and Japanese armies were in the Owen Stanley Mountains of New Guinea with the coast of Australia almost in sight.
>
> Japan had driven the British fleet from the Indian Ocean and the Pacific; she had sunk almost every American battleship in the Pacific Fleet; and at the end of April

Japan had lost nothing bigger than a destroyer. In May
1942, Corregidor surrendered and the Philippines fell;
Japan invaded the Solomons. She had swallowed Southeast Asia and the islands of the South Pacific; she had
crushed all allied strength in the western ocean.

Our battleship Navy lay at the bottom of Pearl Harbor
and it was a "battleship war" that had been contemplated
by the top Navy strategic planners in Washington. Indeed,
in the master strategic plan the submarine and air arms
of the Navy had been relegated to the relatively minor
roles of scouting for the battleships.[6]

May 1942 was perhaps the low point for the allies in World War II.
Along with the success of the Japanese war effort, Nazi Germany
had conquered most of Europe, and German U-boats had sunk
almost 500 ships right off the North American coast.

Shortly after docking in Pearl Harbor, Jim reported to Submarine Fleet Commander Admiral Robert English and was handed an
official commendation for "the U.S.S. *Grunion*'s gallant rescue of
the survivors of the U.S.A.T. *Jack*."[7] English praised Jim's seamanship and his crew's performance under tough conditions. Singled
out for additional praise was Danny Cullinane.

Kay Abele and the boys learned of the rescue on June 27, when
a letter arrived on from George Drew. He wrote,

Dear Kay,

While I cannot provide the particulars [because of
wartime censorship] I want you and your sons to know
that Jim risked his life to rescue me and 15 others a few
weeks back. I have never been so happy to see anyone as

Jim under the circumstances. Not that you don't already know, but your husband is just the man in a pinch....

My love to you and the boys,
Cousin George[8]

A JOKE In Honolulu the crew of the *Grunion* received ten days of top-secret training along with the crews of the subs *Gato*, *Growler*, *Triton*, *Tuna*, *Trigger*, and *Finback*. Although many of the exercises several miles off Honolulu were torpedo drills, the crews loaded and fired the "old fish," not the expensive new MK 14 torpedoes.

Jim likely spoke at length about the MK 14 with two skippers who were old friends—his Annapolis classmate Lieutenant Commander Howard Gilmore of the *Growler*, and Lieutenant Commander Chuck Kirkpatrick of the *Triton*—and was disturbed by their take on the weapon. Their blunt comments no doubt mirrored those of fellow submariner Clay Blair, who would write that "by the end of March [1942] almost every Pearl Harbor submariner who had fired a torpedo in anger believed that the MK 14 'Exploder' was defective."[9]

Gilmore and Kirkpatrick had filed complaints about the MK 14 with Admirals Thomas Withers, Robert H. English, Allan R. McCann, and Charles W. Styer, but they refused to listen to the skippers' suggestions and criticisms. Torpedo expert Anthony Newpower writes in *Iron Men and Tin Fish*, "With so few patrols in the books, senior commanders hesitated to believe what they heard from [Lieutenant Commander Tyrell D.] Jacobs" and other skippers. Newpower adds, "Jacobs's superiors thinly masked their displeasure with his actions" and assigned him to transport duty.[10] With the admirals insisting that any problems were caused by poor marksmanship by undertrained crews, skippers understood that they were to keep their mouths shut and use the costly torpedoes sparingly.

Art Taylor, the skipper of the USS *Haddock*, voiced the frustration of submariners with the Navy brass in a poem widely circulated throughout the fleet:

Squat Div One

[derisive term for the sub fleet's "desk jockeys"]
They're on their duff from morn til nite;
They're never wrong they're always right;
To hear them talk they're in the fight;
Oh yeah?
A boat comes in off a patrol,
The skipper tallies up his toll
And writes it up for all concerned.
He feels right proud of the job he's done,
But the staffies say he should of used his gun!
Three fish for a ship of two score ton?
Outrageous! He should have used but one!
A tanker sunk in smoke and flame—
But still he's wide open to blame.
His fish were set for twenty right—
That proves he didn't want to fight!
Oh Yeah?
The freighter he sunk settled by the stern
With depth set right she'd split in two!
So tell me what is the skipper to do?
He's on the spot and doing his best
But that's not enough by the acid test.
The staff must analyze his case
And pick it apart to save their face.
Just because you sink some ships
Doesn't mean you win the chips—

You've got to do it according to Plan;
Otherwise you're in the pan!
So here's to the staff with work so tough
In writing their endorsements guff—
Whether the war is lost or won
Depends entirely on Squat Div One.
Oh Yeah?

The verse enraged Admiral English,[11] who, according to naval historian Anthony Newpower, felt that "culpability for the attack failures lay with the men doing the attacking not their weapon."[12]

Jim probably discussed the MK 14's problems with Gilmore, the *Growler's* skipper. The hope was that the Exploder's defects had been addressed by its designers in Newport and that he and Jim were being sent out to test a revamped MK 14 in combat. But it did not instill confidence when Fleet Command informed them that because of the cost of the allegedly improved Exploders, all "live-fire submarine exercises" off Hawaii would use 1930s-vintage torpedoes. Clay Blair, who served aboard the USS *Guardfish* and became a well-known journalist and historian after the war, pointed out, "At the very least, Sub Command could have expended a few days conducting live tests against an expendable target with the torpedoes we were about to go out with—shortage or no shortage."[13]

English's directive that crews were to fire only two torpedoes rather than the standard three was both galling and dangerous. Every experienced submariner knew that firing torpedoes in a "3-spread" was crucial to compensate for any small errors in the firing angle.

Jim received orders to paint the *Grunion* black on June 23, 1942; at that time every American submarine went out on patrol painted black and with no recognition markings of any kind. As Japanese subs were also painted black and as Radio IFF (Identification, Friend or Foe) gear was not yet available, surfaced subs were vulnerable not only to enemy aircraft but their own. On June 28, 1942, the *Grunion* and the *Gato* received orders to depart Pearl Harbor for the Navy base at Dutch Harbor, Alaska, where they would join Task Force 8, North Pacific Force. The fleet commander instructed Jim to patrol the waters between Alaska's Aleutian Islands and Japan. Japanese troops had seized and occupied the islands of Kiska and Attu, on the western tip of the Aleutians, earlier that month, and Japanese warships and supply ships traveled along that route.

Most Americans had no idea the enemy was already on American soil. The U.S. Naval counteroffensive in the Aleutians was slow to get started and equally slow to gain momentum; nevertheless, the action comprised America's first retaliatory campaign in the Pacific, preceding the Guadalcanal campaign (which began August 1942) by two months. A total of seven fleet boats, including the *Grunion*, headed to the Aleutian theater along with nine older, smaller S-type submarines (one of which, the *S-31*, Jim had previously commanded).

On June 30, 1942, the *Grunion* pulled away from the Pearl Harbor sub pens and began the long voyage to its "assigned area westward of Attu Island on routes between the Aleutians and the Japanese Empire."[14] In the storage rack in the fore and aft torpedo rooms sat twenty-four MK 14s. Although Jim had been ordered to "use torpedoes judiciously rather than aggressively,"[15] he intended for the *Grunion* to go on the offensive. His last stop before the Aleutians was for refueling at Midway Island—the site of the stunning Navy victory that had sent the cream of Japan's aircraft carrier fleet to the bottom of the ocean just twenty-four days earlier. The crew of the *Grunion* headed for the Bering Sea cheered by the sense that the tide of the war might be turning in America's favor.

CHAPTER SIX

THE ENEMY AWAITING THEM

———◆◆◆———

Despite the victory at Midway, the crew and officers of the *Grunion* knew that the Japanese were still a formidable enemy. And the seas where they would meet that enemy were themselves a life-threatening danger to the submariners. As Japanese Captain Seiichi Aiura, already operating near the Aleutians, would write, the waters there "have the worst weather in the world…dense fog and heavy weather harass every ship no matter the time of year."[1] Seiichi's vessel, the freighter *Kano Maru*, had been part of Admiral Yamamoto's fleet at the Battle of Midway and had been reassigned to the Aleutians after the debacle.

Also already in the Aleutians was Japanese Sub Chaser Squadron 13, including *CH-25*, *-26*, and *-27*. Japanese Commander Shinoda Isamu, skipper of the *CH-27*, noted the double danger—from the enemy and from the deadly weather: "All of our ships must suffer a submarine threat throughout this 'Devil Sea,' and in the vicinity of the islands there exists the additional threat from aircraft. Furthermore, once a ship sinks and one is thrown into this North Sea even in summer one cannot survive more than a few minutes."[2]

Shinoda's career was a remarkable mirror image of Jim Abele's. The Japanese commander, born just a year after Jim, had been ordered to take command of the sleek, brand-new sub chaser *CH-27* at the Kure shipyard in early December 1941, at just about the same time Jim Abele was appointed skipper of the spanking new USS *Grunion*. Like Jim, Shinoda had been at sea for much of his adult life. And his career in the Imperial Navy had followed a path as unconventional as Jim's in the U.S. Navy. Just like Jim, Shinoda had become a naval officer by an indirect route that showed his resourcefulness and refusal to give up when circumstances did not favor his ambitions.

Shinoda Isamu, a short, muscular man with dense dark hair and a formal, commanding demeanor at sea but a cheerful, frank, and friendly countenance off duty, was born in Gifu City, Japan, the sixth of eight children. His family was well-off, descended from aristocratic landowners. Shinoda's hometown lay almost directly in Japan's center, a city of more than 400,000 located on the fertile plains above the Nagara River, which flowed to the Sea of Japan, only some thirty miles distant, and visible from atop Mount Kinka, which Shinoda and other local boys climbed. Shinoda loved the water, learned to fish and handle small boats in the river, and—like young Jim Abele a world away—set his sights on a naval career.

He graduated first in his Gifu City High School class and promptly applied to the Imperial Naval Academy. Shinoda achieved a high score on the entrance exam and was athletic, but all Imperial

Naval Academy candidates had to stand five feet, six inches. Shinoda was just under the requirement.

Just like Jim, Shinoda refused to surrender his dream of commanding a ship. In an echo of Jim Abele's unconventional choice to get a place at the Naval Academy by first enlisting in the Navy, Shinoda Isamu decided to apply to merchant seaman school, where cadets embarked on a grueling academic curriculum and physical regimen that led to skippering vessels as diverse as coastal freighters and luxury passenger liners; and in times of war, the best of them could be chosen to command warships—regardless of height.

Accepted by the Kobe Nautical College (today, Kobe University), Shinoda distinguished himself as one of the most promising cadets and was selected to also train as a naval auxiliary officer at the Imperial Navy Gunnery School. His status as an auxiliary officer guaranteed that if called up for duty he was slated for an officer's rank commensurate with what he earned in the merchant marine.

By 1931, the twenty-six-year-old Shinoda was serving as 3rd officer and chief navigator on the international trading liner *Taketoyo Maru*, voyaging all over the globe. By just a decade later, his superior navigational and command skills had earned him his captain's qualification. The promotion jumped him into line to take the helm of a combat vessel. While proud to serve his nation, Shinoda, unlike many of his countrymen, did not welcome the prospect of war. He was married, the father of four children (three of whom had survived), and he did not believe that Japan had the necessary resources to embark on a vast war of conquest in the Pacific.

In June 1941, he was commissioned an auxiliary ensign in the Imperial Navy. His first berth was as Chief Navigator and Division Officer of the auxiliary gunship *Katori Maru*. He was aboard when the news of the attack on Pearl Harbor came and sent jubilation racing through his fellow officers and crew. At home, his eldest son Kazuo remembers,

> At the day when the Pacific war began, I was [in] second grade of Kinomoto national elementary school. I still remember that morning. The teacher told us that Japan had begun the war against the United States and England, attacked Pearl Harbor before the dawn and sank the British battleship *Prince of Wales* and the [British battle cruiser *Repulse*] in the southern sea. He explained by drawing figures on the blackboard and added that President Roosevelt and Prime Minister Churchill were very evil men.[3]

After the attack, Shinoda received orders to report to the Yokosuka Navy District and take command of a fast new sub chaser, *CH-27*. It was just under 168 feet long, was powered by two powerful diesel engines, and boasted a 3-inch deck gun, two 13 mm machine guns, and a 25 mm antiaircraft gun. It also carried an innovative depth-charge thrower, two depth-charge rails, and Japan's latest sonar, radar, and hydrophone technology to detect enemy subs below the surface.

As most Japanese children in January 1942 did, Kazuo had in his bedroom "a map of Southeast Asia...and I pasted small hinomaru flags [the famed 'Rising Sun' battle flag] where Japanese forces occupied new territories."[4] Shinoda spotted the map and told his son he would soon be pasting more flags, including in Hong Kong and Manila. Later, however, Kazuo overheard his father saying to his mother that Japan could not win a protracted war against the United States.

From February to May 1942, Shinoda readied the *CH-27* for combat, taking the ship through maneuvers and depth-charge and gunnery drills in Tokyo Bay and at Saeki Navy Base, at Kyushu. Rumors of a large-scale naval operation swirled throughout the fleet. Shinoda had no inkling just how ambitious the plan that Admiral Isoruku Yamamoto, the mastermind of the Pearl Harbor attack, had devised was.

Yamamoto, Commander in Chief of the Combined Japanese Fleet, had argued for months to the Imperial General Staff for the occupation of Midway, an American atoll 1,100 miles northwest of Pearl Harbor and a key naval base. He hoped to lure the U.S. Pacific Fleet—including its aircraft carriers—to the outpost's aid and into a battle in which the Japanese Combined Fleet, with far more firepower and carrier-based aircraft, would demolish the Americans. Yamamoto asserted that gutting the American fleet might force the United States to accept a negotiated peace.

In the first week of April 1942, Japan's Naval General Staff, most of whom believed that occupying Midway would prove useless if the U.S. Pacific Fleet did not respond, debated Yamamoto's plan. Yamamoto won the debate with his conviction that the American carriers and screening ships would rush to the atoll's aid. On April 5, 1942, his bold plan was approved. He quickly made a key addition to the massive operation: an air attack on the small, remote American base at Dutch Harbor at Unalaska, followed by the invasion and occupation of Attu and Kiska Islands, at the western edge of the Aleutian chain. Yamamoto's feint in force toward Alaska was intended not only to peel away American submarines from Pearl Harbor to the Aleutians, but also to land a psychological blow, as the Aleutians were part of Alaska and therefore actual American soil.

If Yamamoto's plan succeeded in destroying or crippling the U.S. Pacific Fleet, the occupation of Midway, Attu, and Kiska would create a formidable barrier to any American actions in the Pacific even if America refused to negotiate. Japan's Imperial General Headquarters issued Navy Order No. 18 on May 5, 1942, ordering

Yamamoto to work with the Army to finalize preparations and logistics for the sprawling offensive against the American Navy, Midway, and the western Aleutians.

On May 17, 1942, exactly a week before Kay and the boys last saw Jim at the Naval Officers Club in Groton, Connecticut, Shinoda Isamu received orders to join a flotilla of destroyers, cargo ships, and troop transports heading from northern Japan to the Aleutian Islands. Shinoda was part of Sub Chaser Squadron 13. At the Kure dock the next morning, he gave his wife Chiyo a formal hug and kissed each of his children except for Kazuo, who could not be excused from examinations at his school. Shinoda stepped back and looked at Chiyo. "I entrust our children to you," he said.[5]

He turned and climbed down a rope ladder into the waiting launch. Sitting in the craft's bow, he watched his family until he reached the *CH-27*. Chiyo saw him raise his hand and wave. Then he pulled himself onto a swaying gangplank several feet above the oily water, walked up to the gunwales, and disappeared from his family's sight.

Sakae Nakano, a seventeen-year-old radio operator on the *CH-27*, handed Commander Shinoda a message as soon he stepped into the bridge's control room. The sub chaser was ordered to get underway at 10 a.m.

Moored a short distance from Shinoda's sub chaser, the *Kano Maru*, an 8,752-ton freighter carrying munitions and provisions, pulled at its thick anchor chain. The cargo ship's captain, Seiichi Aiura, had already said good-bye to his wife and five children; the forty-year-old officer, a career maritime man like Shinoda Isamu, had orders to set out with the huge fleet bound for Midway.

Neither Seiichi nor Shinoda knew that just three weeks later Japan would be reeling from a spectacular defeat at the Battle of Midway. Even less could they have guessed the course of events that would bring their vessels back into proximity with each other again in the Bering Sea—and into contact with Jim Abele's *Grunion*. Of the three ships—and the three captains—only one would survive the Aleutians.

——————◦◦◦——————

On July 15, 1942, the *Grunion* lurked near the mouth of Kiska Harbor as Japanese Sub Chaser Squadron 13—including *CH-25*, *CH-26*, and Shinoda's *CH-27*—swept the waters for American subs. Jim and his men readied their torpedoes, the sub's silent course close to the island's shore and just outside Squadron 13's sweep area. Jim peered through the #2 scope in the control room, waiting for the sub chasers to come within 4,000 feet.

The *Grunion* had twenty-one torpedoes left. Five days earlier, a Japanese destroyer had picked up the sub on sonar thirty-five miles northwest of Kiska and steamed after her. Jim had fired three torpedoes from the aft tubes in a defensive action and taken the sub down 300 feet. For the next hour, the crew had sweated out a depth-charge attack before the destroyer gave up. Two of the *Grunion*'s torpedoes had apparently missed the destoyer. The third ran past and under the vessel's hull and exploded just ten yards astern of it.

Now, as the trio of sub chasers came into the periscope's cross-hairs at 4,000 feet, Jim again gave the order to "fire torpedoes."

Matsushima Minoru, the commander of *Sub Chaser 26*, and Horita Kyo, the squadron's chief medical officer, spotted the wakes of six torpedoes "running fast at them."[6] Two torpedoes passed directly beneath the *CH-26*, but the magnetic detonators failed.

CH-25 and *CH-27* were not so lucky. One torpedo exploded directly beneath the hull of *CH-25*, which simply vanished into the sea; *CH-27*, commanded by Shinoda Isamu, exploded from the impact of another torpedo and sank engulfed in flames. There were no survivors from either ship. Matsushima was stunned by the effectiveness of the attack. For Jim and his crew, however, the twin kills had taken six torpedoes, and fewer than half of the "fish" had done the job. The *Grunion* submerged, the *CH-26* fled into the safety of Kiska Harbor, and only an oil slick testified to the lives sent to the bottom of the Bering Sea.

CHAPTER SEVEN

A MYSTERIOUS MESSAGE

———◆—◆—◆———

At 5:47 a.m. on July 30, 1942, Jim trained the *Grunion*'s #1 periscope on a large freighter emerging to the starboard from the
fog a few miles off Kiska Island. He had a decision to make. For
the past week the *Grunion*, the *Growler*, the *Finback*, and the *Trigger*
had all reported a high level of anti-submarine activity off the Aleutians; on July 28, the *Grunion* had fired three torpedoes in a defensive clash with a Japanese destroyer and had endured a depth-charge
attack.

The *Grunion* had radioed a message to Task Force 8 headquarters in Dutch Harbor just over two hours earlier, at 3:35 in the morning of July 30:

> With visibility four hundred yards heard echo ranging
> ships near Sirius Point which dropped numerous depth

charges. Evaded those vessels in hopes of contacting [Japanese] convoy. Now believe vessels were merely assigned protection [of] harbor [Kiska].... Have ten torpedoes forward remaining.[1]

Task Force Command had ordered the *Grunion* and all other subs off Kiska and Attu to return to base at Dutch Harbor. But the *Grunion* did not depart for Dutch Harbor. Possibly she never recieved the message. Or Jim and his crew may have been engaged in heavy action again.

Edward L. Beach, the communications officer on the *Trigger*, reported decoding a second message from the *Grunion* before dawn on July 30—sent by Billie Kornahrens, a good friend of Beach's from the Naval Academy. Task Force Command never received the message, which Beach believed to be the very last communication sent from Jim's boat:

FROM GRUNION X ATTACKED TWO DESTROYERS OFF KISKA HARBOR X NIGHT PERISCOPE SUBMERGED X RESULTS INDEFINITE BELIEVE ONE SANK ONE DAMAGED X MINOR DAMAGE FROM COUNTERATTACK TWO HOUR LATER X ALL TORPEDOES EXPENDED AFT...[2]

According to Beach the message decoded perfectly up to that point—then turned into an unintelligible jumble. The transmission had gone out before dawn of July 30, 1942.

Now the *Grunion* lay submerged in the frigid waters five miles off Kiska Harbor. Every night in the Aleutians was fraught with dangers for the submariners. Lieutenant Commander Jim Abele must have surfaced a few hours earlier to refill the sub's air tanks and recharge her batteries. Unless sonar detected Japanese ships nearby, Jim took the sub up at staggered times every night; one officer and fourteen sailors—four lookouts and the crews of the *Grunion*'s .50-caliber machine gun and 3-inch deck gun—clambered out of the conning tower and foredeck hatches into the cold night in watertight oilskin slickers and caps with fleece-lined ear flaps. The lookouts perched themselves in the bridge's four corners to train their binoculars on the water and sky, scanning for enemy ships and planes. The *Grunion* needed three hours to fully charge her batteries.

Sailors lurched in thick-soled rubber boots along the steel-plated deck, waves slapping against the hull and dousing each man topside. The machine gunners detached their weapon on the conning tower's bridge to take it below decks for a thorough cleaning and replace it with the second machine gun, which they had taken apart, scoured, and reassembled the previous night. Snapping .50-caliber belts into the weapon's chamber in case a plane swooped through any opening in the fogbanks, the gunners silently counted off the long minutes.

Below the tower, the deck-gun crew swabbed the muzzle and put every working part of the cannon through its movements to prevent the salt air from rusting it and ice from jamming the mechanism. Several men chained a case of seventeen-pound antiaircraft shells to the weapon's stanchion in case of attack.

"Each minute on top was sheer hell," Executive Officer Charlie Tate of the *Grunion*'s sister sub *Gato* recalled. "Especially in the Aleutians, because the Arctic skies don't get that dark at night and Japanese seaplanes could dive at you through any break in the cloud cover."[3]

The crew of a submarine feared every moment she lay exposed on the surface as much as they agonized deep under water during enemy depth-charge runs that shook every inch of the sub and promised certain death if one of the "trash-cans" scored a direct hit.

With anxiety tingeing even the most stoic submariners' breaths as depth charges' concussive waves pounded the boat's steel skin, the rancid air that blowers recirculated throughout the sub made every man willing to risk nightly trips to the surface to refill the air tanks.

Since American submarines had orders to break radio silence at random hours after nightfall and the *Grunion*'s radio antenna only worked on the surface, Jim recharged the boat's batteries and sent and received transmissions at the same time. On the night of July 29–30, a coded transmission from Dutch Harbor should have crackled in the earphones of the *Grunion*'s radioman, who then typed it into the translation machine, a printer-sized device that spit out a teletype tape with the translated message. The codes changed daily—sometimes as often as five times a day—to hamstring Japanese cryptologists listening to American radio traffic around the clock.

If the *Grunion* did in fact receive the transmission from Task Force 8, communications officer Lieutenant Billie Kornahrens would have hustled to the ward room to show Jim the decoded communiqué. The message ordered the *Grunion* and five other subs—the *Triton*, the *Trigger*, *S-18*, *S-32*, and *S-33*—operating off Kiska and Attu islands to return to the U.S. base at Dutch Harbor "with all due speed"[4] in advance of a planned American air attack on Kiska.

But it's not 100 percent certain that the *Grunion* received the message. We don't know for certain whether Jim was able to take the orders that the *Grunion* should return to Dutch Harbor into consideration as he peered through the periscope at the single large freighter—all by itself. The *S-33* received the missive at 2:20 a.m. Three of the other boats acknowledged the transmission, but not until several hours later. And the *S-18* did not receive the order until 5:45 a.m. With all of the submarines noting a lot of noise from Japanese radiomen zeroing in on the Americans' radio signals and garbling them, and with stormy weather creating severe radio static, both Dutch Harbor and the subs off the Aleutians had to keep resending messages, and each boat was required to acknowledge all incoming transmissions. In all likelihood, heavy Japanese interference thwarted Lieutenant Kornahrens' attempts to respond, but it's possible that the message never got through to the *Grunion*—like three communications of a very different sort that went out that same day to Jim Abele, one from his wife, and two from his sons.

Kay wrote,

> Dearest Sweetheart, have no doubt that I've toasted your birthday here, and Bruce, Brad, John, and I had a little party for you, with cake and ice cream. Remember that we are with you no matter how distant the miles. Remember that we love you, miss you, and wait for the day you come back to us. . . .

From Bruce's pen came,

> Dear Jim . . . Today we went on an all day picnic with our cousins and played kick the can. Keep em sinking, Japanese, German and Italian. The reason that this letter is short is that we want to save paper for the war drive. . . . Love, Bruce and John

On the back of the same sheet of paper, Brad wrote,

> Dear Jim . . . I caught a perch yesterday, and while I was on the water, I closed my eyes and thought about where you might be on the water with your sub. . . . I can't wait

to go fishing with you again and to go on another ride on the *Grunion*. Keep sinking Jap ships! Love, Brad.[5]

CHAPTER EIGHT

"AS WE WAITED FOR THE END"

———◆◆———

At 8 p.m. on July 29, 1942, the Japanese freighter *Kano Maru* was drifting in dense fog twenty miles from Kiska Harbor. She had lost her sub chaser escort, the *CH-26*, in the mist between Attu and Kiska Islands, and Captain Seiichi Aiura did not dare steer his 8,875-ton ship—packed with medical supplies, sacks of rice, and lumber for the Japanese troops dug in at Kiska—toward the island until visibility improved. The forty-year-old captain, his creased face testifying to his twenty-two years at sea, did not trust his outdated Imperial Navy navigational charts with their 1930s depth readings for McArthur Reef. Until the weather cleared, he could steer nowhere near those hull-splicing volcanic outcrops jutting just beneath the surface off Kiska. No one could last more than a minute in the 34-degree waters around them.

Seiichi also worried about another danger lurking near the harbor. American submarines prowled the waters. He knew that just two weeks earlier one had sunk two sub chasers, the *SC-25* and the *SC-27*, near the harbor in less than a minute in a blinding ball of flame and smoke—though of course he could not know it was the *Grunion* that had been responsible, or that the very same sub would soon be threatening his own ship.

Peering out from the freighter's bridge beneath his dark-blue, black-visored officer's cap, Seiichi searched for any break in the slate-gray fogbank. The 680-foot-long *Kano Maru*, a former passenger liner on the Kobe-Marseilles-New York route, offered submarines an inviting target with her high prow and six-story superstructure. Every second adrift without a sub chaser in sight and with the safety of Kiska Harbor still miles away was an hour of suspense that unnerved every man aboard the *Kano Maru*.

Gaps opened in the fog just after midnight, and Seiichi ordered the helmsman to set an anti-submarine zigzag course of fifteen knots toward the harbor. The freighter's engines surged back on, their rhythmic hum a heartening sound to the anxious crew.

The *Grunion* must have waited beneath the surface from the moment that the sub's two sonar systems picked up the target. The "passive" sonar man, perched in a cubicle in the conning tower, tracked a sound that was "like the slap of a shaving brush in a sink"[1] in his thick, padded earphones. In the control room, just beneath the tower, the "active" sonar man's amplified headset rang with a steady series of pings that allowed him to calculate a bearing and distance for the target.

Counting the slaps with the aid of a metronome, the passive operator calculated the speed of the vessel he was tracking and relayed it to Jim and Executive Officer Millener Thomas, who huddled over the tower's plotting board and waited for the active sonar man in the control room to send up his initial bearings and distance for the target. Then they marked the coordinates on the board with a grease pencil, and Jim called down to the control room, where Quartermaster Elmer Schumann typed the data into the TDC, the torpedo data computer (one of the earliest computers), to calculate the best angle to the target.

Jim must have known already that the target was a big one. With sonar continuing to pick up just one set of heavy propeller screws, he would have ordered Schumann to raise the #1 periscope, gripped the retractable handles, pressed his eyes against the rubber-rimmed lenses, and confirmed that the target, a hulking cargo ship, was plowing westerly toward Kiska—alone.

Jim had a decision to make—weighing the fat and solitary freighter in his sights against the risks (as well as his orders to return to Dutch Harbor, if he had received them). Torpedo explosions would echo to Japanese forces on and around Kiska, but Jim could dive deep and slip away ahead of scrambling destroyers and planes if he took the target down fast. For Jim, sinking enemy vessels trumped all. He chose to strike.

He would have snapped the handles back into their slots, cueing Schumann to lower the scope—then ordered the helmsman to nudge the sub into a prime firing angle of 30 degrees or less from the Japanese cargo ship, taking the *Grunion* from the contact phase to the approach phase of action. The torpedoes needed 450 yards just to arm their warheads, and with any range less than 850 a gamble with the erratic detonators, Jim always placed the *Grunion* 1,000 yards or more from his targets unless fighting a defensive action in which he had no time to plan, only react.

The order to "man battle stations" always sent adrenaline rushing through every officer and crewman. As each wrestled with his nerves to focus on his assigned task, the skipper mapped out an

escape path—just in case. In the cramped conning tower, where the
blinking gauges and dials bathed the fire control team in an eerie
reddish-white glow, the passive sonar man continued to track the
target's course and speed for Jim. He was still detecting just the
single vessel in the wash of heavy screws and the pings. And neither
he nor the active radar man in the control-room was detecting the
higher-pitched pings that would betray the presence of Japanese
sonar. The freighter's skipper had no idea that an American submarine was stalking it for the kill.

The *Grunion* had six "tin fish" loaded in the forward torpedo
tubes, four in the storage racks, and none in the stern. Jim ordered
the torpedo men to "open all outer doors forward" and "stand by for
final bearing." Near 5:45 a.m., Jim gave the order "down periscope."
Seconds later came the command to "fire!"

Two jolts shook the *Grunion*'s 312-foot length as a pair of torpedoes surged from the forward tubes with a teeth-rattling *whoosh*.

After thirty seconds, the passive sonar man would have reported,
"Fish running straight and hot."

All Jim and his crew could do for the next minute was wait and
hope to hear their torpedoes explode against the target.

On the *Kano Maru*, twenty-two-year-old Medical Sublieutenant
Rikimaru Nakagawa stepped from his starboard cabin near 5:45
a.m. and climbed a steel ladder onto the ice-slicked deck. Shivering,
he pulled his fur-lined cap over his closely cropped scalp and almost
over his eyebrows, tugged the flaps close against his ears, and tightened the white woolen scarf and long blue greatcoat on his stocky
frame. He removed his waterproof sealskin gloves for just long
enough to light a Benson & Hedges cigarette from one of the millions of cartons the Japanese Army had seized from the surrender-
ing British troops at Singapore. Bracing himself against the gunwale,
he squinted at the fog.

As he took a deep drag, he reflected on how far away from his medical school studies, from his fiancée, Atsumi, and from his family he now stood. Of all the postings an Imperial Navy officer could pull, "Devil Sea duty" in the Aleutian theater ranked as the worst. "Give it back to the Americans," sailors griped. Still, though homesick and far more frightened than he would ever admit to his shipmates, Rikimaru believed in his nation and his Emperor, and he was determined not to dishonor his family by showing cowardice.

As he turned to look to starboard, one of the whitecaps appeared to be moving toward the freighter. Putting both hands on the gunwale, Rikimaru peered through the icy, stinging mist at the trail of the oncoming torpedo. Another bubbled just a few yards behind the first.

First Sergeant/Signal Master Ahiro Wakisaka, whose short, slight frame belied the fear that his martial-arts prowess and rigid adherence to shipboard discipline evoked from the *Kano Maru*'s crew, stood alongside Captain Seiichi. Ahiro trained his binoculars to the starboard side. Spotting the same two wakes as Rikimaru, Ahiro gaped for a moment as they plowed toward the freighter.

He shouted, "Torpedoes! Starboard fore!"[2]

Seiichi immediately ordered, "Full power and full turn starboard!"

The *Kano Maru* shuddered as her huge engines surged from 15 to 25 knots. All too slowly for every man aboard, she swung to the right as the torpedoes rushed closer. Seiichi mouthed a silent prayer and watched the seething wakes in what he was to call "the longest, most intolerable moments of my life."

The first torpedo dipped beneath the vessel with a hiss. Seiichi grabbed the bridge's chest-high, bolted-down brass compass and waited. Nothing happened.

Seconds later a searing yellow flash burst along the cargo ship's hull. An explosion thundered upwards, the concussion sweeping from bow to stern and knocking Seiichi and Ahiro to the steel floor-plates. On the starboard deck the impact tossed Sublieutenant Rikimaru backwards against a bulkhead.

Captain Seiichi wobbled to his feet and again steadied himself against the compass. Pain tore through his left arm—his wrist was shattered. Blood streamed down Ahiro's face from a deep gash on his nose.

Three rumbling vibrations convulsed the *Kano Maru*. As the captain, "shocked by the hellish force from below," ordered a radioman to send out a distress call, a frantic voice stammered on the bridge intercom: "Ensign Murikami—direct hit to engine room. Water coming in!"

"Seal off starboard bulkheads!" Seiichi ordered the helmsman.

The intercom grated again: "All engines out, Sir. Two men dead, several wounded."

The *Kano Maru* listed and drifted in a clockwise direction, her rudder locked into the same hard starboard position where it had been at the moment the second torpedo had hit.

Seiichi switched on the ship-wide intercom and bellowed, "Battle stations!"

The ship's lights flickered and went out with a sudden gasp, and crewmen on the bridge grabbed for flashlights. The generators, inside the engine room, had shorted out.

On the deck, Sublieutenant Rikimaru, his left eardrum punctured by the blast, staggered upright as sailors scrambled past him to man the 3-inch guns on both the stern and the bow and the ship's several .50 caliber machine guns. Even without electricity, the crew could operate the deck guns manually. Several sailors grabbed the stern gun's manual winch and twisted, but it did not budge. Grunting and cursing, they futilely yanked it again and again. The explosion had jammed the weapon, leaving the stricken freighter with only one deck gun.

Below the surface, a muffled boom jarred the *Grunion*. The sonar operator would have informed Jim, "Screw count zero." The freighter's propellers had stopped. Jim had another quick choice to make: how to finish the freighter off. If the stricken vessel had managed to radio Kiska, he had perhaps thirty minutes before Japanese aircraft would swoop onto the scene.

Seiichi had no idea if the distress call had reached Kiska. Using his binoculars to follow the MK 14 torpedoes' telltale wakes, which lingered several minutes atop the surface, Seiichi spotted a periscope 1,000 yards away from the *Kano Maru*'s starboard bow.

Jim had made his choice. The *Grunion*'s plates shuddered again as a forward tube launched another torpedo. The MK 14 sped fifty yards to its "reach distance" and suddenly veered onto the course calculated by the sub's computer. Somewhere between 450 and 850 yards, the torpedo should have automatically armed itself.

It homed in on the crippled freighter's starboard hull at 5:57 a.m. Again Seiichi held his breath, the crew tensing for impact.

The torpedo vanished beneath the surface just a few yards from the ship's bridge. After several seconds the wake reappeared to port and trailed away from the *Kano Maru*. Seiichi muttered to Ahiro, "How lucky we are—for now."

Awaiting the next spread of torpedoes, Seiichi sent a sailor scrambling to the aft deck to gather some crewmen and attempt to launch the freighter's seaplane, a Mitsubishi F1M, which swayed beneath a derrick's hook. With the freighter's electricity out and the derrick's controls useless, the sailors unhooked the aircraft and dragged the nearly 5,500-pound biplane to the crane at the freighter's open stern. They tethered it to the crane and shoved the plane into the sea.

The young pilot, Lieutenant Rasawa, crawled across the slippery pontoon with waves breaking over him and pulled himself into the cockpit of the "Pete" (the Americans' code name for the plane). If Rasawa got the Pete airborne, he could drop his two 132-pound bombs on the sub and then dash the ten miles to the Kiska base for help.

His teeth chattering, Rasawa tried to gun the powerful 820-horsepower radial engine. It sputtered but would not catch as the seaplane, still attached to the crane, bobbed helplessly in the swells.

Seiichi grimaced at the Pete's rasps and tracked the American sub's periscope, which "sometimes appeared and moved from the stern to the portside." The sub was inching closer, for the kill.

The deck gun on the bow poured dozens of 3-inch shells at the elusive periscope, joined by the steady but useless chatter of the Kano Maru's machine guns. Seiichi thought that he "had no way but to accept his fate and go down fighting for the Emperor."

In the sub's conning tower, the attack party readied the third salvo. At 6:07 a.m. three torpedoes sped at the freighter. Sublieutenant Rikimaru, who had stumbled to the aft deck to help with the seaplane, froze as cries of "torpedoes port" pealed across the ship. Seiichi "found it hard to breathe."

The first torpedo slammed against the Number 2 cargo hold. The MK 14's head snapped off, and the body floated tail down less than ten feet from the hull. A moment later the second torpedo crashed dead center against the *Kano Maru*, bounced off, and floated harmlessly a few yards from the ship.

The third torpedo slipped beneath the stern as Rikimaru, along with other horrified crewmen, grabbed for railings or flung themselves to the deck. After a few seconds he opened his eyes. Fifty yards or so past the freighter, the torpedo was still churning in the choppy gray waves and circling in an arc that would take it well clear of the *Kano Maru*.

With the MK 14's wake marking a trail back to the sub, the Japanese were able to spot the *Grunion*'s periscope. Seiichi was baffled that two direct hits had not detonated, and wondered "if the American torpedo men had forgotten to unlock the firing pins." He also wondered if the American commander had any torpedoes left and, if he did, whether he would risk staying any longer.

To the horror of the Japanese crew, the sub's periscope stayed up and knifed through the surface only some 1,500 yards to port. Seiichi marveled: "How calmly the American captain tracked us, not knowing if our planes, destroyers, or sub chasers might come from Kiska at any moment. I knew this was a brave man."

As the forecastle gun hurled one 3-inch shell after another at the darting periscope, Seiichi and his crew "watched them hit nothing but water and clenched our fists as we waited for the end." The machine guns also spat away at the target, the bullets only kicking up small water spouts near it.

A large ripple suddenly appeared around the periscope. Seiichi thought the American skipper was coming up to finish off the freighter with his deck gun. So, too, did Rikimaru, who reached inside his greatcoat, pulled out a small black-and-white photo of his fiancée, and with his hand shaking, kissed the picture. "Good-bye, Atsumi," he murmured.

The deck gun kept firing. Its eighty-fourth round vanished into the ripple, or "washing wave," around the periscope. Suddenly a column of water masked the periscope, and a "dull water explosion sound" pealed toward the *Kano Maru*. As oil spread where the sub had been, a long black rod burst above the viscous surface and plunged back into the sea.

CHAPTER NINE

"MISSING AND PRESUMED LOST"

———— ◆ ————

Jim and Kay Abele had decided to rent the house in Mystic, Connecticut, only till the end of the boys' school year, no matter when the *Grunion* was ordered out on its first war patrol. During the summer of 1942, Bruce, Brad, and John lived in a rambling converted barn on the Tiverton, Rhode Island, estate of relatives with their uncle Doctor Bill Stevens, his wife, Fran, and their three children. Kay, meanwhile, headed to Boston to search for a house to rent near the city and close to her sister's family in Brookline.

As the summer unwound, Kay and the boys wrote frequently to Jim. Weeks went by with only two replies from him, but that was to be expected, as they knew the *Grunion* was likely in action. In early August 1942, Kay excitedly wrote to Jim that she had rented a spacious house in Newton, Massachusetts, a Boston suburb, a "steal" at $70 per month and a home in better shape than any in which the family had lived before. She added, "…Bruce says every little while— 'Wouldn't it be wonderful if Jim should surprise us and walk in.'"[1]

The family still heard nothing from or about Jim and the *Grunion* as September arrived and the boys started school in Newton. Then, on September 30, the yellow Western Union telegram that families all across America dreaded was delivered to Kay. The message had been forwarded from Tiverton, which Jim, not knowing how long it would take Kay to find another house, had listed as his official address with the Department of the Navy.

She called for the three boys, tossing around a football on that sunny fall day, to come inside to the living room. Telegram in hand, she told them that their father was "missing following action in the performance of his duty and in the service of his country."[2] Across America, sixty-nine other families, those of Jim's crewmen, received the same notice.

Brad and John said nothing, but twelve-year-old Bruce, the oldest son with the most memories of Jim, let out a gasp before collecting himself quickly. The boys trudged outside to play rather listlessly, still hoping that missing in action did not mean Jim was lost, hoping against hope that he was still out there alive somewhere. Nine-year-old Brad reasoned that his father had been gone longer than four months on previous cruises and simply could not get word to them yet. Over the next few weeks, Bruce, a budding basketball player, would spend hours shooting free throws and telling himself that if he just sank ten in a row, then another ten, and did it again and again, then somehow Jim would be safe. Kay viewed the *Grunion* as "not definitely lost"[3]—not without irrefutable confirmation by the Navy.

In the months after the arrival of the telegram, Kay wrestled with fear and sputtering hope. A week after the telegram arrived at the

Abele home, the *New York Times* ran a story that an American submarine and its crew had been captured "somewhere off the Aleutians."[4] Then an Annapolis friend of Jim's told Kay that an American aircraft had mistaken the *Grunion* for a Japanese sub and sunk her, but later he told her he was mistaken. The boys noticed that their mother especially hated a war poster that showed an American fighter plane attacking a submarine with the slogan, "We See Em, We Sink Em."

The families of the *Grunion* crew experienced shock, denial, despair, or some gut-wrenching blend of all these emotions. Many clung to the hope that unless the crew was officially declared KIA—killed in action—the *Grunion*'s crew might have been taken prisoner or beached on some desolate island and awaiting rescue. The three Abele boys took to heart their father's words that "good soldiers never cry."[5] They embraced the traditional Yankee stoicism of both their mother's and their father's families.

A second telegram arrived for Kay on October 1, 1942. While it restated that the Navy believed Jim to be missing, a new sentence added, "However, no proof has been received that it was the result of enemy action."[6]

The Navy's contention that there was nothing to indicate the *Grunion* had gone down in combat belied both logic and fact. Task Force 8 headquarters at Dutch Harbor was fully aware that the missing submarine had engaged Japanese vessels off Kiska throughout the last two weeks of July, sinking at least two sub chasers, firing at destroyers, and enduring at least one depth-charge attack. The *Grunion*'s last transmission up the chain of command—relating that she had just encountered and escaped a Japanese destroyer—would normally have led Navy officials to conclude that the submarine had gone down in action in an active battle zone.

In all fairness to the Navy in the fall of 1942, the two telegrams'
omission of any information about the *Grunion's* last known position was and is not suspicious. The Navy's official policy was to
maintain total secrecy about American submarine losses for two
reasons—to deny the Japanese and the Germans any chance to
confirm their "kills," and to avoid demoralizing the American public during the dark opening years of the war. Admiral Gene Fluckey
wrote in his submarine history *Thunder Below*,

> Admiral [Charles] Lockwood was adamant that subma-
> rine operations not be publicized for at least sixty days
> afterward. For instance, known losses of our subs were
> not listed as "overdue and presumed lost" until *two
> months later*. Admiral Nimitz understood and insisted
> upon this procedure. As one of our earliest submariners,
> he would never forget the secret briefing at Pearl that
> went awry and cost us 10 subs. A politician had informed
> the press that the Japanese were not setting their depth
> charges deep enough to sink more of our submarines. A
> war crime![7]

While Lockwood did not take command of ComSubPac [the U.S.
Pacific submarine fleet] until Admiral Joseph English was killed in
a plane crash in early 1943, Lockwood—a daring and effective submarine skipper—merely continued the policy of listing lost submarines as "missing in action." The only hard information that could
be gleaned from the many front page newspaper articles that followed the two telegrams was that the *Grunion* was missing, that Jim
Abele was its commander, and that the submarine had been assigned
to the "Pacific Theater of Operations."

In mid-October 1942, scant weeks after Kay Abele received the
second telegram, she opened a letter from Fran McMahon, the wife

of John McMahon, a lieutenant on the *Grunion*. Fran had learned "through the Navy's notoriously accurate grapevine" that the *Grunion* had been lost "in the Kiska area of the Aleutian Islands."[8] The information was more specific than any detail the Navy would offer for some sixty-five years.

Once the story of the *Grunion's* disappearance hit the newspapers and magazines in bold print, the Abeles' neighbors rallied around the family of a bona fide Naval hero. Brad remembered how they were "new to the Newton neighborhood, and these gestures were very much appreciated. The country was in a very patriotic mood in those days and even though we had apparently lost our father, we were all very proud of the fact that he had been a submarine commander, defending his country…."[9]

The *Grunion* was removed from the Naval Register on November 2, 1942. She was simply listed as "missing and presumed lost." On March 11, 1943, Kay received a letter from the Bureau of Naval Personnel informing her that Jim had been awarded the Purple Heart and the Navy Cross—the latter, the service's highest award— for "extraordinary heroism as a result of the actions of the *Grunion* from June 30 to July 24 1942."[10] He was credited with sinking three Japanese Towlekju-class destroyers. (After the war this was reduced to two Japanese sub chasers and damage to a third.) His name was added to the Navy's Roll of Honor. While at that time only commanding officers of submarines were awarded the Navy Cross, Kay felt that the sixty-nine men who had set out under Jim's command deserved recognition as well. From the Department of the Navy in Washington, D.C., she obtained the names and addresses of the next of kin of each *Grunion* officer and crewman. She wrote a letter to each family, offering them empathy for their uncertainty and anguish over their loved ones' fate.

The replies poured back—as they would for years to come—from wives, fiancées, and parents. The writers shared their grief. Many of them also expressed their frustration with the lack of details about the crew's fate.

"Mrs. Abele, I've let myself go all to pieces," wrote one mother, six months after the *Grunion*'s disappearance. "Do you feel there is still hope? I just can't make myself believe that all are gone.... Please forgive me if I upset you, but I can't help myself."[11]

Kay answered each and every letter, year after year.

As the wife of a commanding officer, she at least received some sort of acknowledgement from the Navy from time to time. The Navy offered little but silence to the relatives of the crew. Cornelius Paul's mother beseeched officials again and again, writing that she "just wants to know what happened to my son."[12] She never received a reply to the more than thirty letters she wrote.

One of the most interesting communications Kay Abele received from the Navy was this cryptic letter, dated October 9, 1943:

Died: 2 August 1943; (Officially reported missing as of Aug 1942, having been attached to the U.S.S. Grunion when that ship was lost in the Aleutian Alaskan area. In compliance with Sec. 5 of Public Law 490, as amended, death is presumed to have occurred on 2 August 1943.)

Place: Alaska—Pacific area; Cause: Loss of ship—not enemy action.[13]

While the Navy did acknowledge that the submarine had been lost in the Aleutians, "the Aleutian Alaskan area" covered a broad swath of ocean and islands. The "rumor mill" had given Fran McMahon much more specific information—that the *Grunion* had gone missing off Kiska Island. But what was far more interesting and problematic was the Navy's terse line that the loss of the submarine had *not* been the result of enemy action. What did the Navy know at that early juncture? Without specific information that they were unwilling to share with the families, how could they be justified in saying that the submarine had not been lost to enemy action—when they knew the *Grunion* had indeed seen heavy action for two weeks in late July 1942?

While life might have proved easier if Kay Abele had accepted the $10,000 death benefit from the government, she returned the stipend. She believed that if she cashed it she bought into the deal that Jim was dead, and she refused to do so without genuine proof from the Navy. Kay's explanation to her boys was that their father was missing, not dead, and that other families needed the check more. Meanwhile, she had three young boys to bring up as the breadwinner—a situation that more and more young mothers faced every day of the war.

Kay filed for and received the one year's pay for servicemen who were reported as MIA, and in August 1942, Congress authorized a bill to pay to MIA submariners' families 150 percent of base pay "because of the hazardous nature of this duty." Naval aviators had received the same rate much earlier. The families of the *Grunion*'s crew would receive an increase in pay for the upcoming year, but then the payments would end, with no pensions or survivors' benefits for men lost in action. Jim's foresight in taking out a $10,000 government life insurance policy entitled Kay, as the beneficiary, to receive $46.40 per month for the rest of her life. But even when she was able to surrender to the loss of her husband to the extent of accepting the death benefit, Kay would still need to augment the family income. A trained violinist and music teacher, she began by giving private lessons in the Newton house; she was soon hired to provide both group and private lessons at nearby grade schools.

Bruce, Brad, and John pitched in to help with the family finances—and the war effort—by tending a Victory Garden and digging potatoes at local farms to bring some extra money home.

With $3,000 she saved from her job as a music teacher, Kay bought a house in Newton. The family was slowly learning to make do without Jim, but they never forgot him. They never would. The questions about what had happened tore at the boys and their mother. The same held true for other *Grunion* families.

———————◆———————

Half a world away, Shinoda Chiyo in Japan was also grieving her husband's death and struggling to raise three children without Isamu, who had gone down with his ship, the *CH-27*, when the torpedo from the *Grunion* hit it on July 15, 1942.

The last letter Chiyo had received from Isamu was dated eight days before his death, "from husband at war front." He assured her that "I am safe" and asked for every detail she could think of about their children. He could not reveal his location was Kiska Harbor, but did describe the island's snow-crowned volcano and beautiful white, yellow, red, and purple flowers. Hinting at the dangers he faced, he wrote that "occasionally this beautiful scene instantly changes to [an] awful hell."

Shinoda's final words to his wife were, "Tell Kazuo to study much. I send flowers of this place to you with my heart."[14]

In November 1942, Chiyo and her children received the official Navy Ministry notice that her husband had been killed in action and a military funeral was to be held at the base at Kure. Then the family would hold a private service at their ancestral temple.

As heavy snow fell on Kure, a member of Japan's royal family and several high-ranking officers presented Chiyo a white wood box with a photo of Isamu. When the service ended, the Shinodas boarded a train for the return trip from Kure to Gifu, and at the station, a throng of friends and family greeted them and formed a solemn procession that wound its way through the snow to the

Shinodas' home. There, all of Kazuo's classmates and teachers stood in neat rows, their heads bowed, their lips murmuring prayers for a fallen hero. Inside the box, Chiyo placed the lock of hair that Isamu had left as a keepsake before his ship departed.

Chiyo faced an uncertain future, but with the aid of family and friends was determined to raise her children as Isamu would have wished. Unlike Kay Abele, Chiyo had ironclad eyewitness reports that her husband had died in action in the Aleutians. But the Shinoda family endured an even harder struggle for physical survival during and immediately after the war. Chiyo raised her fatherless children amid bombings by American planes and meager food supplies, as the conflict turned against Japan—displaying a stoicism in adversity like Kay Abele's.

————◆◆◆————

In 1944 Kay Abele, with her sons, christened the destroyer USS *Mannert L. Abele* at Bath, Maine. The ship was hit by a kamikaze attack several months later and went down with nearly all hands.

Danny Cullinane's family christened a new sub at New London in 1945. Kay still wouldn't accept that Jim, Danny, or the other crewmen were dead—not without official proof.

CHAPTER TEN

MAKING DO WITH LESS

K ay Abele's dogged pursuit of information about her missing husband and his submarine continued into the postwar years, which were fraught with many other challenges for the Abele family.

John had begun to show signs of illness not long after the *Grunion* vanished, but he was not correctly diagnosed until he was seven. He had contracted osteomyelitis of the hip, a bacterial infection of the bone marrow. For seven years, John endured casts from leg to hip, numerous surgeries, and stays in Boston Children's Hospital—becoming one of the first Americans to be treated with penicillin for the infection.

With his family's staunch support, John overcame incessant pain and learned how to turn adversity into opportunity—a trait that would infuse his entire life and career. "Self-pity was not on the program in a 'Yankee' family,"[1] John Abele recalls. He refused to allow his condition to keep him housebound, learning to use his crutches so well that he could outrun other neighborhood kids.

His mother's stoic attitude—Kay believed that problems existed to be solved—took root in all three of her sons. For the three brothers, the loss, pain, and survival forged a bond that would never weaken as the years and decades passed.

Bruce and John Abele assert that despite the hardships the family faced, the three boys "enjoyed a classic boy's life in the postwar era."[2] According to John, "We did more with less. We invented things."[3]

The boys whose father had vanished at sea shared his love of the water, and in the basement of their Newton home they fashioned their own "aqualung" and a "pneumatic spear-gun." All three boys, like Jim, loved to tinker with ideas and machinery.

Kay, meanwhile, not only wrote to Navy sources, but also continued her correspondence with family members of the *Grunion*'s crewmen. No matter how tired she was from work, and from dealing with three high-spirited boys, she spent countless evenings at her desk, answering every letter she received. The loss of the *Grunion* had opened up gaping wounds in many lives.

On September 30, 1942, Carmine Parziale's mother, who had no phone, had received a yellow telegram via Coppollo's Grocery Store in Weedville, Pennsylvania. It was the same message on yellow paper that Kay Abele had received, and the words first tore at Louise Parziale. Then she simply refused to accept them without proof. She never gave up on Carmine's return. For years, one of her children always had to go to meet the morning train because she believed that Carmine just might be coming home.

Julia Pancoast never even received the yellow telegram for her husband, Jack. Julia was caught up in a nightmarish day-to-day struggle to survive in and around Japanese-occupied Manila. She had hid her boy, Jackie, with an aunt and uncle in the countryside, always fearing that Japanese soldiers might discover he was the son of an American sailor and throw him into a prison camp. Her last communication from her husband was a December 1941 letter. Jack's parents had no way to reach her in Manila and tell her that the *Grunion* was missing. In February 1945, months after General Douglas MacArthur's army had liberated the Philippines from Japan, she wrote to the Navy and learned that her husband was listed as "deceased." Later in that same year, Julia and Jackie left the Philippines for San Francisco and headed by train to Pittsburgh to visit the Pancoast family. Julia and her son were in the United States for good, and she began to carve out a new life in America— but without the submariner she had fallen in love with in Manila.

When the family of *Grunion* crewman Sy "Ken" Kennedy received the Department of the Navy telegram in August 1942, they did not share the news with his fiancée, Evelyn, nor was she invited to attend the Requiem Mass celebrated for him. Evelyn waited for Ken's return for many years. When she finally realized that the man she loved was not coming back, she had built up such a fantasy about their life together that no other man could ever live up to her dreams. Although the pretty, vivacious Switzer had an active social life and boyfriends, she never married.

Trudie Kornahrens could never get over the loss of her husband, Lieutenant Billie Kornahrens, who had apparently sent out the *Grunion*'s last transmission on July 30, 1942. Their daughter, Nancy, born after the submarine disappeared, remembered a childhood of being the only one of her classmates who had never known her father. While she often wondered what had happened to her father, her mother seldom spoke about him, except to say how much they had loved living in New London in their "*Grunion* days."[4]

Genevieve Cullinane never remarried either. Danny Cullinane had escaped death so many times in his life. When the sub was lost his family and the sailors and officers he had served with couldn't help believing that he and the *Grunion* would somehow reappear. A year after the *Grunion* went missing, eighteen-year-old John Cullinane had enlisted in the Navy to "avenge his father."[5]

The Abele sons attended prestigious colleges, married, raised families, and carved out successful careers in business and science. Bruce, an engineer, co-invented the Polaroid Instant Camera. Brad, who had served in the "brown-shoe Navy" as a fighter pilot on an aircraft carrier, built and owned a large management-recruiting firm.

After graduating from Amherst College, where he double-majored in physics and philosophy, John Abele eventually went to work for a small medical-supply company near Boston. When he and Peter Nichols, another innovative young businessman, decided to form their own business to develop state-of-the-art medical technologies such as the balloon catheter and the stent, the result was Boston Scientific Corporation, a company that went global and made John Abele one of America's wealthiest men.

Two things that never changed for John, Bruce, and Brad Abele were their tight bond with each other and their admiration for their mother.

The mystery shrouding the fate of the *Grunion* gnawed at the Abeles even as the years lengthened between their last glimpse of their father and the successful present. One of the few scraps of information they had was the rumor Fran McMahon had written to Kay about in 1942—that the submarine had been lost near Kiska in the Aleutians.

Kay Abele, who had never stopped looking for answers about her husband's fate, died in October 1976 without ever knowing what had happened to Jim and the *Grunion*. Her sons continued to wonder, but no clear starting point for solving this most personal of mysteries suggested itself—even to men whose "can do" approach to life had brought them success.

As the years passed, memories of Jim would emerge without warning. On Sunday, December 7, 1981, the forty-fifth anniversary of Pearl Harbor, Bruce, his wife, Susan, and their two sons, Kurt and Karl, sat down to supper in their Newton, Massachusetts, home. Bruce had been watching a television special about Pearl Harbor and found himself talking about the months following the "Day of Infamy." His voice caught as he reminisced about the May 24, 1942, dinner at the Naval Officers Club in New London. Brushing away tears, Bruce said, "Jim left the next morning, and we never saw him again...."[6] His wife and sons were stunned by the anguish in his voice—Bruce had never spoken to anyone but his brothers with such obvious grief for his father.

On a business trip to Japan in the early 1990s, John Abele listened sleepily as the pilot mentioned that they were passing over the Aleutian Islands. John started and peered out the window. Even though he could not see much from that altitude, he reflected that he might well be flying over the spot where his father and the *Grunion* had vanished.

Meanwhile Brad Abele, without telling anyone except his wife, had begun as early as the 1980s to dig for any clues at all about the *Grunion*. He researched and wrote a personal manuscript entitled *Jim*, detailing his father's life. Brad pored over what little information was available about the *Grunion*'s first and final patrol and about the torpedo woes that plagued Jim and other submarine skippers in 1942–1943. To his surprise, Brad discovered that the *Grunion*'s official "War Diary"—its logbooks up until the time it left for the Aleutians—and all Naval documents about the sub were still classified material, fifty years after the end of World War II. Several attempts to declassify the material through Freedom of Information filings failed.

Brad Abele wondered if one of the Japanese mini-subs in the waters of Kiska had gotten off a lucky shot and sunk the *Grunion*. Research turned up nothing concrete about mini-subs, and Brad next turned his focus to the rumors that "friendly fire" had accidentally sunk his father's submarine. With the Navy offering no help whatsoever in response to any of Brad's requests for information, he wrote,

> As I thought about it, one type of "operational loss" that the bureaucracy might have known about and would undoubtedly want to keep a top secret was the loss of the *Grunion* through..."friendly fire." There was a realistic concern on the minds of all submariners during World War II about this. The brother of an aunt of ours was stationed in the Aleutians in 1942 and wrote that he had heard a rumor to the effect that a U.S. sub had been accidentally sunk by one of our Army antisubmarine planes. We've since learned that the Army field where he was working and heard the rumor was not built until the end of August 1942, so even if the rumor were true, it would not have involved the *Grunion*.... Nevertheless, had such a thing happened at that time, it would have very likely been kept top secret.[7]

Moreover, numerous submariners of the World War II era told Brad that it was general practice to dive immediately when any plane was sighted—and there were many instances throughout the war when American subs were fired upon by American planes, in several cases even after the identifying flares had been fired. The submarine USS *Dorado* was lost with all hands in the Caribbean theater after being fired upon by an American plane. War patrol reports of submarines operating in the Aleutian theater in 1942 relate that there were several incidents of their being fired upon by American planes in these reports.

Brad posited that with the battle of Midway having been fought and won only three weeks prior to the loss of the *Grunion*, the Navy would not want to undermine public morale with the news that one of the newest and costliest fleet submarines had disappeared. He speculated that the command up and down the ranks "probably would rather have kept a thing like this quiet to protect their own careers."[8]

In 1998 Brad finished *Jim* and presented it to the family.[9]

Brad had contacted retired Commander Edward Beach—by this time a well-known author and submarine historian—and Beach sent him the decoded, garbled July 30, 1942, message, apparently the *Grunion*'s final transmission, which placed her somewhere off Kiska. Still, no one knew the exact spot—except the Navy, which remained silent.

It seemed the sub had simply vanished, taking the secret of her fate with her. There was nowhere to start a search.

No one could even imagine that in a Denver, Colorado, antique shop sat a piece of paper that would set in motion a stream of implausible events and change everything.

CHAPTER ELEVEN

A CHART, A CLUE, AND A CHANCE MEETING

⬤◆⬤

Far from the Abeles' homes in New England, far from the Aleutians, far from any conceivable connection to the *Grunion*, a trim man with close-cropped graying hair was browsing a Denver, Colorado, antique shop in 1998 when he spotted a piece of paper among cluttered World War II artifacts. Retired Air Force Lieutenant Colonel Richard Lane, an avid military-memorabilia collector, picked up the document. It was filled with Japanese characters and showed a wiring diagram for the deck winch of a cargo ship named the *Kano Maru*. Lane studied it for a few minutes. Then he handed the store owner the asking price—$1—took the paper home, and forgot about it.

Lane came across the diagram again in the summer of 2001. His curiosity stoked, he searched the internet for any information about the *Kano Maru*. Unable to find any, he posted images of the wiring diagram on the website J-aircraft.com, popular with fellow military history buffs, on September 7, asking if anyone had information about the ship. He did not expect a response any time soon.

But the very next day, Lane found a message from Japanese historian and journalist Yutaka Iwasaki, who wrote that the *Kano Maru* had been a supply ship. Yutaka also included his translation, with his own notes, of an obscure article by the ship's 1942 commander, Captain Seiichi Aiura. The piece chronicled a July 30, 1942, battle off Kiska Island between the *Kano Maru* and an American submarine.[1]

Seiichi wrote that the sub had fired at least six, possibly seven, torpedoes. One had crippled his freighter, three had missed; two others had struck the *Kano Maru* but failed to detonate. According to Seiichi, the sub had then attempted to surface—perhaps intending to use its deck gun to finish off the stricken freighter. The rough translation read, "*Kano Maru's* forecastle gun fired; fourth [apparently this was a hasty mistranslation for the eighty-fourth] shot hit the conning tower of the sub. It is thought the last of *Grunion.*"[2]

Seiichi also reported hearing a "dull but loud thud"[3] seconds after the shot from the freighter's 3-inch deck gun hit the submarine. The significance of that "thud" caught no one's attention yet.

Lane posted Yutaka's material on a U.S. Navy website, COM-SUBPAC, which had a *Grunion* page, realizing that it could be important to families of the lost crew members.

Although the Abeles had seen bits and pieces about the *Grunion* on various websites and were even aware of the COMSUBPAC page, nothing on the internet had ever shed any real light on the mystery of the sub. But in late February 2002, Alicia Hale, the fiancée of Bruce's son Kurt, showed the *Jim* manuscript that Brad had written to her boss at Qwest Communications. A World War II history buff fascinated by the mystery of the *Grunion*, he suggested that Bruce look at five websites mentioning the sub. Though Bruce had seen them all before, he took another look. He went to COMSUBPAC— and was astonished by Yutaka's post.

After so many years of wondering, the Abeles finally had something concrete about the *Grunion*'s fate. They launched a web search for the translator of Seiichi's account and found an email address for Yutaka Iwasaki. John sent an email relating that he was a son of the *Grunion*'s commander and asking if Yutaka was the man who had translated the article by the *Kano Maru*'s captain. On March 7, 2002, John received a reply from Japan: "I am he. I pray for the repose of your father's soul."[4]

Yutaka quickly sent the Abeles his translation of the original article and his notes. The search was now underway—not only for the truth about the *Grunion*'s final moments, but also for her final position, her possible resting place. Even with Seiichi's account, pinning down the actual coordinates of the battle between the sub and the freighter appeared a remote possibility at best—and without a precise location, the Abeles couldn't realistically think of an actual physical search for the wreck.

Over the following months and years, the Abeles, Yutaka, and a growing group of former submariners and history buffs from all walks of life intrigued by the story began to search for any information about the sub and to share what they found with the Abeles. In Japan, Yutaka continued to dig through official archives for more documents on the *Kano Maru* and the *Grunion*. Although the Navy had run the article by Seiichi on the COMSUBPAC site, officials' only response to the Abeles was that "the U.S. Navy has no information about the disappearance of the U.S.S. *Grunion* and no way to corroborate the Japanese account."[5]

As the "*Grunion* collaborative"—John Abele's term—continued to expand, a chance meeting in January 2005 between John Abele and the world's foremost oceanographer and underwater explorer, Robert Ballard, changed everything. John heard Ballard—the man who had found the *Titanic*, the German battleship *Bismarck*, and the remains of *PT-109*, as well as over 150 other historic wrecks dating from the Bronze Age to World War II—speak at a conference in Florida and was intrigued by Ballard's lecture on the technical challenges of hunting a sunken ship. The thought that a deep-sea search for the *Grunion* might just be possible compelled John to set up a meeting with Ballard at Boston Scientific's headquarters outside Boston in October 2005 to discuss that long-shot possibility.

The Abeles knew that Ballard had not only the expertise but also the *Nautilus*, a state-of-the-art research vessel equipped with two ROVs (Remote Operated Vehicles) that could descend 20,000 feet below the surface. At the meeting with all three Abele brothers, Ballard went over Seiichi's account of the battle between the *Kano Maru* and an American sub. The explorer had already pored over sonar images of known World War II wrecks off Kiska, as well as commercial fishing vessels' sonar maps of the Bering Sea off the island.

Ballard pointed out that Seiichi's article provided only a general position of the action, and that an actual search would have to stretch some twenty square miles—making the *Grunion* the proverbial needle in a haystack. While he concurred that the sub Seiichi Aiura had encountered was likely the *Grunion*, he was concerned that volcanic outcroppings had probably ripped the boat to pieces as it sank. If so, the chances of the sub being in one piece—or even two or three—were poor.[6] Even if the sub lay in one identifiable piece, Ballard warned that the brutal winds and waves of the Bering Sea could destroy sonar equipment or an ROV in an instant. They could also sink a large ship. After hearing Ballard's well-intentioned but disheartening estimate of their very slim chances of success, the

Abeles were certain that he would not take on any search for the *Grunion*.

Another worry was that a private search for the *Grunion* might possibly fall afoul of maritime regulations—about, for example, wartime wrecks being treated as graves. "The concern," according to Bruce, "was not that that we would end up in jail but rather the very real likelihood that after we had committed a great deal of time and money that the project could be stopped by some obscure bureaucratic regulation."[7]

Ballard surprised the Abeles. He said that he would be willing to put together a sonar search off Kiska, but that unless a promising "target" was found, risking an ROV in the Bering Sea was not viable. The only possible time for a search was in August, when there might be a day or two of calm waters and winds off Kiska. "Might," Ballard noted, was the most optimistic view. For the chance to enlist the *Titanic*'s discoverer in a search for Jim and his men, John Abele agreed to underwrite the costs of a sonar expedition to the Aleutians.

In the weeks immediately after the meeting with Ballard, the Abeles' elation at the explorer's offer turned to concern when he grew vague about actual dates and details. Then, in December 2005, he told the Abeles that he had already committed to *National Geographic* to search for ancient shipwrecks in the Black Sea in summer 2006 and could not take on both expeditions. While he assured the Abeles that he would provide advice if they decided to go ahead with an expedition, he could not lead it. He offered his assistant, Cathy Offinger, to help the Abeles find a boat sturdy enough to withstand the Bering Sea and large enough for sonar equipment. But the Abeles would be on their own in finding sonar equipment and sonar operators, as Ballard had no choice but to take his own equipment to the Black Sea. The brothers contacted several other well-known underwater explorers and institutes, but were told that they would

never find the *Grunion* and that the risk to the costly search equipment was too high.

John Abele had not become a billionaire by aversion to risk. He
had always trusted his instincts; in co-founding Boston Scientific,
he had ignored warnings that he could not possibly compete with
established international medical-device companies. Now, despite
the logistical obstacles to a search for a vanished submarine off
Kiska, and despite the gloomy assessments of underwater experts,
he persuaded his brothers that "we can do this without Bob Ballard."[8]

The Abeles' long-shot expedition faced a number of hurdles at
the start of 2006. They needed a ship, sophisticated sonar equipment,
and a plan to get that expensive, cumbersome equipment to Kiska.
The logistics, to say the very least, posed an immense challenge. Plus,
the price-tag would be high; however, John Abele was willing to
spend the millions of dollars required to search for the *Grunion*—for
the chance to solve the mystery of Jim's fate and that of his crew.

Over dinner in January 2006 with neighbor Linda Lowney,
Bruce's wife Susan was discussing the possibility of a search for the
sub off Kiska. Linda's son Pete Lowney was a commercial fisherman
who had just returned from a stint aboard a crab boat in the Bering
Sea. Susan suggested that Bruce talk with Pete.

Bruce called him that same night, and Lowney urged him to
contact Kale Garcia, a savvy and resourceful Alaskan fisherman and
skipper. Lowney, who had worked as a crewman aboard Garcia's
165-foot crab boat, the *Aquila*, raved about Garcia's experience in
the remote and treacherous waters off the Aleutian Islands.

All three of the brothers called Garcia, who was enthralled by
the audacity of a search for the sub and the chance to unravel a
World War II mystery. He was also moved by the fact that the three
brothers "wanted to find their dad."[9] Garcia tentatively agreed to
take on the job—so long as the Abeles could find the proper sonar

equipment before mid-May 2006. Without a commitment by that date, Garcia would have to accept a commercial-fishing contract for the summer.

The Abeles' search for sonar equipment led them first to a well-known Massachusetts outfit suggested to them by Kale Garcia. While that company's sonar did not have the capacity to search deep enough to reach any potential resting place of the *Grunion*, they advised the Abeles to contact Seattle-based Williamson & Associates. By early March, John and Bruce were in serious talks with Art Wright, a former submarine officer, about his putting together a Williamson team to search the waters off Kiska with the company's side-scan sonar, which had the capacity to explore the necessary 3,000 feet down or deeper.

Wright did not underestimate the logistical difficulties of hauling the winches, a mile or more of steel cable, the sonar towfish, and other equipment 1,700 miles by sea from Seattle to Dutch Harbor, Alaska, the commercial fishing port that would have to serve as the jumping-off point for an expedition to the remote Aleutians. Besides the distance that the heavy equipment would have to travel, Wright knew that the Bering Sea off Kiska could damage or even destroy the towfish.

He also worried about the size of the search area where the *Grunion* might lie. Even with Yutaka's translation of Seiichi's account of the battle between the unknown American sub and the *Kano Maru*, the potential grid the sonar would have to search could cover anywhere from 20 to 200 square miles.

But a growing number of people from all corners of the globe were captivated by the story and connected through the internet. The Abeles sought their help in pinning down any additional information. They needed to narrow the coordinates of the sub's last reported position to have a chance of finding it. They sent flyers to all of

Alaska's ports in hopes of turning up any scrap of information about the sub and attempted to obtain "snag reports" of potential wrecks detected by the sonar of massive commercial fishing vessels off the Aleutians, but to little avail.

The one aspect of the search that was set in stone was the time frame. The expedition had to reach Kiska in August, the only month offering any seas calm enough to attempt a sonar search. Even then, hull-splitting waves and 100-mph winds could rise at virtually any instant.

The Abeles faced yet another time limitation—an intensely personal one. By early 2006, Brad was experiencing neurological symptoms affecting his speech and balance. He was diagnosed with PSP—Progressive Supernuclear Palsey, and the prognosis was bleak. Brad's dogged, meticulous research and writing of the manuscript he called *Jim* had really been the start of the brothers' quest for the *Grunion*. Although his illness compelled him to turn over all of his research material to Bruce, Brad remained an integral part of the unfolding quest for the *Grunion*. John and Bruce were more determined than ever to mount a search for the wreck while all three brothers could still take part.

The Abeles kept talking with Wright and Garcia. Then a series of fortuitous developments unfolded, beginning in early May 2006. When John Abele happened to be in Northern California on business, he learned that Kale Garcia had anchored the *Aquila* in Seattle. John flew there to talk with both the skipper and Art Wright about taking the crab boat off Kiska to use it as a platform for Williamson's side-scan sonar—with no guarantee that Wright and Williamson & Associates would be willing to risk the equipment on a vessel that was the antithesis of a sleek research vessel.

John believed the words he had told his brothers: "We can do this."[10]

CHAPTER TWELVE

LOGISTICS OF A LONG SHOT

In early May 2006, Art Wright—competitive rower, former submariner, and Williamson & Associates sonar expert—pulled his way across Seattle's bustling harbor to check out both the *Aquila* and her captain. The 165-foot *Aquila*, battered from months at sea, bore no resemblance to Robert Ballard's state-of-the-art research ship, the *Nautilus*, and the crab boat would need major refitting to handle Williamson & Associates' sonar equipment—if it ever reached that point. Unless the no-nonsense Wright could be convinced that the fishing-boat captain was up to the job, the towfish would not be en route to the Aleutians.

The skipper who greeted Wright as he clambered aboard the crabber was a wavy-haired, muscular man with the deeply burnished features acquired in a life spent at sea. Born in Portland, Oregon, and raised in California, forty-year-old Kale Garcia had originally planned to become a geologist, but when, as an eighteen-year-old, he started working summers aboard a commercial fishing boat in Alaska, he fell in love with the dangerous but lucrative profession. The job appealed both to his lifelong love of the water and to his adventurous nature.

In a profession where experience meant everything, Garcia's early success—he was skipper of his own boat by age twenty-two—was far from the norm. In the beginning, he admits, he was considered "green" and had to earn veteran crewmen's respect. A navigational knowledge far beyond his years helped to win their trust, as did his gregarious but tough demeanor.

Wright took Garcia's measure and approved of what he saw and heard. Over dinner that night Garcia, Wright, and John Abele decided that an expedition could be put together. Williamson and Garcia were on board—literally—by mid-May, and the contracts were signed.

Garcia planned to dock the *Aquila* at Dutch Harbor by August 1, 2006, after a commercial trip to Cold Bay. The Abeles and Wright decided that the only way to ship the sonar equipment to Dutch Harbor safely was to lug it aboard a giant barge for the long trip from Seattle to the Alaskan port.

Wright started to assemble his team for the expedition. Topnotch electronic engineer Jay Larson agreed to join the search, as did Richard Graham, a gifted sonar towfish navigator. The Abeles hired Pete Lowney to represent them on the *Aquila* throughout the sonar search, and also to film the voyage on high-resolution video cameras that would send back real-time updates to the family.

Back in Massachusetts, a string of improbable developments added new dimensions to the search. Sue Abele, a museum curator and librarian, read through all of Kay Abele's long correspondence with the families of *Grunion* officers and crew and sorted and collated it into loose-leaf binders. Sue's binders would prove a treasure trove, not only a record of that remarkable correspondence, but also a tool in another search—the one for the relatives of the *Grunion*'s men.

In June 2006, a local newspaper, the *Newton Tab*, ran a story about the Abeles' evolving search, and a man in Israel—a submarine expert named Michael Mohl—contacted Bruce after reading the piece. Mohl introduced Bruce to Charles Hinman, Director of the USS *Bowfin* Submarine Museum and Park, and to the Eternal Patrol (lost submarines) website. As news of the story began spreading globally, Pete Lowney and computer wizard Newman Lanier set up a website (ussgrunion.com) to chronicle every aspect of the Abeles' search for the *Grunion* as it was actually happening.

As preparations for the expedition intensified in July 2006, Yutaka Iwasaki, the Japanese naval architect, writer, and World War II researcher who had first brought Seiichi Aiura's account of the *Grunion*'s fate to the attention of Richard Lane and the Abeles, combed through Japanese Defense Ministry archives for any additional scraps of information about the freighter *Kano Maru*. Working alongside Yutaka was a naval researcher named Minoru Kamada. The pair's sleuthing at the Ministry had been set in motion when Dr. Robert J. Cressman, Head of the Ships History Branch at the Naval Historical Center in Washington, D.C., suggested to the Abeles that Minoru, a Japanese colleague who had access to the National Institute of Defense Studies where Defense Ministry records were stored, contact Yutaka.

In the voluminous files they came across the *Kano Maru*'s logbook, which had been misfiled—including a chart that Seiichi had drawn shortly after the clash between his freighter and the submarine. He prepared to send the material he had discovered to the Abeles. In gratitude for all the help they were receiving from Japan, the Abeles decided to expand the planned search off Kiska to include

not just their father's sub, but also the two Japanese sub-chasers—
CH-25 and *CH-27*—that the *Grunion* had sunk, and the *Arare*, a
Japanese destroyer that had been torpedoed in the same waters by
the *Growler*.

Meanwhile, the Abeles' discussions with a federal judge assuaged
concerns about bureaucracy or civil or military regulations hamper-
ing the expedition.

On July 17, 2006, as the barge laden with the side-scan sonar
towfish and its cumbersome equipment and portable control room
slowly made its way from Seattle to Dutch Harbor, Yutaka emailed
the Abeles a large batch of material—270 files. No one noticed anything special about one file amid the 270. Not at first. Then, when
they opened that file, everything changed. For it contained the chart
that Seiichi Aiura, commander of the *Kano Maru*, had drawn shortly
after the clash between his freighter and the submarine. Seiichi had
recorded the coordinates of the *Grunion*'s last engagement.

There is no way to exaggerate how key a find Seiichi Aiura's chart
was. The Japanese captain's record of the engagement was a Rosetta
Stone for the Abeles—the clue no one had even imagined.

The chart narrowed a search area of at least twenty to as much
as two hundred square miles in the rough Bering waters, to a target
zone of some *four* square miles. The proverbial haystack had just
shrunk to manageable proportions.

Although the task remained imposing, the chances of success
had soared. John Abele called Robert Ballard with the news; Ballard
replied that it was still a long shot, but looking a bit better.

A storm that delayed the barge's arrival at Dutch Harbor had
everyone's stomach in knots—there was such a short span of time
in August to get out to Kiska before the weather made a search too
risky. Finally, on August 1, 2006, the team could begin the difficult
task of moving the side-scan sonar equipment from the barge and

converting the thirty-year-old *Aquila*, just finished hauling a load of salmon, into a research platform. As quickly and securely as possible, the team aboard the vessel had to set up winches able to handle a mile or more of heavy cable, the towfish, the control room, and a j-crane from which to launch the towfish.

Joining the *Aquila*'s skipper Kale Garcia for the expedition were his wife, Anj, and their two children, Tanner and Kenzie. Kale and Anj's courtship and married life were hardly conventional. Anj, born and raised in Oregon, had gone to the Oregon Institute of Technology to study physics, specializing in a new field called laser electro-optic technology. Working full-time to pay for school, she decided to take a year off to make enough money to devote all her energy to her tough major when she returned to school. Anj took a job at an electronics firm in Corvallis, Oregon, but chafed at the staid routine. Meanwhile, she was competing for the Miss Oregon beauty crown, which would bring scholarship money if she won. If she did, she planned to remain in Corvallis and return to college.

Anj did not win the pageant, but when she was offered a job as a bookkeeper and computer operator aboard an Alaska-bound crab-processing boat, she jumped at the chance for a "little adventure"[1] before heading back to school. Kale, skipper of the *Chevak*, a 126-foot crabber, was anchored in Port Moeller, Alaska, in the summer of 1990, and friends told him he should try and meet "the beautiful computer gal"[2] aboard the floating processor where all the local skippers brought their catches. Since he needed to order some steering equipment for his vessel and planned to do so aboard the processing ship, he took their advice.

The attraction between the young skipper and the adventurous physics major was immediate, and even though company strictures banned Anj from dating clients, she and Kale found ways around the ban. Over the next five months, they saw each other at every opportunity, and when the *Chevak* was out at sea, she used the processing ship's radio to talk with Kale. In 1991 she finally left her job, enrolled at the University of Fairbanks, Alaska, and moved in with Kale. She went out on a crabbing expedition with him that same year, and when she became pregnant in 1992, the couple married. Daughter Kenzie was born in November of that year, and son Tanner four years later. [3]

Art Wright and his team were taken a bit aback at the prospect of going to Kiska with Garcia's wife, teenaged daughter, and eleven-year-old son. But they soon saw that all three were experienced and savvy sailors: every summer, when the Bering was relatively calm though fickle, Anj, Kenzie, and Tanner went to sea with Kale—Anj handled the cooking for the crew, but she was also adept at the vessel's helm. The children worked alongside their parents on the *Aquila*, Tanner and Kenzie able to perform virtually any shipboard task.

The storm that had delayed the arrival of the *Aquila* and the barge to Dutch Island forced the team to work round the clock to ensure that the crabber could leave in time to catch the "weather window" in the Aleutians. The presence of survival suits for everyone on board testified to the dangers of the frigid waters beneath which the *Grunion* might rest, and of the unpredictable weather above them.

CHAPTER THIRTEEN

"WE HAVEN'T SEEN THE WORST OF IT YET"

———— ◆ ◆ ◆ ————

A s the *Aquila* pushed through choppy swells into Kiska Harbor at
6 a.m. on August 10, 2006, only the glowing orange crest of a
9,000-foot volcano hinted that an island was hidden within the fog.
Tash and Gromeko, Aleut fishermen who had shipped out with
Captain Kale Garcia on the 1976-vintage vessel for a decade, looked
up from the ship's prow to the wheelhouse, awaiting a thumbs-up
from the skipper to lower the crabber's two anchors with electric
deck-winches.

Gromeko, his shoulder-length black hair billowing out from
beneath a tight woolen watch cap, turned and flashed a gap-toothed
grin at Art Wright, chief of Williamson & Associates' deep-water
sonar team, assuring him that Garcia knew every inch of the waters
below and had just guided the boat over shoals capable of cutting
a vessel in two.

Wright simply nodded. In Seattle a month earlier, he had grasped that Garcia was a seasoned hand at the helm in the world's roughest waters. Also in Seattle, John Abele had decided that even if the dour Wright and the personable commercial fishing captain loathed each other, they would have to work together: both were the right men to lead the expedition.

Gromeko and Tash, their yellow pull-over slickers glistening with spray, hit the switches at Garcia's signal. The *Aquila* jerked as the anchors hissed from their casing, splashed into the sea, and sank until their chains stiffened at twenty fathoms.

"We're here,"[1] eleven-year-old Tanner Garcia piped up in the wheelhouse. Jay Larson, one of the electronics and engineering experts for Wright's team, tousled the boy's hair and said, "Too bad we can't *see* 'here.'"

As spray from six-foot swells and fifty-mile-per-hour gusts slapped against the thick wheelhouse windows, the fog conjured images for team members who knew about the "Aleutian Turkey Shoot." In late July 1943, fog had cloaked Kiska so densely that 5,183 Japanese troops and civilian workers had been successfully evacuated from the harbor without tipping off the oncoming U.S. invasion fleet. All American aircraft were grounded. Three weeks later, 35,000 American Marines and soldiers realized—after eight days of stumbling across the fog-swathed island—that Kiska was deserted. By the time the murk lifted, at least twenty-four Americans had been cut down by friendly fire, and scores more wounded on Kiska's slopes.

Garcia glanced at the fog again hiding those same crags, and then at the barometer. He gauged that the damp veil would break in twenty-four hours.

Most of the Williamson team—the exceptions were Larson, Wright, Graham, and former nuclear submarine navigator Bill

Heath—had never sailed in waters as wild as the Bering Sea. Though all of the Williamson team had deep-sea experience, some of them were having a hard time acclimating themselves to the choppy, swollen sea and had been retching and groggy ever since the *Aquila* had lumbered out of Dutch Harbor.

At 6:00 the next morning, August 11, the team members whose stomachs could handle a full breakfast downed scrambled eggs, ham, bacon, toast, and coffee served up by Anj and Kenzie Garcia. Other men only dared to put a little coffee and juice in queasy stomachs. Kale Garcia poked his head into the galley and suggested that they come up onto the deck to take a look at something.

The sonar team rushed out of the galley and gathered along the starboard gunwale. A cavernous opening in the fog revealed the peaks and plateaus of Kiska, treeless but carpeted by brilliant yellow and purple wildflowers. On wind-bent shore grass beyond a shelf of black volcanic sand sat a rusted Imperial Navy mini-submarine. Japanese antiaircraft guns still pointed skyward along the ridges, and long-abandoned machine gun barrels jutted from algae-encrusted pillboxes peering down at the beach. Deep divots from American bombs and Naval shells pocked every hill. No one called Kiska home anymore, not since World War II.

Pete Lowney, his weather-beaten Red Sox cap turned backwards like a catcher's, trained his digital video camera on the aging relics of the long-forgotten theater of war, Jim Abele's war. As on every night since the sonar team and the *Aquila* had gathered at Dutch Harbor, Lowney planned to email video and still photos to Jim's sons. Tonight Bruce, Brad, and John would have their first glimpses of the rugged island and sheltered harbor that had filled their father's periscope lens so many years ago.

As Lowney's camera whirred and leaden waves washed over abandoned concrete docks and sea-plane ramps at the harbor's

North Head, Garcia pointed at a reddish-brown mass poking at least a dozen feet above the surface. "That's the bow of the *Nazima Maru*," he said. "Our planes got her. American and Japanese wrecks all over the place around here."

Richard Graham, the chief navigator of the unmanned side-scan sonar submersible "towfish," hoped they could at least get it into the water soon.

The latest weather report was predicting seventy-mile-per-hour winds and twelve-foot waves moving in, and Garcia and the Williamson team could not risk the costly towfish in open waters that rough. Still, Garcia pointed out, the front would probably not hit Kiska for five or six hours.

Graham and Wright asked Garcia to join them in front of the squat, windowless steel navigation shack that the engineers had constructed in the *Aquila*'s stern. As usual, Tanner bounded along at his father's side. The skipper suggested that he take the ship just outside the harbor mouth so that the Williamson team could lower the towfish over the side and test their equipment for a few hours before the weather turned.

Wright asked if they could get a quarter mile out to check their electronics with a quick peek for the sub chasers—and the destroyer that had been torpedoed by the *Growler*.

Garcia agreed to try, but warned that at the first sign of heavy winds and swells, the towfish had to come up immediately and the *Aquila* rush into port. He also warned that they had to watch for any hint of a "williwaw." Pointing at the volcano's smoldering crest, he explained that williwaws were sudden winds that gathered around the peaks and shot down the cliffs at a hundred or more miles per hour to kick up monster waves—even in August.

At 10 a.m. Garcia throttled up in the wheelhouse, and the anchor chains squealed back into their casing. Graham and Heath huddled inside the windowless, corrugated steel walls of the control shack, checking the high-resolution computer screens that would grid images from the towfish as the pair maneuvered it in beneath the surface. A sophisticated GPS system apprised them of the side-scan sonar's depth and distance from the *Aquila* at every moment. On another screen shone a sonar grid that mapped twenty square miles, spreading west from the harbor's entrance.

The *Aquila* headed from the relatively calm waters of the harbor into choppier ones a few miles southwest of Kiska. In the wheelhouse, Garcia scanned the waves from the helm, and Tanner kept his eyes on the *Aquila*'s own sonar screen. Wright, Kelly, Lee, and Beck were arrayed in front of Williamson's huge ICIS computer and sonar monitors in the chart room, just below the wheelhouse, no intercom necessary for them to talk with Garcia. As soon as the team winched the towfish into the sea, sonar images would stream onto the chart-room screens.

Jay Larson, Tash, and Gromeko removed the padlocks from the lid of the 30-foot-long, 5-foot-wide steel container bolted just in front of the control shack. A 2-ton, 40-foot-high j-crane that Williamson engineers had designed specifically for the *Aquila* loomed over the container and in front of the starboard aft rail. They tugged open the lid. As Tash remarked, the gleaming, freshly painted towfish inside looked just like a big yellow torpedo.

Tash and Gromeko each moved in front of the electric deck winches normally used to cast king crab and black-cod nets over the side and deep into the Bering Sea. On this trip, though, three miles of 5/8 inch-thick steel cable were wound tightly in each winch's mammoth spool, one line for the towfish only, the other link attached both to the towfish and the j-crane.

Tash pressed the switch and carefully released just enough cable for Larson to feed into a large eye-hook on the front of the yellow submersible. Once Larson locked the line into place, Gromeko released enough steel strand for Larson to wind through a second eye-hook on the towfish and clamp onto the j-crane.

Larson stood and flashed both thumbs up. With a deafening rasp of hissing cable winding up the winch, the j-crane lifted the towfish, and it rose from its container and swayed above the stern. Graham popped out of the shack, stared for several long seconds at the dangling submersible, nodded at Larson, and vanished back inside the control hutch.

"Let her down!" he hollered.

Squealing metal cable pealed along the *Aquila* again. Slowly, the towfish descended from the crane and splashed into the whitecaps behind the ship. The submersible's powerful propellers thrashed to life, kicking up spouts, and the towfish began to pull away to starboard as line from the second winch dipped into the sea. Graham plotted the submersible's course on his screen and nudged the joystick. "Surface current's not too bad," he said to Heath, who tracked the images of the towfish on the visual monitor. "She's responding about three seconds from each prompt."

"Surface images clear," Heath said.

Underwater currents can be tricky anywhere, but in the Bering Sea they will shift in any direction without warning. As Larson watched the lines for any possible snags and the towfish bobbed a hundred feet away, Graham flicked the joystick to take the towfish down.

Bubbles rippled around the towfish as it vanished beneath the surface, and then only a fleeting trail of foam was visible. Two minutes later, Graham leveled the submersible at thirty feet below the surface, the currents swirling but not heavy.

Controlling the position of the towfish to the *Aquila* and keeping the cable aligned was challenging even in these calm waters. If the sea grew stormy—a guarantee at some point—disaster loomed. The cable could jam or catch on something underwater and become tangled, and it would be impossible to lift the costly towfish from the waves back aboard the *Aquila*.

In the wheelhouse, Wright's gruff voice sounded pleased that they were "getting good feeds from below, but picking up some 'drop-outs' on the audio."

The drop-outs meant sudden silence amid the sonar "pings" that the towfish was sending up. A steady stream of sound waves was supposed to allow the computers to create maps and images of every seabed undulation, underwater outcrop, ridge, slope, and ship-wreck. Interruptions in the sonar waves emitted by the towfish would distort the images. A large rock or even a dead whale might look like a sunken vessel, or vice versa.

But now a loud and steady series of pings filled the monitors with sharp images of what lay underwater just outside the harbor. Amid dozens of trawling nets torn loose by rocks and swift currents, two large masses appeared twenty yards apart. Garcia made several passes over them. Lowney speculated that the image might be the two halves of the destroyer *Arare*, broken in two when the torpedo hit her.

But then another rash of sporadic breaks in the signal obscured the objects on the feed. Wright frowned, deciding that they could come back to the spot later once they cut the noise.

For the next several hours, the *Aquila* towed the side-scan sonar southwest of the harbor, adjusting the audio to deal with the shifting currents that Wright and his team believed to be the source of the drop-outs. Garcia guided the ship back to Kiska at 7 p.m., and after the winches lifted the towfish smoothly onto the deck, everyone piled into the galley for a dinner of grilled salmon with papaya sauce, mashed Yukon potatoes, and grilled acorn squash. Over dessert, homemade chocolate mousse and ice cream, compliments to Anj and Kenzie gushed before the serious business of mapping out the search strategy for the following week.

With the dishes cleared from the galley's long table, they sipped coffee as Wright and Garcia spread out an enlarged color copy of Seiichi's chart of the clash between the *Kano Maru* and the *Grunion*. As the team gathered around the chart, Wright remarked that even though the chart narrowed the search area from two hundred to four square miles, finding the submarine was still a long shot in such rough waters. He picked up a map pointer and moved it along a bright red line on the chart, Seiichi's line tracking the *Grunion*'s path. The chart showed the location and direction of each of the six, perhaps seven, torpedoes she fired.

Wright ran the pointer along a solid black line that showed the various positions of the sub's periscope relative to the *Kano Maru*. At the end of this path, Seiichi had marked where the 3-inch shell fired from his ship had hit the wave caused by the sub's conning tower.

Carter Lee asked if that was the same spot where the Japanese had later heard an explosion and seen oil on the surface, to which Wright nodded.

Graham wondered out loud about the dotted line that ran from the Japanese ship to the sub's last location, speculating that it might mark a bubble trail showing the torpedo path that the Japanese had used to find the sub and open fire on her.

Garcia added that Seiichi's report mentioned a black bar that shot out of the water near the sub and fell back in at the end of the bubble trail. He suggested that it might not have been just simple debris, but what else it might have been, he had no idea.

Wright had no answer, other than to say the black rod or bar might have been the flagpole on the sub's prow.

Garcia then related that the forecast for the following day had changed; the weather was now looking good enough for them to head out early with hopes of staying out for a significant length of time; the critical spot was only about five miles away, close enough to get back to the harbor fast if the weather turned. Wright and the team members laid out a schedule of 24/7 shifts, most of the Williamson men to work six hours on, six off. Meanwhile, Tash and Gromeko would spell Garcia in the wheelhouse, with Anj, Kenzie, and Tanner taking turns at the fishing boat's own sonar screen, and the crewmen would also split shifts with Wright's team on the winches. Target analysts Mike Kelly and Kevin Beck decided to take twelve-hour shifts in front of the monitors.

Later that night, Garcia sent Bruce, Brad, and John Abele an email: "We had a good day. Art and the boys worked out some kinks in the sonar, and it was running smooth by nightfall. I'm taking them out for the heavy lifting tomorrow and will keep at it till the 19th, or unless the weather turns bad. My gut? I can get them right on top of the spot on Seiichi's chart. These guys know what they're doing."[2]

Wright had written to the Abeles earlier about the problems with the sonar equipment on the towfish: "We have had some problems today with noise in the sonar system from various causes, but they seem behind us after three sessions on deck for investigation and tuning. We have no sunken ships yet but we do have a possible large, rectangular object in two pieces about 50 x 20 meters. Could be the Japanese destroyer *Arare*, but I'm not willing to go that far yet.... Right now, the wind is NNW 20–30 mph. We are in a lee in Kiska Harbor so seas are only 3–5 knots. Temps are in mid-forties with some sporadic snow and sleet in the squalls. Weather is very variable."[3]

A third email, from Pete Lowney, went out with video images and a few sonar pictures to the Abeles that night, his words filled with excitement and anticipation: "I jumped the gun in thinking we saw the *Arare*, so I'll leave the sonar analyzing to the pros. It is really amazing here."

The weather tempered even the high-spirited Lowney's words, though: "Since dinner and our strategy session, the winds have started to gust, and the rigging is starting to howl from it. I am sure we haven't seen the worst of it yet, but Kale knows what he's doing in any kind of conditions."[4]

CHAPTER FOURTEEN

"THAT LOOKS LIKE A SUB"

At 5 a.m. on August 12, the *Aquila* set out from the almost glassy waters of Kiska Harbor and slipped southwest. The plan, set forth in email from Garcia to the Abele brothers, was to "run lines near McArthur Reef and work our way through the sonar grid out to the spot on Seiichi's battle map."[1] Garcia, pleased by the slow, rolling swells and the 68-degree temperature, throttled down the engines into neutral three miles from the harbor, and the Williamson team winched the towfish into the waves. It submerged with barely a ripple, and seconds later clear sonar images surged onto the screens in the shack and the chart room.

Suddenly Kenzie cried with delight from the starboard rail, pointing down the towfish line. Several sleek black mink whales leaped out of the water and over the cable, plunged, and resurfaced to vault over the line again and again, their loud splashes dousing everyone on deck.

As the submersible descended to nearly 3,000 feet, rocky outcrops, underwater ridges, and several sunken trawlers came into view. Slowly and meticulously, Kale Garcia navigated the *Aquila* over dozens of "boxes" or "squares"—of the grid mapped onto the computers by the target analysts—on the ocean floor. The search edged ever closer to McArthur Reef, a low, telltale bulge of dark volcanic rocks covered in kelp and gulls and terns arrayed in neat ranks. In the waters surrounding that mass lay the sharp edges of submerged volcanic peaks—and dozens of wrecks.

Two sets of images flowed up to the *Aquila* from the towfish; one series was 30 khz low-resolution used for large areas; the other, high-resolution at 60 khz. Scrutinizing and cataloguing the scans, lead target analyst Mike Kelly was pleased by the images' clarity; the underwater currents were not causing much distortion. "If the *Grunion*'s down there and the pictures stay this good, we've got a strong chance,"[2] he told Wright.

Wright immediately emailed an update to the Abeles:

> John, Brad & Bruce—There are a lot of survey days between now and 19 August; we will have a lot of results by then to show you, and I urge you to come to Adak, which is less than a day from here and has the only airstrip big enough for a Gulfstream, to go over the pictures we're getting. At that time you can tell us your priorities for further search or target evaluation or we could call it a day. I think a trip out here makes a lot of sense for you. The food here's excellent, and the Garcias are eager to host you. Of course, it all hinges on whether we find the sub first.

The sonar is working well. We have been clearly imaging even crab pots over 3,000 feet down. We already have about 15 targets to evaluate. A few are destroyer or sub chaser size. None are deeper than 400 meters yet, and the waters where the *Kano Maru* was are a lot deeper than that. If there's a submarine-size target there, we will see it. It may be difficult to see on a rocky surface, but it would show up in post-processing of the images.

As always, we watch the weather as closely as the screens. Old Neptune's cooperating right now. The visibility is over 1,500 feet, and the water's almost flat calm with small, slow passing swells. We've done lots of searching today and will stay out all night. I believe we are now in the high probability area near McArthur Reef.

Again, John, Adak has a landing strip more than big enough for your Gulfstream.[3]

Near midnight, the *Aquila* was cruising at a mere three knots, her prow rising and dipping in long but gently rolling 4-foot swells. Even under ideal weather conditions, making turns without the tow lines swinging wide and pulling the submersible off course was a daunting piece of navigation, but Garcia's deft work at the helm allowed slow, steady turns even as the crabber and the towfish inched nearer to the menacing outline of McArthur Reef.

"Moving into the high-priority squares," Graham announced from the shack. The winch lines grated and squealed as he nudged the towfish deeper.

As the submersible reached 2,200 feet below the ship, the images on Kelly's screen turned grainy. "Some currents down there?" he asked Graham through the intercom.

"Yeah, swirling a little," Graham replied. "I'll take her back up to 1,800 and see if it's calmer."

Larson, manning the depth-control winch line, hit the "up" switch as Graham's voice came over the headset. The spool rotated clockwise, tugging against the pressure below to pull up the line fifty feet a minute.

A sudden clang bellowed from the winch, then a vibration that jarred the *Aquila*. Larson instantly killed the power and shouted, "Cable jam!"

Wright and Garcia raced out of the wheelhouse, pounded down the narrow steel ladder to the deck, and joined Larson, who pointed to a thick snarl of cable at the winch's crest. Everyone else except Graham, in the shack, and Tash, who had taken the helm for Garcia, gathered within seconds at the winch. No one had to say what they all knew: a $5 million submersible was floating helpless nearly 2,000 beneath the surface of the Bering Sea.

At just the wrong time. The weather was not going to cooperate with their efforts to retrieve the towfish. The swells were starting to roll higher and faster, the winds were picking up from the north, and the temperature was about to plummet.

Larson and Gromeko climbed into the buoyant but cumbersome fluorescent-yellow survival suits and gingerly scaled the steel rungs on both sides of the winch, weighed down further by their tool belts. Garcia strained to keep the ship from lurching in the gathering swells as spray crashed across the *Aquila*'s decks and burst over the two men, who hooked themselves to the winch forty feet above the deck and the waves.

Larson cursed softly as he studied the snag. It was the size of a basketball, the thick steel strands so gnarled that each was indistinguishable from the next. Even worse, friction had frayed the cable a few feet beneath the knot. If it snapped, the towfish went to the bottom with it. The mission would end then and there.

Larson spoke into his wireless headset. "It's bad, but if we can run just enough line to lower the knot to the deck, we can work on it there. Problem is, there's a chance that even that will snap the cable. Your call, Art."

Garcia turned from the helm to Wright. Both knew that if they did not lower the line, it would give anyway. Garcia began steering the boat in tighter circles to give the line more slack and buy some time.

Wright instantly calculated that Garcia's maneuver would decrease tension on the snarled cable, but it would also decrease control of the submersible from the ship—and thus increase the risk that the sonar would ground on a rock or slope. The more slack in the swing of cable between the towfish and the *Aquila*, the harder for Graham to navigate the vehicle.

Carter Lee and Kevin Beck waited at the winch's switch, listening intently on their headsets.

Larson instructed them to let the cable out no more than twenty feet.

The winch shuddered, the cable jerked downward, and Lee cut the power nearly as fast as he had turned it on.

The tangle of cable clattered onto the deck at the base of the winch. The frayed section was less than a foot long, but every second the towfish tugged on the line below, the chances that it would break mounted. Beck twisted clamps just above and below the shredded steel fibers as Larson and Gromeko clutched the slippery stanchion, unhooked themselves, and eased back onto the deck.

In the shack, Graham said that the towfish was responding, but that he was watching for anything that could rip into it down there, and instructed Kelly, on the monitors in the chart room, to holler if he saw *anything*.

Everyone heard the quaver in the normally laconic navigator's voice.

Larson and Gromeko took turns yanking at the maze of twisted line with a 3-foot wrench and a crowbar, while Lee and Beck alternated working with another wrench to straighten every loosened bit of cable. It was dangerous work; the steel strands could wrap around a finger—or a hand—and slice it off in an instant.

With winds rising to forty miles an hour and whipping up 7-foot waves, Tash tethered life-deck-ring lifelines to all four men and himself. Graham strapped himself into his swivel chair and struggled to control the towfish—keep it steady and guide it away from the rocks and ledges that were appearing in its path with increasing frequency as the swells pulled the *Aquila* closer to McArthur Reef.

Over an hour had rushed by since the cable jam, as the crew members frantically attempted to untangle the cable. Anj Garcia gave her husband a nudge that no one else in the wheelhouse saw. He nodded. She knew the waters nearly as well as Kale. They both realized that time was running out for the Williamson team. Kale Garcia would not sacrifice his family, his crew, and the Williamson men on the reef no matter how valuable the towfish was. Glancing at his watch, he decided to give Art Wright just one hour more, till 2:30 a.m., before cutting the submersible loose, turning back to Kiska, and ending the mission.

Ten more minutes evaporated. Then Larson's voice burst through the wheelhouse intercom: "Line's free. Get ready!"

The spool shuddered and began to turn. With a screech the cable tightened and hissed upward. Graham manipulated the joystick to keep the towfish level in the shifting underwater currents and avoid outcrops that could snag either the vehicle or its cable. The line continued to stream up from the depths, the towfish rising fathom by fathom.

"C'mon," Graham muttered.

At fifty feet per minute, the submersible would break the surface in forty minutes, leaving less time than he wanted for the team to haul it back aboard before Garcia needed to take the *Aquila* about and head back to Kiska. He asked Wright if the Williamson crew could "still pull the thing out of the water if I turn around as soon as it breaks the surface."

Wright, who had been deployed on several voyages near McArthur Reef in his days on nuclear subs, realized that Garcia was cutting it close by waiting even that long to navigate away from the rocks. He agreed, but urged Garcia to "start slow.... Five knots till we have her alongside the crane."

Garcia told him that it would have "to be seven to ten in these winds."

Wright inhaled sharply and nodded. The line continued to come up to the spool.

Shortly after 2 a.m., the surface roiled and bubbled thirty yards to starboard. "There it is!" Tanner yelled in the wheelhouse.

The yellow submersible rode the rising swells as Graham shut down the vehicle's propellers. Larson cut the winch's power, and Lee started up the other winch, the one with the tether line running from the towfish to the j-crane. The submersible bobbed back to the *Aquila*, bumped against the hull, and rose from the ocean to dangle from the j-crane above the ship. Carefully, Lee swung the crane over starboard gunwale and lowered the towfish to the deck.

The *Aquila* turned to the northeast, fighting headwinds while the Williamson team chained the submersible to several deck rings. They would have to wait until they were back at Kiska to check it for damage.

"Jesus Christ," said Graham, who had just emerged from the shack. The navigator pointed at the towline's winch. A long strand of cable dangled and twisted in the gusts. The cable had snapped, most likely just as the submersible had broken the surface and Lee switched power to the tether. If the steel had torn free even seconds earlier, the towfish would be spiraling to the bottom of the Bering Sea.

"Maybe this sub does want to be found," Larson said, shaking his head as the ripped cable clanged over and over against the winch.

Back in the harbor, they discovered that the winch's spool had lost about 150 feet of steel cable, but by 10 a.m., Larson had the machinery running smoothly again. It still contained nearly five miles of line, more than enough for the 3,000- to 6,000-foot depths over the key search area during the next few days. If Seiichi's chart was accurate, the *Grunion* lay somewhere along sonar-grid squares 100–117. But those four square miles, Kale Garcia warned, would prove more challenging than the other sixteen boxes of the surrounding 20-square-mile grid. "The area where the chart has the *Grunion* going down is usually one big rip-tide," he told Wright.

Over coffee in the galley that morning, Garcia and Graham, drained but with adrenaline still churning, pored over Seiichi's chart and Garcia's sonar maps to gauge a course adapted to the currents in the target area, five miles from Kiska and ten from Segula Island. Figuring that 8-foot waves and the undertows would pull the cable at least 300 feet away from the *Aquila* at any given point, the skipper and the navigator settled on moving the ship in long, slow circles that would not place her directly above the spot Seiichi had marked, but would allow Graham to maneuver the towfish to the target location. Three hundred feet—the length of a football field—could make all the difference between finding and missing the sub if she rested in one or two pieces. If she had been torn apart by rocks on her way down, as Bob Ballard suspected, they would never find the *Grunion*.

After thirty-six hours pinned in the harbor by a storm after the near-disaster with the towfish, Kale Garcia guided the *Aquila* back out in the early evening of August 14 and set course for the area where the *Grunion* had last been seen. The fishing boat slogged through 25-mile-an-hour headwinds five miles out, and as the towfish was lowered into the swells, Graham stood ready to bring it back up if the waves rose higher than ten feet. "We could use one of those glassy calms the subs recorded here in 1942," he quipped to Lee.

Graham nestled the towfish down to nearly 6,000 feet, just short of the ocean floor, and as the *Aquila* crisscrossed the grid in long, choppy loops, Graham piloted the submersible uphill along slopes and ridges in alternating east and west runs. "Data looks clear," Kelly said in the chart room.

Twelve hours later, at 9 a.m. on August 15, frustration gnawed at the team. The towfish had made passes over 96 percent of grid squares 100–117. As the sonar pings remained steady but did not increase in speed or loudness (the twin signals of a hit) Wright, sitting next to Kelly in front of the target monitors, emailed an update to the Abeles.

> We are running E-W lines from south of a large slope to its top in sloppy weather without a prominent sub-sized target. Analysis and processing continues. Waves over 9 ft can prevent the search so we are on the border line of bad weather.
>
> We have completely covered the southern portion of 100-117, and the current search area includes part of the location indicated by the Seiichi Battle Map. Today we will cover the northern half of the slope.
>
> This search is not going to be easy, and there is no guarantee.[4]

In the early afternoon, as Garcia started the first pass above the northern slope, the waters on the surface calmed. He leaned toward the intercom in front of the helm. "Richard, how fast are the currents at 3,000 feet?"

From the shack came the navigator's voice: "Not that bad, surprisingly."

Garcia suggested that Graham pull the towfish up to 3,000 feet. "It's worth a shot to see if we get lucky and pull the sonar right over where Seiichi last saw the sub. No more than three knots."

"Go for it," Graham said.

An hour went by, and Garcia was nearing the crucial point on the map, but the pings were still soft. Mike Kelly leaned in close to the target monitor in the chart room, studying every contour of the underwater slope.

Suddenly, a louder ping echoed from the chart room up to the wheelhouse, followed by another.

"Hold her steady, Kale," Kelly called up. "Richard?" The pings grew louder.

"Hearing it, too," Graham replied. "I'm at 3,600 feet. Do you see that shelf at about 3,200? Let's take a look."

The pings intensified, pealing through the intercom to every corner of the *Aquila*. Anj, Tanner, and Kenzie materialized in the chart room. Gromeko rolled from his bunk in the bow's sleeping quarters and raced up to join them.

As Wright's fingers softly drummed on the back of Kelly's chair, Pete Lowney flipped on his video cam and trained it on Kelly and the monitors. The entire team, except for Graham and Lee who were hunkered down in the shack guiding the submersible, crowded the chart room.

"We're at 3,300," Graham intoned, the pings coming faster as the still-grainy outlines of a flattened slope danced in the screens.

No one said a word, the only sounds their quickened breathing, the muted thrum of the engines, and the insistent pings.

Graham announced, "3,200 feet."

On the computer screens in the chart room and the shack, a long, tubular silhouette began to emerge as the sonar signal reached a crescendo. Graham pulled the towfish to a virtual stop above the shelf where the object rested. The pictures sharpened.

He said, "Target is sitting upright on the shelf. Looks to be about 280 feet long, 27 wide." He paused. "That looks like a sub."

Wright peered at the target. "The width's right, but the *Grunion* was 312 feet long…"

Graham shouted: "There's the conning tower and the periscope–that's a sub!"

Cheers and high-fives erupted in the chart room. Kelly grinned and shook his head. "The exact spot where Seiichi said she'd be."

In a solemn voice, Graham said, "There are seventy men down there…"

Quiet filled the wheelhouse again. Then Wright pronounced, "We've got a lot more passes to make over her. We need a look at what's left of the bow."

At 2 a.m. on August 16, 2006, in Newton, Massachusetts, an email popped up on Bruce Abele's computer. Bruce, unable to sleep after the earlier message from Art Wright, was sitting in the living room with the television turned on low to the History Channel. He leaned toward the laptop on the end table. His breath caught for a second at the subject line: "WE FOUND SOMETHING!"

Bruce opened the email and gaped at six sonar images. He read the message, the words effusive and excited for the usually gruff Art Wright:

I am 95% certain that we've found the *Grunion* a few
miles north of McArthur Reef. The object shows a conning tower and periscope. This is certainly the sub, and
exactly where the Japanese chart said it would be. Part of
the bow appears to be blown off or buried in the mud.
You can see part of her slide path behind her. More later.
We will be making runs over the sub for the next two days.
You need to get out here. I'd suggest that you think about
getting an ROV out here to film what we've discovered.[5]

Bruce walked upstairs to the bedroom and gently awakened Sue.
"We've found Jim..."[6] He fought back a sob as the phone rang on
the nightstand. On the other end was John.

CHAPTER FIFTEEN

"DON'T LET YOUR DESIRE FOR THIS TO BE THE RIGHT TARGET FOOL YOU"

———✦———

Off Kiska, the unusual "target image" picked up by the side-scan sonar at 3,200 feet sparked excitement and, soon, debate. The narrow oblong silhouette lay almost exactly at the spot where Sei-ichi Aiura and the crew of the *Kano Maru* had last seen an American sub's periscope and the eighty-fourth shot from the *Kano Maru*'s deck gun had reportedly struck the sub. But with a sonar image, there was no way to tell if the round had even damaged the *Grunion*, let alone sent her to the bottom. Only video or photographs could determine that or rule it out.

———✦———

As the *Aquila* towed the side-scan sonar in the Bering Sea in search of the *Grunion*, another search was underway, one that had been unfolding for several years—the hunt to find the families and piece together the life histories of every man lost on the *Grunion*. The historical detectives were three remarkable women employing not sophisticated tools such as side-scan sonar, but their ordinary computers, telephones, and extraordinary resourcefulness—Rhonda Raye, Vickie Rodgers, and Mary Bentz, known fondly to the rapidly growing "*Grunion* community" as the "Sub Ladies."

The saga of the Sub Ladies had its ultimate beginnings back in the early years after the *Grunion* vanished, with Kay Abele's long-running correspondence with *Grunion* wives, mothers, and sweethearts. But as with so many aspects of the search for the submarine, the internet played a pivotal role in expanding the *Grunion* community and bringing to light more clues and facts about the men who had served under Jim Abele.

Bruce Abele's wife, Susan, had read through and organized the letters Kay had saved, and she also discovered Rhonda Raye, the first Sub Lady, through one of Raye's genealogy posts about crewman Paul Banes, her great-uncle. The other two Sub Ladies were also related to crewmen who had vanished with the *Grunion*. Vickie Rodgers was the great-niece of Merritt Graham, and Mary Bentz the niece of Carmine Parziale, of Weedville, Pennsylvania.

Raye, Rodgers, and Bentz, working closely with the Abeles, had been digging into birth and marriage records, Social Security files, obituaries, probate records, telephone books, and countless websites. The women wanted to find answers for what had happened to each and every *Grunion* crewman and to provide those answers to the families. Mary Bentz would persuade numerous newspapers across America to run stories about *Grunion* sailors. All three Sub Ladies were driven by a determination that the men of the *Grunion* would receive their due, would be recognized for their sacrifice.

The Abele Family Portrait, fondly known as "the Adirondack picture" because of the Adirondack chairs on which Jim and Kay are sitting. The boys from left to right: Brad, John, and Bruce. Taken at Tiverton, Rhode Island, 1941. *Courtesy of the Abele family.*

Older brother Trescott Abele and younger brother Jim Abele (batting) in Quincy, Massachusetts, around 1910. *Courtesy of the Abele family.*

Captain Arthur Abele, Spanish American War hero and Jim's uncle, watching Jim, a varsity soccer star for the U.S. Naval Academy, on the practice field at Annapolis in the early 1920s. *Courtesy of the Abele family.*

The *R-13*, Jim Abele's first command. (On the conning tower, note the E for excellence. The *R-13* was the only sub at the time, 1938, to receive that honor from U.S. Submarine Base, New London, Connecticut.) *Courtesy of the Abele family.*

Shinoda Chiyo, wife of Shinoda Isamu, the commander of Japanese sub chaser *CH-27*, holding the couple's first child, son Kazuo, in 1935. *Courtesy of the Shinoda and Abele families.*

Father and son—Kazuo and Isamu in 1941. *Courtesy of the Shinoda and Abele families.*

The *Grunion* (*SS-216*) slides down the launching ways on December 22, 1941, at the Electric Boat Company in Groton, Connecticut.
Electric Boat Company photo courtesy of John Crouse, St. Mary's Sub Museum, for ussgrunion.com.

The crippled Japanese freighter *Kano Maru* off Kiska Island, 1942.
Courtesy of Lieutenant Colonel Richard Lane (retired).

Kay Abele, now a war widow raising three boys on her own, 1943. *Courtesy of the Abele family.*

31 Mountfort Rd
Newton Highlands, Mass
Oct. 28.

Dear Mr Hutchinson

As the wife of the captain of the Grunion I have been thinking very much these days of the families of the men aboard. I know how very anxious we all are for any satisfaction to the men to

Catherine T. Abele
(Mrs M-L. Abele)

One of the individual condolence letters sent by Kay Abele to the families of every man lost aboard the USS *Grunion*. *Courtesy of the Abele family.*

The homefront. The Abeles' Victory Garden, summer 1942. The family lived in the barn (background) until Kay Abele rented a house in Newton, Massachusetts, later that summer. *Courtesy of the Abele family.*

Young Bruce Abele and John Abele (in cart), after the loss of the *Grunion* and their father. *Courtesy of the Abele family.*

Bruce and Brad (on Bruce's shoulders), 1943.
Courtesy of the Abele family.

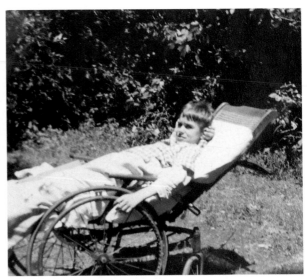

John Abele, battling osteomyelitis and the full-length cast that went off and on for seven years. *Courtesy of the Abele family.*

The *Aquila*, the commercial fishing boat that was a far cry from the sleek, sophisticated research vessels that typically hunt for shipwrecks, but proved up to the task of finding the USS *Grunion* in the dangerous Bering Sea. *Courtesy of the Abele family.*

Preparing the *Aquila* as a makeshift research platform for a sophisticated sonar search for the *Grunion*, members of the 2006 sonar search discussing how to mount the winch they would need for the towfish (the side-scan sonar vehicle). *Courtesy of the Abele family.*

The 2006 sonar search team and crew. (All members are identified in the photo.)
Courtesy of the Abele family.

The side-scan sonar, or towfish, that would be lowered into the Bering Sea in search of the USS *Grunion*. *Courtesy of the Abele family.*

Yutaka Iwasaki, flanked by John Abele (left) and Bruce Abele (right), gave the Abeles the two key clues for discovering the *Grunion*—Seiichi's battle report and the chart that narrowed the search area in the Bering Sea from 200 to 4 square miles. *Courtesy of the Abele family.*

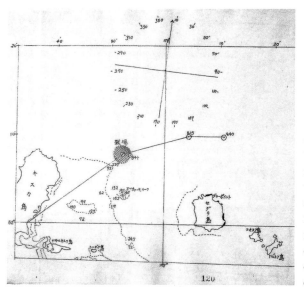

Seiichi Aiura's map, the "Rosetta Stone" of the search for the *Grunion*, narrowed the target area from 200 to 4 square miles—though finding the sub was still a massive longshot, given the dangerous winds and currents of the Bering Sea. *Courtesy of the Abele family.*

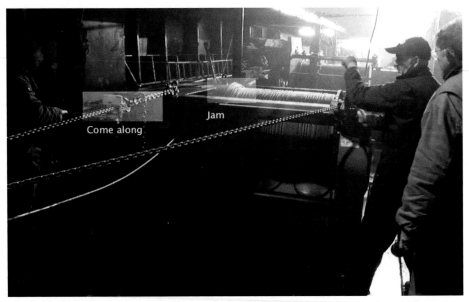

Come along

Jam

The cable jam that nearly ended the sonar search before the *Grunion* could be found. *Courtesy of the Abele family.*

One of the difficult-to-read sonar images from August of 2006 that convinced team leader Art Wright that they had "almost certainly" found the *Grunion*. *Courtesy of Williamson & Associates and the Abele family.*

Aboard the *Aquila*, the Max Rover ROV (Remotely Operated Vehicle) that found the *Grunion* on a volcanic shelf 3,000 feet down in the Bering Sea off Kiska Island, providing the first visual images since 1942 of the vanished sub. *Courtesy of the Abele family.*

The 2007 ROV search team and crew. (All members are identified in the photo.) *Courtesy of the Abele family.*

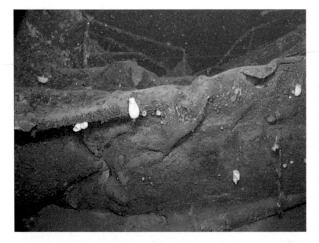

A ghostly ROV image of the wreckage of the *Grunion*'s forward torpedo room. The pictures from the Max Rover were the first visual images of the *Grunion* since her disappearance sixty-five years earlier, on July 31, 1942.
Courtesy of the Abele family.

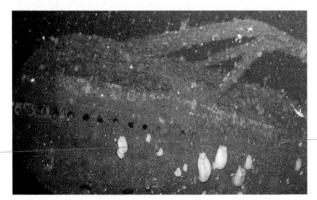

Max Rover footage of the *Grunion*'s propeller guards, affixed to the stern. This key part of the puzzle was strong proof that the wreck could be no other than the missing submarine.
Courtesy of the Abele family.

The *Grunion*'s prop guards as they looked during her construction in 1941–42, and on her first and final war patrol. *Electric Boat Company photo courtesy of John Crouse, St. Mary's Sub Museum, for ussgrunion.com.*

ROV image of the *Grunion*'s deck gun. *Courtesy of the Abele family.*

The *Grunion*'s stanchion, sixty-five years after she sank. *Courtesy of the Abele family.*

On the *Aquila*, John Abele prepares to spread wildflowers from Kiska Island at the exact spot where his father's submarine went down sixty-five years ago.

The ship's bell of the USS *Grunion*. John Abele arranged for the bell to be flown from Greenville, Mississippi, to Cleveland, Ohio, for the 2008 USS *Grunion* memorial service, on Columbus Day weekend 2008.
Courtesy of the Abele family.

Grunion families, friends, and media gathered at the USS *Cod* Museum, Cleveland, Ohio, for the 2008 memorial services and associated events over the Columbus Day weekend. Mary Bentz was one of many people who read names from the honor roll of the *Grunion* crewmen and officers before a hushed, reflective crowd.
Courtesy of the Abele family.

Shinoda Chiyo, seen holding flowers from Kiska sent to her by the Abeles. In February 2012, Chiyo passed away at the age of 101. *Courtesy of the Shinoda family.*

The USS *Volador* survived a circular-run torpedo that lodged in the conning tower but did not detonate. *Courtesy of National Archives, Naval Branch.*

The *Grunion* on the Thames River in the spring of 1942, as she would have looked on her way to her first and final war patrol on May 24, 1942. *Electric Boat Company photo courtesy of John Crouse, St. Mary's Sub Museum, for ussgrunion.com.*

The realization that their father's submarine might well have been found and a desire to sit down in person with Art Wright and his Williamson team to analyze the intriguing sonar images compelled the Abele brothers to board John's private jet and head to Alaska. Although Brad was suffering from pronounced neck soreness and other symptoms of his illness, he insisted on making the trip.

The Abeles planned to meet with Wright and company at Adak Island, some 240 miles east of Kiska and some 1,300 miles from Anchorage. The flight did not go as planned.

On August 20, the jet approached Adak—only to find a dense fog shrouding the island and its airstrip. Fuel was dwindling, but attempting a landing could prove lethal. The brothers, at the pilot's strong suggestion, made the decision to head to Cold Bay, the site of a 10,420-foot runway. They were taking the risk that the fuel gauge might hit empty before they completed the more-than-600-mile flight, but it was a risk they had to take.

They made it to Cold Bay with the fuel gauge hovering just above "Empty." But as the jet touched down, ice on the runway sent it skidding. It spun to a stop just a few yards from the ocean.

The Abeles, shaken but undeterred, hoped they would be able to refuel the plane—and meanwhile, find a place to stay—on this remote, rugged outpost. And luck was with them—after their harrowing near escape from the icy waters, they were fortunate enough to find lodging at the Cold Bay Lodge, where proprietress Mary Martin made certain they had everything they needed—including, to their surprise, wireless access. And the aptly named Frosty Fuels would be able to replenish the jet for the run back to Adak. Now, all they could do was wait and see if the fog there would lift. The Abeles checked in constantly with people in Adak, glad to have found refuge in the Cold Bay Lodge but eager to be where they could go over the sonar images with Art Wright's team.

The unexpected wireless access put John Abele in touch with wreck-recovery expert Bob Ballard by email. Ballard had read a front-page *Boston Globe* story about the sonar hit—reporter Ralph Ranalli happened to interview Bruce Abele the very morning following the discovery—and viewed several of the images the Abeles had posted on their *Grunion* website. Ballard urged caution over emotion in scrutinizing the images. Art Wright had evinced "95 percent certainty" that he had found the submarine, but Ballard had several concerns about the images. He was most bothered about "the target's shadow, which looks much more like a surface ship than a submarine."[1]

Ballard also speculated that "the forward portion of the image shows a high mast that appears to be too far forward to be the submarine's periscope and conning tower nor does it look like that."[2] Still, he did not dismiss the possibility that "if the submarine crashed into a hard bottom, you may be looking at a buckled (modified) bow and an overall shortening to the sub's length."

He viewed the possibility as unlikely, though: "It is my belief that you have found a surface ship."[3]

Ballard suggested that if the brothers were leaning toward a second expedition, another sonar search, not a Remotely Operated Vehicle, would be advisable. But for the moment, the fog cloaking Adak was the Abeles' chief concern. The Abeles had not yet even discussed a second expedition—not before they had even had the chance to sit down to look at all the side-scan images from the first one.

The fog finally cleared enough for the Abeles to fly to Adak on August 21. Wright and his team were waiting.

Together they pored over two series of towfish images, both the low-resolution 30 khz images of large areas and the other high resolution images at 60 khz. The towfish could send low-resolution images from close to a half-mile in either direction, for a total one-mile swath.

It would look left and right, roughly parallel to the seabed. If there was a hill or rock in the way, everything behind it would be shadowed, or hidden. As a result, Art Wright had substantially overlapped the vehicle's passes. The team had enjoyed remarkable luck because the area of the bottom where the target was found was largely free of any rocks or other objects that might distort the image. (Later, in the search for the two sub chasers sunk by the *Grunion* and for the destroyer *Arare*, protrusions and rocks would make conclusive readings of the sonar images impossible.)

Even though the sonar images of the main target Wright's team had identified showed protrusions that could be a conning tower and a periscope mast, the entire object appeared to be some twenty to fifty feet shorter (it was difficult to estimate length with the towfish) than the 312-foot *Grunion*. The range—twenty to fifty feet— reflected the difficulty of estimating length with the towfish. The debate about the "superstructure" of the object led several team members to agree with Ballard that it was likelier to be a surface vessel than a sub.

Complicating the team's interpretations, one of the potentially best images had been distorted by winch movements as the side-scan sonar had passed by the target. The images were so difficult to read that skeptics could argue the target might be a dead whale or a large chunk of cold magma from Kiska's volcano. Even if it was a wreck, the shape might be a sunken surface vessel, especially since it did not appear to have the propeller-guards that had been affixed at the *Grunion*'s launching so many years ago. The debate over the prop guards—a crucial part of the profile of a Gato-class submarine like the *Grunion*—would continue long after the meeting at Adak. Team member Richard Graham asserted that outlines of a propeller guard were present, but Art Wright and several other Williamson experts vehemently disagreed.

Still, it might be the sub. Graham could be right about the prop guards, and it was feasible that that part of the submarine's bow had been buried or blown off, making the wreck appear shorter than the 312-foot sub.

The Abeles sensed that they might have beaten the odds, that some sixty-five years after the *Grunion*'s final transmission, they might have found their father's submarine, 3,000 feet deep in the Bering Sea. For Jim's sons, the Sub Ladies, and the ever-expanding worldwide ranks of people mesmerized by the search for the *Grunion*, the desire to find out for certain pushed the implausible project forward.

"At the very least," John Abele said, "the sonar images gave us something to go after."[4]

Now, as John, Bruce, and Brad flew back home, no one knew exactly what the next step would be.

Bob Ballard had advised the Abeles, "Don't let your desire for this to be the right target fool you."[5] No matter how instinctively they believed that the towfish had discovered the *Grunion*, clearer proof was needed. In the weeks and months following the brothers' return from Adak, they consulted numerous experts, who scrutinized the sonar images.

Many of them believed that the sonar image could not be the *Grunion*. They agreed with Ballard that a submarine would have broken into pieces on the rugged volcanic terrain in the waters off Kiska.

Scientists and nautical experts were naturally skeptical of the Abeles' quixotic quest. Critics scoffed at the possibility that three inexperienced sons of a sub's commander, funding an expedition to some of the most dangerous waters in the world in an old crab boat, had discovered the long-vanished *Grunion* nearly two-thirds of a mile down. In Las Vegas, the odds against success for such a venture would have been off the proverbial board.

But the Abeles were impressed by the fact that the target they had found lay exactly where it should according to Seiichi's account and the *Kano Maru* logbook.

Ongoing study of the sonar images continued. In November 2006, John Abele commissioned Art Wright to create a computerized 3-dimensional collage of the sonar images. Wright enhanced the images' background, accounting for topography and shadows and focusing on the slide path—the "track" that led to the target site on the underwater slope. Augmenting Wright's work, Bruce Abele took a model sub and photographed it on a gravel slope for comparison to the target lying on the underwater slope off Kiska.

John Abele showed Robert Ballard additional images, but the discoverer of the *Titanic* was still wary of accepting that the target Wright and Garcia had found was the *Grunion*. Meanwhile, the Abeles pondered their next move—whether to mount a second expedition to Kiska and, if they did, whether to use sonar again, or a Remotely Operated Vehicle such as the one that had discovered the *Titanic* in her North Atlantic grave.

A key element in identifying the target as the *Grunion* was the existence or absence of the propeller guards. The guards, armatures of welded pipes that cantilevered away horizontally from high on the vessel's stern, kept mooring lines from fouling a sub's propellers when she was in port. At the Adak meeting, Richard Graham had raised the possibility that several of the sonar images indicated prop guards. If the target did indeed have them, the chances that it could be any other vessel than the *Grunion* were virtually zero.

But even if there were no prop guards on the target, it still might be the *Grunion*. Did the *Grunion* set out on her first and final patrol with the prop guards affixed? And were they still attached when she pulled out of harbor at Midway? Several Naval experts pointed out that in 1942 an order was issued to remove prop guards before

American submarines sailed into action. When historian and retired Naval officer Captain John Alden dug into the issue, however, he discovered that the order had been issued in *September* 1942—well after the *Grunion* had disappeared.

So the Abeles had something very specific to go after. If actual video of the target taken from an ROV were to reveal prop guards, she absolutely had to be Jim's missing submarine—they would have found the final resting place of their father and his sixty-nine crewmen.

The Abeles decided to locate a Remotely Operated Vehicle and go back to Kiska in August 2007. When the brothers had considered an ROV for the 2006 expedition, they had discussed the possibility with Deep Sea Systems International of Falmouth, Massachusetts; however, the logistics of flying out more than 30,000 pounds of costly equipment had seemed too daunting. On Ballard's advice, the Abeles had chosen to send out the *Aquila* with the towfish instead. Now the necessity to film the target, which they believed was their father's submarine, not only compelled them to mount a second expedition, but also to use the ROV.

CHAPTER SIXTEEN

BY LAND, SEA, AND AIR

———◆———

Art Wright, who hoped to operate the Remotely Operated Vehicle, suggested the Mohican, a submersible owned by Seattle-based Northwest Underwater Construction. John Abele, who would have to pay to use an ROV, and also to insure it, had qualms about letting Wright pilot the vehicle—Wright's experience was with sonar. Bruce Abele, agreeing with John, contacted another outfit, Submersible Systems of Louisiana. One of the deep-sea experts there pointed out that the Mohican was well suited neither to the Bering's rough conditions nor to the depth where the target rested. Although Submersible Systems offered a better-suited ROV for the 2007 expedition at a reasonable bid, the Abeles decided that the Louisiana company was not the right fit for the job either.

Over Wright's objections, the brothers went back to Falmouth, Massachusetts, and Deep Sea Systems International (DSSI), a division of Oceaneering. John and Bruce struck a deal in March 2007 to bring DSSI's state-of-the-art Max Rover to Kiska, and for DSSI's own team to travel to Alaska to operate the vehicle. When John and Bruce told Wright that he was welcome to come back for the second mission to handle the sonar that would accompany the ROV, Wright brusquely refused.

Richard Graham, whose expertise had proven so vital in the 2006 side-scan sonar search, had left Williamson & Associates after clashing with Wright. Graham asked if he could be part of the ROV search—he wanted the chance to see if his theory that the target did, in fact, have prop guards was accurate. The Abeles immediately rehired him.

The new team included DSSI's ROV experts Chris Nicholson, Joe Caba, and Toshi Mikagawa, and Woods Hole oceanographer Dave Gallo. Gallo, a Ballard protégé, related that his Woods Hole scientific colleagues put the chances of finding the sub at "zero."

It seemed especially fitting that the Japanese Toshi was a pilot on the ROV, for the venture would never have been possible without Japanese help. From Japan—not the U.S. Navy—had come the key clues, Aiura's account and chart, which chronicled the last actual glimpses of the doomed sub. Every time the Abeles contacted the Navy, they hit a stone wall.

The DSSI/Oceaneering vehicle that the Abeles hoped would capture the target was the ROV Global Explorer, which was outfitted with a sophisticated, high-quality HD video camera and a 3- to 4-megapixel digital camera. The ROV's powerful lighting equipment meant the images it sent back from the ocean floor would have an expected clarity of thirty to forty feet. The team also hoped to use a bathymetric navigator, which could provide a 3-D image of the ocean bottom, the target, any nearby debris, and the three Japanese wrecks.

Hiring the DSSI team was one thing. Getting some 36,000 pounds—eighteen tons—of equipment from Falmouth to Seattle and then from Seattle to Adak for mobilization in advance of heading out to Kiska again was quite another matter. Kale Garcia planned to dock the *Aquila* in Seattle on July 21, after completing a commercial run in the South Pacific. She would need an overhaul to prepare for the rugged waters off Kiska again, and the Abeles believed that she could be refitted in the three to four days that they hoped it would take professional truck driver Bob Crider and his wife to haul the ROV and other equipment 3,100 miles cross-country to Seattle. The Criders left at 11 a.m. on July 27, hoping to roll into Seattle on July 31.

The expedition's mobilization crew, as well as Pete Lowney, planned to meet up with them and the equipment there on July 30. After three to six days of mobilization to ready the *Aquila* for the ROV and equipment and then carefully transfer it all aboard, the ship would set out for Adak, a voyage of twelve days or so, depending on the weather. As it had been the previous summer, time was a crucial factor. To have any chance of lowering the ROV to the target, Garcia had to navigate the *Aquila* to Kiska no later than the third week of August; even then, everything hinged on whether the rough waters and williwaws of the Bering would wane for at least a few hours.

In Seattle, Garcia and his crew started constructing the necessary sounding pole on July 25. Garcia also reviewed ways of improving communications with two 64k modems with a 128k bandwidth, so that both emails and photos could be sent at a high speed from the Aleutians to the mainland. The plans for the expedition called for three satellite phones aboard the *Aquila*.

Bob Crider reached Seattle with the eighteen tons of equipment, including the ROV, on August 1, after barely missing one of the worst traffic jams in Massachusetts' history on the first day out and passing through Minneapolis two days before a fatal bridge collapse. Chris Nicholson and the DSSI team were ready and waiting on the dock in front of the *Aquila*. Knowing that they were racing the elements in distant Kiska, the team quickly unpacked their equipment and began to assemble the ROV, the winch, and the mission's electronic operating shack in the stern of the crabber.

By August 8, the team had completed the mobilization but still needed to run a key test of the ROV in the harbor. To set out for Adak, let alone Kiska, without testing the equipment would be too chancy. They lowered the ROV into Seattle Harbor and found a small leak in one of the cameras. Fortunately, Nicholson could repair it and subject it to a second trial. As the Abeles now knew, an ROV camera "cost about the same as a small house." The team breathed a collective sigh of relief when the camera stood up to the second test in the harbor.

———————◆◆◆———————

As the *Aquila*'s crew readied her for the trip to Adak and everyone began to scrutinize extended weather forecasts for the Aleutians, the other search for the *Grunion*—back in time—continued in earnest. Sub Ladies Raye, Rogers, and Bentz continued to turn up amazing stories about Jim Abele's crew, their backgrounds, and their families.

"Look at those faces," Bentz, looking at photos of crew members, would tell *USA Today*."They're frozen in time." The Sub Ladies were determined to make the stories behind those pictures come alive. As Rogers would say, "We were just turning over rocks. There was no system or method. Whatever idea we came up with, we ran with it."

According to Raye, "The thing is, Vickie, Mary and I all have various ways of going about the search, and it is that combination that made this a success."[1] Turning over the rocks revealed scores of compelling stories. The crew of the *Grunion* was a microcosm of American society.

One search led to a convent, where a crew member's long-lost sister was a nun. Another led to two sisters who had been given up for adoption as infants. In one of the most poignant stories, Bentz traced Jack Pancoast's marriage to Julia in the Philippines and her harrowing years of hiding their son, Jack, Jr.—blond and blue-eyed– during the Japanese occupation. Not until Mary Bentz put the pieces together, more than half a century later, would the son learn his father's story.

On August 10, as the *Aquila* was poised to head out for Kiska, Rhonda Raye found a nephew of John E. Wilson, a cook on the *Grunion*. The Sub Ladies had now discovered relatives for sixty-eight out of the seventy officers and crew—the trio's hunt had narrowed to the two last crewmen, Moore J. Ledford and Byron A. Traviss.

At 6 a.m. on Saturday August 11, 2007, the *Aquila* pulled from the Seattle dock and headed out for the Aleutians. With luck, Garcia hoped to reach Adak on August 20. Luck, fate, chance, and belief that the *Grunion* somehow "wanted to be found" propelled the Abeles' quest for their father and his crew and for answers to what had happened in July 1942, sixty-five years before.

On August 14, 2007, three days out of Seattle, the *Aquila* was making good time toward Adak, averaging a little over ten knots in the Gulf of Alaska. Kale Garcia informed the Abeles that the forecast for the next several days looked fairly calm, but his mention of the dense fog cloaking the *Aquila* reminded everyone that the winds and waves could change in an instant.

"Clearly," Garcia noted in an email to the Abele brothers, "we're in the hands of Mother Nature at this point."[2]

Garcia had originally planned to dock at Dutch Harbor to stock up on provisions for the expedition members who would meet the *Aquila* at Adak, but on August 18, swells "taller than most houses" and winds at forty-plus miles per hour slammed the vessel from the west and directly on the bow. Garcia told the Abeles, "It's almost like driving a jeep up and down steep hills."[3] To save at least twelve hours of crucial time, he decided to bypass Dutch Harbor and churn straight through the heavy seas to Adak.

For John Abele, who planned to fly on his jet first to Anchorage and then to Adak, tracking the weather in the Aleutians also took center stage. For this expedition, John would himself join the team on the crabber. (Bruce had decided to remain home with Brad, whose health was declining rapidly.) Dave Gallo, Mike Nicholson, Pete Lowney, and Joe Caba would also be assembling at Adak to meet the *Aquila*. Caba was the other ROV pilot, along with Toshi Mikagawa, who had left Seattle aboard the crabber.

And one more man would join the expedition at Adak. Freelance writer Donovan Webster was sailing with the *Aquila* to cover what everyone hoped would be the confirmed discovery of the *Grunion*. Originally, *National Geographic* had wanted Donovan to write the piece, and was also planning to send a photographer on the expedition. But the magazine had backed out of the expedition, the editor dissuaded by the daunting odds, and by Ballard's certainty that the ROV would not find the submarine—that the sonar images were those of a surface ship. When the magazine cancelled the assignment, *Reader's Digest* picked up the Abeles' story.

John Abele intended to fly from Burlington, Vermont, to Anchorage on Sunday August 19, pick up several other expedition members there, and then make the two-hour flight to Adak. If cloud cover around Adak loomed above 1,200 feet, as it had the previous summer, the fall-back landing site was once again Cold Bay.

Potentially ominous news came in—a volcano named Mount Pavlov was stirring. A mere thirty-seven miles southeast of Cold Bay, the volcano was threatening to erupt and spew ash on Cold Bay. Kale Garcia sent John an email: "Be careful, John. Simply put, jets and volcanic ash do not mix."[4]

John Abele's jet took off from Burlington at 8:30 a.m. on August 19. The flight crew received hourly reports about both the cloud cover above Adak and Mt. Pavlov's smoldering conditions.

As the jet soared toward Anchorage, the *Aquila* pushed on toward Adak, slowed by heavy swells south of the Shumigan Islands, off the Alaska Peninsula. About to take the ship into the Unimak Pass, Garcia anticipated "huge seas and lots of current." The good news, Garcia wrote in his log, was that "the winds in the next few days should be keeping ash from Pavlov away from Adak."[5]

More good news came from the Sub Ladies' ongoing search. An article by Mary Bentz on the front page of the *Asheville Citizen-Times*, North Carolina, had garnered a fast response from a niece of Moore Ledford on August 17. Only one name, Byron Traviss, now remained on the Sub Ladies' list of seventy.

On August 20, John phoned Bruce and Brad to let them know that "everybody made it to Anchorage on time." Still, conditions at Adak and the restive state of Mount Pavlov remained problematic. All Bruce and Brad could do was wait and hope that John and company could somehow reach Adak in the next day and a half. Otherwise, the schedule tightened, ratcheting up the pressure to relocate the target in a shorter time.

The expedition caught a huge break that same day. The cloud cover at Adak had proven low enough for the team to fly in from Anchorage. The only missing arrival was Joe Caba's luggage.

Adding to the day's good news, the *Aquila* emerged from "pea-soup fog" and into Adak's harbor around 6:30 p.m. Weather reports indicated that conditions off Kiska would be decent for the next few days. The window for finding the target again and definitively identifying it as Jim Abele's submarine had opened a bit.

To prepare to put out to Kiska, a day's trip from Adak, the team worked fast. Garcia needed to repair the *Aquila*'s main heater; he told John Abele that the "normal, routine stuff—servicing of engines and equipment"[6]—could be done on the way out of Adak to save time. But the DSSI/Oceaneering team wanted to test the ROV, the clump (the tether to which the ROV's sensors, sonar, cameras, and lights were attached), and the depth-finding pole to check for any potential problems before subjecting the equipment to the treacherous waters off Kiska.

They ran the tests just outside of Adak Harbor on the afternoon of August 21, lowering the pole beneath the *Aquila*'s keel, floating the clump over the side, and deploying the Max Rover to a depth of 300 feet. Finally, they put the crucial Max Sea software to the test. It worked, filling the computer screens and video monitors in both the wheelhouse and the ROV shack with crystal-clear images and data.

The *Aquila* pushed out of Adak Harbor near 7 p.m. on August 21. Ahead lay Kiska, which Garcia expected to reach at 5 p.m. or so on the following day—and the target that the Abeles believed was Jim's submarine.

John Abele and the team wanted answers as fast as the weather would allow. With the forecast still a good one, they hoped to map the area the same night they arrived and to lower the ROV early the following morning in the waters where the side-scan sonar had found the enigmatic target. Garcia's words perfectly summed up their situation: the expedition was "in the hands of Mother Nature."

CHAPTER SEVENTEEN

"THERE SHE IS"

As the *Aquila* plowed for Kiska in thick fog, John Abele held a meeting with the team, handing out baseball caps emblazoned with the words "U.S.S. *Grunion*." Toshi Mikagawa presented a search plan to deploy the ROV as soon as possible—that very night, if the always treacherous weather allowed. John Abele reasoned, "My concern is that we could be here two weeks. We've got a crane, we have to lift this ROV and put it over the side, and we can't do that if the seas are too rough. Toshi's right—let's go tonight if we can."

The *Aquila*'s crew laid bets with each other on how long it would take to locate the target. Some had strong doubts the ROV would even find the target from the previous summer, and many believed— as Dave Gallo's fellow scientists at Woods Hole did—that the chances the target that had been located by the side-scan sonar was the submarine were "zero." Gallo had revealed to John that Robert Ballard himself believed the odds were slim at best.

Near 5 p.m. on August 22, volcanic peaks jutted through the cloud cover. Despite their worry that heavy seas might slow down the expedition, the team had reached Kiska in roughly twenty-four hours. As the *Aquila* slipped into Kiska Harbor, they needed a window of calm waters—or at least relative calm—to search for the target. They had the coordinates from the previous summer, but currents—a critical factor in any undersea search—could throw calculations off by as much as a mile in any direction. In short, there was no 100 percent-certain guarantee that the ROV would relocate the sonar hit of 2006.

The team sat down to dinner shortly after anchoring in the harbor. Then they noticed something. "'Holy cow, the sea just got calm,'" John Abele said.

With weather reports indicating that a massive low-pressure system was headed for Kiska, the team had to move fast. John made the decision to start the search immediately. At 7 p.m. the *Aquila* left the harbor and set course for the target area.

At 9 p.m. the ship reached the point at which the coordinates said they should find the target. First, they tested for depth with the sounding pole, and then, for the next hour, they conducted computer mapping of the sea bottom. At 10 p.m., with the waters still flat but the storm system looming, Abele and the team agreed to send down the ROV. If the waters turned rough—inevitable with the oncoming low-pressure front—the equipment would be at risk; however, if they waited they might be pinned in Kiska's harbor for several days with no guarantee that the sea would turn this calm again.

At 10:20 p.m., the team winched the ROV over the side with a "crab-pot crane" that proved ideal for the task. The Max Rover followed its weighted clump of control instrumentation toward the bottom of the Bering Sea, aiming for a GPS point that the operators had labeled "U.S.S. *Grunion*" on their charts.

The team quickly realized just how tricky the job was, with the currents around the *Aquila* and those farther below moving in different directions and at varying speeds. Everyone peered tensely at the video coming up from the ROV's cameras.

By 11:20 p.m., the Max Rover had descended some 3,000 feet. Suddenly, Joe Caba, piloting the vehicle from the control room on the crab boat's aft-deck, radioed the *Aquila*'s wheelhouse: "We've got a target out at 045 degrees and about 80 meters…60 meters now, it's a big target."

The team waited, at least twenty minutes ticking by as Caba and Garcia grappled with the currents that dragged the ROV erratically above the silt and gravel of the bottom. The skipper and the ROV pilot had to counter the sudden shifts of 3,000-plus feet of cable between the ship and the Max Rover second by second.

At 11:48 p.m., everyone's breath caught as an image slowly materialized amid the large orange jellyfish and giant black cod swimming in the cameras' view. A brownish-gray mass filled the *Aquila*'s computer monitors screens. "It looks like kelp," John Abele said.[1]

As the ROV slipped closer, the object no longer looked like kelp. The long, ghostly contours of a battered, partially collapsed submarine's port side took shape. Then, the twisted but unmistakable metal of the sub's conning tower appeared.

Almost miraculously the ROV had discovered the target— unquestionably a submarine—little more than an hour after the Max Rover had been winched into the Bering Sea.

John Abele, staring at the monitor in the wheelhouse, almost whispered, "There she is."[2]

He knew that he was looking at his father's submarine. It was the first time that anyone had seen the *Grunion* since July 1942, sixty-five years before.

For the next twenty minutes, the ROV continued to send up images of the submarine. For a heart-stopping second, the team even caught a glimpse of what might be propeller guards. If they could get a clear image that confirmed the wreck actually had prop guards, they would establish beyond a reasonable doubt that it was the *Grunion*. But at that tantalizing moment, with rising waves starting to slap against the *Aquila*, the sub suddenly disappeared from the monitors.

As the ROV operators scrambled to relocate the sub, the minutes began to pass. It started to look as though she might have vanished again—before the team could prove she was the *Grunion*. John Abele wondered if the string of good fortune that had led them to the submarine had snapped.

Even with the *Aquila* herself more or less over the GPS coordinates, determining exactly where the ROV was in relation to the submarine was a maddening process. Kale Garcia was relying on his knowledge of the waters and his instincts to read the currents and work with the ROV crew to rediscover the sub. Even if the ROV was just 200–300 yards away from the target, the currents could make that seemingly short distance insurmountable. The team needed not just skill, but one more dose of luck, fate, providence, or all three. They would soon learn whether or not, in fact, "the *Grunion* was waiting to be found."

The minutes dragged into hours.

CHAPTER EIGHTEEN

LOST AND FOUND—AGAIN

———◆————

As the clock ticked, little except clouds of crawfish-like krill appeared on the video images streaming up from the Max Rover. Tension in the wheelhouse and the on-deck shack holding the ROV controls was increasing. Everyone knew the sub could not be too far off, but that fact offered little solace as Joe Caba tried to navigate the underwater vehicle back to the target. The luck that had been with the Max Rover when it went straight down to the sub in less than a half hour had vanished. And adding to the anxiety of the crew was the knowledge that the oncoming low-pressure system would bring wind and waves.

If what the team had glimpsed on the quick pass from the submarine's bow to stern was really prop guards, then near-certain proof that the wreck could only be the *Grunion* lay beneath the *Aquila*. The question remained *where*.

Team members argued for some two hours. John Abele said they were "almost feeling like Keystone Cops as we struggled to re-find the sub."

Special sensors installed on the *Aquila*, the clump of control instrumentation, and the ROV should have shown the positions of all three in relation to each other on a computer map, but the sensors failed. The malfunctioning clump sensor posed a particular problem: everyone worried that the tether tying the clump to the ROV might wrap around the control cable in a nightmare scenario that could mean the loss of millions of dollars worth of equipment.

Flying blind, Garcia remained calm at the helm as the debates swirled in the wheelhouse and the ROV shack. He continued to maneuver the *Aquila* over the GPS location; however, he and the team realized that even if the crab boat was directly over the site of the wreck, the Max Rover could still be spiraling 200 to 300 yards away. A few short-range sonar sensors, with only 100 to 150 feet of visibility, were working intermittently and sending "target hits" to the screens. Each hit raised hopes that they had found the sub again, but each turned out to be a false reading.

Even though the ROV was equipped with high-intensity lights, the murky depths surrounding the sub limited the cameras' vision to only twenty to thirty feet in any direction. Unless the ROV came within that reduced camera range of the target, no one would see it. The vehicle could come very close and still miss the sub altogether.

Joe Caba had to draw upon all his skill and experience to maneuver the Max Rover as Garcia gauged how to turn the crabber in the shifting currents around the GPS position to keep the *Aquila*'s keel above the target. Garcia's instinctive seamanship corrected for any drift above the target; Caba had to somehow figure out how far both the ROV and the clump had drifted from the coordinates.

For Caba in the control shack, using a joystick to guide the ROV, every push and tug worked on a delayed reaction that was caused by the currents and the distance between the *Aquila* and the submerged Max Rover. With the clump moving up and virtually hiding each time the crabber moved, Caba constantly had to adjust for the impression that he was driving the Rover sideways. Everyone had one eye on the screens and the other on the clock as take-charge navigator Richard Graham and skilled driver Caba in the control shack struggled with the ROV.

The nerve-fraying wait continued. Then, as Caba pulled the ROV up a hill, suddenly they all noticed something. They had found the slide path that the submarine had gouged out in its descent. That meant the ROV now lay somewhere above the sub. Carefully, Caba started to follow the downhill track.

At 1:59 a.m. on August 23, that same eerie shape materialized on the computer screens. This time, though, the sub's stern came into full view—with the prop guards there for all to see.

Joe Caba positioned the Max Rover just above and behind the sub. Palpable relief filled the wheelhouse and the ROV shack. Dave Gallo said later, "If you were to pick a place to hide from a diving crew, the *Grunion* nearly had it."[1]

Despite that, they had found the sub—again.

The team worked all night, steering the ROV around the wreck, taking hours of high-definition video. The *Grunion* was badly damaged: part of its deck had been sheared off, a 52-foot section of its bow was gone, and the pressure tanks along the entire length of the submarine gaped open. It looked, one crew member remarked, as if someone had gone at the ship with a gigantic can opener. Still, except for the missing bow section, she lay in one piece, her conning tower, deck gun, and—most importantly—the prop guards clearly visible.

To John Abele's relief, the crew on the *Aquila* saw no human remains. At that depth in the calcium-poor water, bones would have dissolved long ago.

Wanting one more look at the conning tower for any sign that the 3-inch Japanese shell had actually penetrated the sub's steel skin, Toshi maneuvered the ROV close to the periscope shears. The team spotted no concrete evidence whatsoever that the shell had punched a hole in the *Grunion,* that the eighty-fourth round from the *Kano Maru's* deck gun had sunk the sub.

It was 4 a.m. when Toshi pulled back on the joystick to nudge the ROV away from the conning tower. Nothing happened. The Max Rover's tether had snarled around the *Grunion's* radio antenna. Again and again Toshi tried to untangle the vehicle from the wreck; but the knot tightened.

John Abele grew increasingly concerned as an hour passed. With the storm moving in and the Max Rover still snared by the sub, the possibility that they might lose the $20 million underwater vehicle loomed. He asked Toshi to let Joe Caba take the joystick.

Caba pulled the ROV backwards from the antenna in ever-expanding loops, battling the strong currents. As the Max Rover started swinging slowly around the antenna in longer and longer circular loops, the knot unfurled. Caba freed the Rover near 6 a.m., and the crew immediately began to winch the ROV from the wreck to the *Aquila.* The vehicle broke the surface at 6:30 a.m. With the waves surging and the wind ripping in at fifty miles per hour and rising, they hauled the costly ROV back aboard and secured it.

Back on the East Coast, Bruce Abele was overcome by the images pouring onto his computer screen from the *Aquila.*

"Sub Lady" Mary Bentz woke before dawn to check the *Grunion* website. When she saw the post from Bruce Abele—"WE FOUND

THE SUB!"—she burst into tears. She was determined to find crewman Byron Traviss's family before the day was over. Bentz called in to a popular Detroit talk show and broadcast a plea for information about the only crewman whose relatives remained a mystery.

Within minutes, a woman phoned in to the show and told the host, "Byron's Purple Heart is hanging on my dining room wall."[2]

The caller was the wife of one of the crewman's cousins. At last, the list was complete: on the same day the *Grunion* was found, the Sub Ladies had met their goal and located the families of the entire crew.

As dawn broke off Kiska on August 23, 2007, and Kale Garcia revved the *Aquila*'s engines for the run back to the harbor ahead of the storm, John Abele stood by the port gunwale and tossed wildflowers from Kiska Island onto the spot where the *Grunion* had disappeared. Then he lowered a large container into the ocean, filled it, and pulled it back aboard.

Toshi Mikagawa, standing alongside John, performed a ceremony for the sailors of the sunken Japanese ships, pouring Saki into the sea.

When John returned home, his plan was to sit down with Bruce and Brad; the three brothers would fill seventy small vials, one for each crew member's family, with water from the container. Then the brothers would place each vial in a handsome leather case with a photo of the *Grunion* and a short note: "The water from this vial comes from the Bering Sea just off the Aleutian island of Kiska. It was taken from over the resting place of the USS *Grunion*. It is a small memento of the gravesite of the crew and a symbol to honor their service and their sacrifice."

Over the next two days, the team took additional footage of the sub and also went hunting for Shinoda Isamu's sub chaser, the

CH 27, and the destroyer *Arare*. Hampered by storms, the team could not lower the ROV into the rough seas, but they did capture several sonar images that might be of the *Arare*. The destroyer had been blown in half by a torpedo from the *Growler* near the mouth of Kiska Harbor, and the *Aquila*'s sonar picked up a "hit" there. The image showed two large masses on the bottom of the sea.

On August 27, 2007, the *Aquila* departed Kiska, passed over the *Grunion*'s resting place one more time, and headed for Adak, where John's jet waited. Still ahead for the Abeles was the fight to get the U.S. Navy to break its long silence and acknowledge that the sunken sub off Kiska was, in fact, the *Grunion*.

And though the *Grunion* had been found, questions about her fate remained unresolved. As experts and amateur sleuths alike began to analyze the underwater photos and video, a contentious debate simmered over what sent the *Grunion* to the bottom.

CHAPTER NINETEEN

FROM BOW TO STERN

———◆◆◆———

Despite the discovery of the *Grunion*, the Abeles' lifelong struggle with Naval bureaucracy was far from over. The Navy would at last—in large part because of the efforts of John Fakan, president of the USS *Cod* Submarine Memorial—officially recognize that the sub off Kiska was the *Grunion*; however, the official Navy position would continue to be that the reason the sub sank remained unknown.

But experts analyzing the Abeles' hours of video footage of the *Grunion*, the hundreds of still images of the wreck, and the Japanese eyewitness accounts of the battle between the *Grunion* and the *Kano Maru* were coming to the conclusion that the cause of the sinking *could* be determined.

What happened in the *Grunion*'s final minutes? What took place just before, during, and after the eighty-fourth shot from the *Kano*

Maru's 3-inch deck gun struck the submarine? Nationwide and internationally, scientists, engineers, and naval historians with scientific and submarine backgrounds continued to analyze not only the photographic evidence but Japanese charts and eyewitness accounts of the action between the sub and the *Kano Maru*, blueprints of Gato-class submarines, drawings and composites of the wreck, radio communications, charts of the *Grunion*, and many other sources. The cause of the *Grunion*'s loss was debated over several years.

The experts agreed on one point early on: the submarine had experienced a total and catastrophic loss of depth control. But from what cause? Different experts proposed different scenarios.

Dr. John Fakan, the president of the USS *Cod* Submarine Memorial and a noted physics, hydraulics, and nautical engineering expert, and engineer Jim Christley had been with the Abeles from early on in the searches. They argued convincingly that after firing torpedoes that disabled the *Kano Maru*, Lieutenant Commander Jim Abele had maneuvered the *Grunion* to open the range to the freighter, both to verify the absence of Japanese aircraft and surface forces, and to load the remaining torpedoes to finish the ship. Seiichi Aiura had written that the submarine "moved calmly"[1] first to starboard and then slightly port and to the fore of the stricken freighter—Jim likely gauging the best angle to increase the chances of the poorly performing torpedoes to detonate. The *Kano Maru*, dead in the water, blazed away at the sub with machine-gun fire, which was utterly ineffective against the submarine's steel skin, and with the 3-inch deck gun, and a lucky shot from the latter must have hit the *Grunion*'s raised #1 periscope.

Cold seawater could have flooded the scope and punched out a lower optic lens. A stream of water would have sprayed into the *Grunion*'s control room. With the scope bent and disabled, the attack party would have had to shift to the conning tower to use the #2 periscope, and Jim Abele likely ordered a hard turn to get away from the crippled freighter's guns.

The *Grunion* was already running at a shallow depth with the #1 scope raised. As she turned, her bow must have suddenly broached—broken the surface—at the worst possible moment. Factors contributing to the sub's broach may have included weight changes from draining the torpedo tubes prior to reloading, and weight shifts due to the movement of torpedoes in the torpedo room. As the *Grunion* broke the surface, her periscope shears were lifted out of the water. And at that exposed moment for the sub, the eighty-fourth round fired from the freighter's deck gun hit just below the shears and exploded near the masthead light. The sub was "blinded" with both periscopes now out, and Jim needed to get his boat out of harm's reach right away. He would have ordered the diving officer to "get the boat down!"

The dive officer would have ordered the stern planesman to take the sub to full dive—only the planes had jammed. Experts poring over the video from the ROV had found that the *Grunion*'s dive planes had jammed, or locked, into a steep position. The planes could have been damaged in an earlier depth charge attack. Just as when a nail is driven into the tire of a car, and later stresses determine whether and when the tire will go completely flat, the damage to the dive planes might not have caused the submarine to go into an uncontrolled dive the first few times Jim took her under the surface. Until the sub started down at a severe downward angle—in the engagement with the *Kano Maru*—no one would have even known the planes were damaged. The planesman would have struggled to control the angle of the dive. Meanwhile, icy water might have started to flood into the *Grunion* through leaks and openings likely caused when the 3-inch shell exploded. As the crew struggled to regain control of the descending sub, the pressure on the hull would have increased with each fathom. So, too, would the submariners' "derangement," or confusion, from the water rushing in, the steep angle of descent, and the chaos, both mechanical and emotional, that overwhelmed the ship from bow to stern.

Finally the sub would have slid to a depth where the hull failed catastrophically. Beginning with the forward torpedo room, a shock wave would have gone coursing through the boat at the speed of sound. All the sub's compartments would have failed in less than a second, creating a massive traumatic impact that killed the crew in an instant. Then the *Grunion* would have sunk ever deeper, spilling a grisly trail of debris and bodies. At 3,200 feet she must have crashed against a ridge top and crunched to a stop, to lie undetected—along with the secret of what caused her to sink—for sixty-five years.

But as other experts pored over the data and images and scrutinized Fakan and Christley's scenario, it didn't seem to cover all the known facts. The crew of the *Kano Maru* had yelled "Banzai" when the eighty-fourth shot hit the *Grunion*; they believed *they* had sunk her. What did they see that convinced them that the hit by the deck gun had a *direct*, in contrast to indirect, effect on the loss of the *Grunion*?

The Japanese sailors had reported hearing a "dull thud" that shook the freighter. They also reported seeing something—a rod or some other piece of metal—shoot above the surface from the sub and spotted "dirty brown liquid" at the place where it went down.

Other hypotheses couldn't explain this evidence, either—or else they were incompatible with other known facts. Terry Terrass, Naval Academy Class of 1948 and former submarine skipper, as well as a retired nuclear industry executive, had focused his attention on the gasket on a torpedo door of the sub. He argued that the gasket had been damaged in an earlier depth charge attack against the *Grunion* and that it gave way and allowed flooding of the forward torpedo room. But Terrass's theory didn't explain the thud that shook the *Kano Maru*, the piece of metal the Japanese sailors saw shooting up from the sub, or the fact that they believed they had sunk her. Also— although a flooded forward torpedo room would have been a desperate state of affairs, the *Grunion*'s crew could still have taken measures to save the sub.

There was also Brad Abele's early theory that an American plane had bombed the *Grunion*, but there was no evidence that an American plane had been present.

And an account that an American destroyer had sunk an American submarine near Kiska in July 1942 could be dismissed as well—it turned out to be a Soviet submarine that was sunk in that case of mistaken identity.

John Fakan and Jim Christley still argued compellingly that the lucky hit by a 3-inch Japanese shell had set off a catastrophic chain of events and sent the *Grunion* to the bottom despite the crew's desperate attempts to control the dive. They asserted that if the round had not hit the sub, Jim would not have ordered such a quick and steep dive. And without a full dive, the pressure on the damaged planes might not have proven enough to jam and prevent the planesman from recovering the angle.

But it eventually became clear: the scenario most likely to be true was that the *Grunion* had been sunk by one of her own torpedoes. The defective MK 14 torpedo had made a circular run back to the *Grunion* and, though it did not explode, it damaged the sub enough to sink her when she dove. The key clues were the "dull thud" and the "black rod" that shot up from the submarine in the eyewitness accounts, and a *Kano Maru* officer's diagram that actually showed the torpedo making a circular run. The torpedo, circling back after missing the *Kano Maru*, slammed into the *Grunion* at or near her periscope shears, but did not detonate. And it was that impact that caused Jim to take the *Grunion* into a deep dive—from which she was unable to recover.

At 7:37 a.m. on July 30, 1942, two Japanese sub chasers, the minesweeper *Ishizaki*, and a tug had arrived to aid the stricken freighter *Kano Maru*. Floating atop the oil slick that marked the sub's last position, they saw "pieces of lifeguard buoys, chips that seemed to be the material of submarine decks, and other many things." The *Ishizaki* confirmed the sinking and radioed news of the freighter's kill to the Imperial Fifth Fleet's headquarters, on Attu Island. Seiichi, the *Kano Maru*'s captain, sent his superiors his battle-chart with the exact coordinates of the engagement, along with his detailed report.

News of the clash was reported to the Japanese Fifth Fleet and the Chief of the Grand Fleet via the Fifth Guard Troop Commander (Kiska Island). And in late 1945, U.S. Navy investigators combing through Imperial Japanese Naval records for information about sunken or missing American ships missed or glossed over indications in Seiichi and Rikimaru's accounts of the possibility of a circular-run torpedo striking an American sub off Kiska on July 30, 1942. The Navy knew that only one of its subs had operated in that spot on that date. For almost sixty-five years, the two reports and Aiura's chart vanished. The *Grunion*'s status simply remained "missing in action and presumed lost."

The Abeles learned of Aiura's account of the battle between the *Grunion* and the *Kano Maru* only in 2002 when they contacted Yutaka Iwasaki. "For the prior 59-plus years," Brad wrote, "we had been of the understanding that the fate of the *Grunion* was unknown and that her crew therefore was officially *missing in action*."[2]

Caught up in the actual search for the submarine from 2002 to 2007, the brothers and others in the so-called "*Grunion* community" did not begin to notice several curious aspects of the Navy's official position until 2010–2012. In 1947, the Japanese admiral who commanded the Aleutian fleet had testified that the *Kano Maru* had sunk an American submarine off Kiska in late July 1942. He cited the *Grunion* by name. Seiichi's detailed account of the clash had appeared in a Japanese maritime magazine in 1963. In 2006, while the sonar expedition to Kiska was the Abeles' chief focus, John Abele received a packet of material from historian and archivist Vernon J. Miller. Miller, who had seen Seiichi's 1963 article, included a detailed account of the *Grunion*'s sinking that he had published in 1981 and had sent to the U.S. Navy's public relations office.

When evidence about the potential circular torpedo emerged, Brad Abele talked with retired Naval commander John Alden, the expert who had settled the issue that the *Grunion* had indeed gone on patrol with her prop guards—which had helped identify the wreck conclusively as Jim's boat. And it turned out that Alden had actually written an article in the April 1988 issue of the *Submarine Review*, which described the battle between the *Grunion* and the Japanese freighter. Acclaimed as "the most respected keeper of submarine records in the country,"[3] Alden took note of the fact that the Japanese observed a large explosion after the 3-inch shell hit the sub's conning tower. He wrote, "Since the conning tower could not have exploded like that, I wonder if it could have been a circular run by a fourth dud torpedo."[4]

The abysmal performance of the Exploder torpedoes carried by the *Grunion* and the other American subs operating in 1942–1943 reached its nadir in several "circular runs" in which the torpedoes missed their target—often because of the weapons' faulty settings— and circled back to slam into the subs that fired them. It has been established that at least three subs were lost in this way. The evidence shows that there was a fourth—which was actually the first submarine to suffer this fate—the USS *Grunion*.

Other experts, including Tuck Weaver and John Hart, had also hypothesized about the possibility that in the fatal engagement with the *Kano Maru*, one of the *Grunion*'s torpedoes circled back and took her down. Weaver contends that a circular torpedo hit the sub's upper conning tower hatch but didn't explode. It did, he asserts, set off a chain reaction of events that sank her. The "dull thud" heard by the Japanese would have been the impact of the circular torpedo. Hart hypothesizes that a circular torpedo slammed into the *Grunion*'s bow, perhaps tearing off the missing section.

Two men have been largely responsible for championing the circular-run solution to the mystery of the *Grunion*. The first, retired submarine commander Charles "Charlie" Tate, speaks from literal hands-on experience. The other, Frederick J. Milford, is one of the world's foremost Naval scientists and experts on Naval ordnance and the author of the groundbreaking work "The Great Torpedo Scandal of 1941–43."[5]

Eighty-seven-year-old Charlie Tate is uniquely qualified to understand both the action on a submarine and that on a cargo ship like the Kano Maru. At the onset of World War II, Charlie served as an enlisted man on a cargo ship carrying materials to Dutch Harbor, becoming familiar with the rough waters and conditions in the Aleutians. He joined the crew of the submarine USS *Gato* in 1943 and eventually rose to become the sub's chief.

Commander Tate's vast submarine experience came into play in examining the last minutes of the *Grunion*. Tate spent considerable time reviewing John Fakan's anaglyph photos (scientists wear special glasses with a range of different-hued lenses that allow the observer to discern details in the 3-D images that can't be picked up by the naked eye) and analyzing Fakan and Christley's "eighty-fourth shot" hypothesis of the *Grunion's* final action. He raised numerous questions and suggested a circular-run torpedo as the cause of the disastrous chain of events that literally drove the *Grunion* to the bottom. One of those events—the jamming of the submarine's dive planes—was something that Charlie Tate had experienced firsthand on the *Gato*.

Tate's contention, which has gained wide acceptance, is that the damage to the *Grunion's* shears could not have been caused by a 17-pound 3-inch shell traveling at approximately 2,700 feet per second. It must have been caused by the much greater impact of a circular-run MK 14 torpedo that did not explode. When that torpedo hit the sub, the men on the *Grunion* must have thought that it was a bomb. The order would have been given to take her down fast. Then when they tried to level out they would have discovered that they had "lost the bubble"—the rear dive planes were locked in a dive position, perhaps as a result of the depth-charge attack the sub had endured. At that point the down angle could have rapidly become so steep that Jim and his crew would not have been able to take recovery action fast enough. The boat would have reached crush depth and imploded.

Tate and numerous scientists now believe that what the crew of the *Kano Maru* saw were the bubbles and oil from the imploded sub. The rod that shot up and fell back was quite likely the 15-foot air tank, or flask, from the circular-run MK 14.

Tate, speaking from his submariner's vantage point, suggests a number of inconsistencies in Seiichi's account. He finds the Japanese officer's statement that the sub was surfacing when it was hit with the eighty-fourth shot especially problematic. Tate and many other submariners point out that unintended broaches were very rare. Tate also notes that the momentum of an MK 14 torpedo would have been approximately six times that of the 3-inch shell. It's more likely that the torpedo caused the "explosion" that the Japanese saw after their shell hit the sub. When the torpedo hit the *Grunion*, the warhead snapped off and likely pushed material in all directions, almost as if there had been an actual explosion. The shell from the Japanese deck gun, which was meant for anti-aircraft action and had a timed detonator, probably would not have exploded. More importantly, it would not have caused the peripheral damage around the shears that the images from the wreck showed.

The *Grunion*'s shears lay fifteen feet below the periscope. If the sub had risen far enough to expose the shears, the crew of the *Kano Maru* would have noted that they saw them. They did not.

In all four translations of eyewitness Japanese accounts, there is clear evidence of massive amounts of oil rising to the surface simultaneously with the eighty-fourth shot from the freighter. That could only have come from the fuel ballast tanks located forty-five feet down, at the base of the sub. Those tanks could not have been penetrated or opened by a 3-inch shell. (The "washing wave"— similar to what one sees at the beach—that the Japanese saw would clearly have been created by the massive bubble from the sub's implosion.)

Why would the Navy have sat on the information they had about the *Grunion*? Frederick J. Milford—an MIT Ph.D. in theoretical physics who is considered by Naval historians to be one of the fore- most experts on torpedoes—contends that at the time the *Grunion* was lost, the Navy was caught up in a bureaucratic, technological, political, and economic morass he has dubbed "The Great Torpedo Scandal of 1941–43." The Navy, Milford argues, did not want the public to know that submarines were being sent to sea with a seri- ously defective and potentially disastrous weapon. Milford points out that Naval brass and contractors were not posing hard questions about the MK 14's design and flaws. Their narrow thinking "was exacerbated . . . by draconian security, which in some cases even excluded the operating forces from full knowledge of the weapons they were expected to use. In this isolated environment, NTS (Naval Torpedo Station)-Newport developed an arrogant 'we are the torpedo experts' attitude, and when problems began to arise, the response was denial—'there is nothing wrong with the torpedoes'—with the result that problems were identified and fixed slowly."[6]

Too slowly to save Jim Abele and his crew. And even after the MK 14's major flaws were addressed by 1943, "the intense polarization that existed between the operating forces and the torpedo shore establishment" remained and would linger long beyond the war's end.

The admirals, politicians, and contractors who sent the *Grunion* and other submarines to war with the MK 14 in 1941–1942 never faced punishment or accountability. After all, to paraphrase former Secretary of Defense Donald Rumsfeld, a nation goes to war with what it has, not what it wants.

Ironically, perhaps, Nazi Germany faced similar torpedo problems, but addressed them in a harsher manner. Milford writes: "This spectrum of problems was not unique to the U.S. torpedo establishment. Almost the same set, defective depth control, unsatisfactory and untested magnetic exploder and a contact exploder that did not work at certain striking angles, occurred in the German navy and many of the responses of the shore establishment to the problems were also the same. . . . The German navy's problems were closed out, however, with four senior officers being tried by court martial, on the orders of Grand Admiral Eric Raeder, found guilty and punished."[7]

CHAPTER TWENTY

"THEY WANTED TO BE FOUND"

————◆◆◆————

On Columbus Day weekend 2008, some fourteen months after the discovery of the *Grunion*, the Abeles—with help of Mary and Richard Bentz and Dr. John Fakan, president of the USS *Cod* Memorial—held a memorial service that was covered by the *Today Show* and major networks and newspapers worldwide. "Sub Lady" Mary Bentz and her husband Richard helped with the ceremony, and John Fakan organized it at the memorial for the *Grunion*'s sister sub, the USS *Cod*. The ceremony, part of a weekend-long remembrance of the *Grunion*, united the crewmen's families in Cleveland, on and around the deck of the *Cod*. Rear Admiral Douglass T. Biesel represented the Navy at the ceremony. Under a brilliant blue sky, two hundred *Grunion* relatives, including two nonagenarian wid- 90's ows of the lost sailors, heard John Abele's wife, Mary, an interfaith pastor, read an invocation from Psalm 107: "They that go down to the sea in ships, that do business in great waters; These see the works of the Lord, and His wonders in the deep."[1]

Speakers offered tributes to the lost men and expressions of gratitude to the Abele family, including Kay, who had died in 1975. At a dinner the night before, Mary Bentz had read a comment left on the *Grunion* blog: "Lt. Commander Mannert L. [Jim] Abele's contribution to his country is evident in his sons." Navy officials had asked John and Bruce Abele to serve as "stand-in captains." As the elegant strains of Samuel Barber's "Adagio for Strings" played in the background, Mary Bentz read each crew member's name aloud. From the deck of the *Cod*, family members tossed a carnation into Lake Erie for each man. The rifle cracks of a 21-gun salute resounded, and a trumpeter played "Taps" as the flowers floated on the surface of the water.

Missing from the ceremony was Brad Abele. The brother who had set the search in motion had passed away in May 2008 with his brothers at his hospice bedside.

Some time after the memorial, the Abeles received a letter from Shinoda Chiyo, the ninety-seven-year-old widow of Shinoda Isamu, commander of the *SC-27* which had been sunk by the *Grunion*. She conveyed her admiration for the Abeles and her belief that "in happier times, Isamu and Jim might well have been friends and were always fathers first, warriors second." (Chiyo passed away in February 2012 at the age of 101.)

"Our families are joined now in honoring each other's loss and healing the enmities of history," Bruce said. "Such an effort of compassion and wisdom makes me think there may be hope for this planet."

———◆◆———

John Abele is often asked why he'd been willing to spend so much money—literally a fortune—to find his father's ship. He always answers, "Because we could." He also says, "Fifty million people died in World War II. Good people, on both sides. This was our way of remembering them." John views the *Grunion* project as the intersection of two curves—the rising information curve created by the Internet and the falling demographic curve of American World War II veterans, who are currently passing from the scene. "We owe it not just to the Greatest Generation, but to those that follow," he asserts.

Jim Abele and his crew remain frozen in time, even as their loved ones have aged. Now at long last the loved ones have answers—answers that emerged from the depths of the Bering Sea sixty-five years after the *Grunion* vanished.

John and Bruce Abele shake their heads at the long series of "amazing improbables" that have driven the *Grunion*'s saga: "The plot is a tapestry of happenstances; pull one thread, and the whole thing may unravel. What if Richard Lane hadn't decided to spend a dollar on the deck winch diagram in that Denver antique shop? What if Bruce's son's girlfriend's boss hadn't been a World War II history buff? What if Yutaka Iwasaki hadn't guessed where the *Kano Maru*'s logbook might be misfiled? Why did the wind die down so helpfully at Kiska, affording a twelve-hour window between gales? Why, every time the crew of the *Aquila* lost track of *Grunion*, were they able to find it again? And why was the water directly over the spot of the wreck preternaturally calm?"

"It was strange," Kale Garcia said later. "As if we had some outside help."

Bruce Abele compares the improbable success of the decades-long quest to "winning the lottery thirteen times in a row." Mary Bentz says, "It was divine intervention. I really believe that."

A man whose entire professional life has revolved around hard facts and science, John Abele has slowly come to see another aspect to the *Grunion*'s story—an inexplicable plan beyond man's hand, one in which there's an incomprehensible design where the improbable crosses into the imponderable. "Something wanted us to find that boat—they wanted to be found," John says. "A higher power."

John and Bruce truly believe that their father and mother would be pleased and proud at the discovery of the *Grunion*. "We all believe that Jim would be pleased to know we made this effort," John Abele said. "You know—'Don't worry, Dad. We'll finish the job here.'"

While the U.S. Navy has finally acknowledged officially that the sunken submarine off Kiska is the USS *Grunion* and that she went down in action, the Navy has yet to name the cause for her loss.

THERE ONE MOMENT, GONE THE NEXT

———◆———

So how did the *Grunion* really sink? How did Jim Abele and his crew die? Some of the details will never be known, but the discovery of the sub and the contributions of expert knowledge and opinion by so many make it possible to guess at the events in their final moments with a fair degree of accuracy. What follows is the story of the sinking of the *Grunion*, as best as it can be reconstructed.[1]

———◆———

It was July 30, 1942.

As the Japanese sailors on the crippled *Kano Maru* waited for the inevitable torpedo hit that would seal their fate, Sublieutenant Rikimaru Nakagawa suddenly saw something unaccountable—a wake surging *toward* the submarine—"a bubble running on the surface and making a half-circle." A desperate hope flared amid his fear—could it be a torpedo?

Captain Seiichi's eyes widened as he spied the same frothing trail.

As the wake rippled closer to the sub, the eighty-fourth shell from the *Kano Maru*'s deck gun clanged against the *Grunion*'s #1 periscope and punched out the glass lens. Freezing seawater sprayed into the sub's conning tower, and Quartermaster Elmer Schumann immediately lowered the damaged scope to cut off the leak. Jim and the attack party climbed down the hatch from the conning tower to the control room and sealed it. The sub was blinded, but had not been critically damaged by the lucky shot.

The moment everyone was safely out of the conning tower, Jim ordered Diving Officer Sam Dighton to "level her off," intending to keep the *Grunion* submerged. With the coordinates to the freighter set, he did not need another peek at his target to sink it. He could fire another salvo at the freighter, take the *Grunion* down deep to wait out any Japanese counterattack from the sea or the air, and then slip away to Dutch Harbor, in accordance with his orders.

The Japanese blazed away at the "washing waves" where the sub's periscope was receding fast. The onrushing wake of the malfunctioning torpedo bubbled just yards away from the spot where the submarine lay submerged.

In the *Grunion*'s control room, a racket erupted in the sonar operator's earphone—"High-speed screws coming in!"

An instant later something smashed into the upper shears at the rear of the conning tower, rocking the entire boat. The thunderous impact bent the shears forward, lifted up the deck around the tower, and ripped off the connecting bolts. Unbeknownst to the men on the *Grunion*, it was their own torpedo coming in over the sub's stern and crashing against the tower's shears that had shaken the *Kano Maru*'s deck.

The massive thump of the torpedo's impact echoed across the water and shook the *Kano Maru* as a towering wall of gray water and foam cloaked the submarine's periscope. Above the spray burst a thin black bar—which no one on the *Kano Maru* recognized as the air flask of one of the *Grunion*'s torpedoes (the warhead having broken off undetonated when it hit the sub). It hovered for a second, plummeted back into the sea, and vanished.

Neither Jim nor the sonar man could have guessed that the *Grunion*'s own 3,500-pound torpedo had circled back on her at forty-five miles per hour—it had *never* before happened to an American submarine. The only thing Jim knew for sure about whatever had struck the *Grunion* was that it had not exploded. With no other Japanese ships in the area and the *Kano Maru*'s 3-inch deck gun and machine guns useless against the sub's thick, double-plated steel skin, Jim would likely have deduced that a Japanese aircraft had spotted him at periscope depth and had dropped a bomb—but it was a dud. Fearing that another was coming, he ordered the diving officer to "take her down!"

Jim ordered the bow and stern planes placed on full dive and the engines "all full ahead." To speed up the descent, crewmen instantaneously opened the negative tank to allow 20,000 pounds of water to fill it and temporarily eliminate the sub's natural buoyancy. As seawater gushed into the tank, the planes tilted down and the propellers drove the *Grunion* down.

The crew had practiced for an emergency dive numerous times. They were trained to blow the negative tank dry at sixty-five feet, and they knew that it should take some fifteen seconds before buoyancy returned. Fifteen seconds passed after the tank was emptied, and still the *Grunion*'s angle steepened. She drove down 100 feet.

Tension always tightened crewmen's faces the deeper a sub went, but unless the boat reached 300 feet, few stared at the depth-pressure gauge. The *Grunion* could go down to 315 feet before sudden metallic groans and squeals began to hint that her 9/16-inch steel plates were edging into "crush depth." Jim gave orders for the standard counter-action—"full rise" on the bow and stern planes and then "all ahead 1/3"—expecting the *Grunion* to right herself and stop her descent at 150 feet.

What Jim did not know was that the submarine's stern planes were jammed on full dive. A planesman shouted the three most chilling words to any submariner—"We've lost the bubble!" They meant that he could not budge the planes. The sub's downward angle tilted to 30 degrees or more, tossing the crew around wildly in every direction. The *Grunion* picked up speed and plunged even deeper.

Jim tried the sole last-ditch recovery action left: to put the engines in "all back full" and blow the forward ballast tanks in an attempt to restore buoyancy and control. All of this had to be done in seconds, and the slightest delay or mechanical disruption meant catastrophe.

Nothing worked. They could not pull the submarine out of its dive. The planes would not unlock. The *Grunion* was going down.

Somewhere past 315 feet the hull began to buckle from the pressure with ear-splitting shrieks. Foredeck rivets weakened by the torpedo's impact popped, and at least fifty feet of the bow tore loose "like someone had used a can opener on the sub."[2]

As the sea poured into the gaping forward-torpedo room, batteries exploded in a spray of metal and acid, sending deadly chlorine gas seeping through the sub. With every light shorting out, she slid deeper in pitch blackness, now scraping along a rugged volcanic slope. Rivets and plates began to crack. Dazed, panic-stricken officers and crewmen wading toward the sub's rear strained to seal hatches and bulkheads against the rush of water.

Oil from the *Grunion*'s three imploding fuel tanks rushed to the surface. A viscous brown slick spread where the sub's periscope had bobbed just a few minutes ago. Shouts of "Banzai" went up from the *Kano Maru*, crewmen thrusting their fists in the air, hugging each other. Some wept. Nakagawa described the enormous sense of relief: "I in spite of myself cried out, 'Good, You got what you deserved!'"[3] Most of his shipmates believed that the 3-inch shell had sent the Americans to the bottom. They were wrong.

As the Japanese cheered their deliverance, the *Grunion* was still hurtling into the depths beneath the oil-choked surface. But the crew was already lost. With each fathom further down, the submariners' movements had slowed, their thoughts becoming cloudier with every chlorine-choked breath. Then the submarine hit crush depth. Suddenly a shock wave ripped through the submarine at the speed of sound. Every compartment failed in less than a second, and massive traumatic impact engulfed the crew. The men lost consciousness as the interior of the imploding sub slammed into them and the sea rushed into the *Grunion*.

Jim Abele, Billie Kornahrens, Danny Cullinane, Carmine Parziale, Cornelius Paul—seventy men never knew what hit them. One minute they were struggling to save their sub. The next instant, they were gone.

APPENDIX

———◆◆◆———

Through interviews, telephone calls, and e-mails with family members of USS *Grunion* crewmen, and through exhaustive research of U.S. Navy records, Mary and Richard Bentz have compiled brief biographies of all the officers and men of the submarine, as well as photographs of all but three of the crew. The accounts below of the lives of the crew members whose stories have not already been told above are edited versions of the Bentzes' biographies. Many of these bios contain snippets of letters to Kay Abele and to the Navy from grief-stricken family members of the *Grunion* crewmen begging for any scraps of information—for some sort of closure. These achingly painful letters make clear why the search for the *Grunion* has such broad emotional resonance.

The search for family members of the sub's crewmen, parallel to the Abele brothers' search for the *Grunion* herself, began in late spring 2006. Susan Abele, Bruce Abele's wife, who had been surfing the web looking for anything *Grunion*-related, came across a note from a woman named Rhonda Raye who had been searching for information about her uncle Paul Banes, a *Grunion* crewman. Susan told Bruce about Rhonda, and he wrote to her,

> This is a stab in the dark. I am under the impression that you are a relative of somebody who was on the *Grunion*. My name is Bruce Abele and I am the son of Mannert Abele, who commanded the *Grunion*. This August the three sons of Mannert Abele are sponsoring a search for the *Grunion* based on new evidence that has been provided because of a Japanese history buff. It is quite a story. Go to ussgrunion.com for the details. If we are right I think you would be interested.

Rhonda replied,

> Well your "stab" hit home. Glad to see your site. I just sent it on to more of my relations that I know will be interested in seeing it...

Raye, of Cartersville, Georgia, turned out to be the first of three remarkable women later dubbed the "Sub Ladies," who eventually located relatives for the entire crew. She was soon joined by Vickie Rodgers of Mayfield, Kentucky, and Mary Bentz of Bethesda, Maryland. Rodgers's great-uncle, Merritt Graham, had gone down with the *Grunion*, and so, too, had Bentz's uncle Carmine Parziale. Bruce Abele marvels that the three women "used every tool imaginable—plus some you'd never imagine" to find *Grunion* family members. Searching for the family of the ship's executive officer, Millener

Thomas, Rodgers pored over genealogical trees, marriage records, Social Security death files, newspaper obituaries, probate records, and telephone books. When she learned that Thomas's widow had remarried and that his son, Peter, had been adopted by his stepfather and renamed Peter Stephens, Rodgers wrote to every Stephens in Allentown, Pennsylvania, and struck pay dirt when a letter reached Peter Stephens's daughter and she passed it on to him.

Bentz describes what it was like to call people out of the blue: "They usually thought you're a bill collector or trying to solicit funds for something or other. Then they're usually shocked. 'How did you find me?' And then it turns to elation. And every once in a while, a family doesn't even know they're related to that person.... But we all consider ourselves a family now."

The search for relatives yielded some unexpected treasures— including the bell of the *Grunion*. In June 1942, the bell was left at Pearl Harbor when the *Grunion* set out for the Aleutians (submarines do not use their bells at sea because a bell would add to the risk that the enemy could detect the sub by sonar). About the time of the Korean War in the early 1950s, the Reverend T. Russell Nunan, a Navy chaplain, was wandering around the Pearl Harbor Navy base and spotted a large bell in a scrapheap. He contacted the Navy authorities to see if he could buy it and received a negative answer. He then wrote a letter to the Admiral of the Pacific Fleet, outlining his request. Some weeks later, while aboard the USS *President Jackson*, the cleric received a 100-lb package, the *Grunion's* bell.

When the Reverend Nunan retired in 1972, he planned to spend his latter years in either Grenada or New Mexico, but he decided first to make a visit to his hometown, Greenville, Mississippi. At a hamburger joint there he bumped into friends Robert May and his wife, and the couple persuaded him to give Greenville a tryout for retirement and offered him temporary accommodations at a pastor's house. The Reverend Nunan was highly respected in Greenville, so much so that some time later several individuals, all tugboat men, offered to purchase him a permanent residence. He accepted.

The Reverend Nunan, aware that *Grunion* crewman Edward Knowles had come from Greenville, donated the submarine's bell as a memorial.

As the news of the *Grunion*'s discovery spread, a Greenville man named Fred Kendrick, a relative of Knowles, sent the Abeles a photo of the bell. John Abele took on the project of getting the bell to the USS *Cod* Museum in Cleveland for the *Grunion* Memorial on Columbus Day weekend 2008. The Greenville Visitor's Center agreed to lend the bell to the Abeles, and John arranged to fly the bell to and from Cleveland.

As the name of each *Grunion* crewman was read aloud, the very bell that had once been on their submarine tolled.

Lieutenant Commander Mannert Lincoln Abele, Commanding Officer
39 years old
Quincy, Massachusetts
married with three sons

Frank Elgin Alexander, Signalman Third Class
27 years old
Elyria, Ohio
single

Born on January 15, 1915, in Lorain, Ohio, Frank Alexander enlisted at the Navy Recruiting Station, New York, New York, on August 9, 1940, for six years. He joined up to learn a trade and graduated from Submarine Training School, New London,

Connecticut, on January 13, 1941. Assigned to the *Grunion* permanently in April 1942, Alexander, remembered by cousin Bob Berrington as kind, funny, friendly, and adventuresome, "spoke highly of the crew and their faith in one another."

Daniel Emery Allen, Signalman Third Class
19 years old
Salem, Indiana
single

Dan Allen, born on February 23, 1922, in Canton, Indiana, enlisted at the Navy Recruiting Station, Louisville, Kentucky, for six years and planned to make the Navy his career. In June of 1941, while serving on the submarine *O-8*, he wrote a letter home about his sub's sister ship, *O-9*, which sank on a test dive off the Isle of Shoals: "They've [the thirty-three men on the *O-9*'s crew] closed their hatch for the last time.... Whether you pass out 440 feet down or in bed, doesn't alter the fact that you still have God to handle your accounts." On November 23, 1942, in a letter to Kay Abele, Allen's mother lamented, "It breaks my heart to see young men die who have so much to expect from life, my boy Dan was a good Christian boy and was such a happy likable boy, I just don't see how I'll ever get used to the idea he is dead."

Herbert Joseph Arvan, Mess Attendant Second Class
No Photo Available

18 years old
De Quincy, Louisiana
single

Herbert Arvan, one of two African-American sailors serving as mess attendants on the USS *Grunion*, enlisted for four years on December 16, 1941, in New Orleans, Louisiana, and completed basic training in Norfolk, Virginia, on January 21, 1942. One of eight children, he joined the Navy to learn a trade and was assigned to the *Grunion* on May 23, 1942. On September 29, 1942, his father received the dreaded Western Union telegram from the Navy. He, Arvan's girlfriend Gwendolyn Vavassesn, and Arvan's brother Felton all wrote to the Navy for more information.

On September 16, 1943, the Certificate of Death was sent to Arvan's father, and later the Purple Heart and official Navy commendation for meritorious conduct as a member of the crew of the USS *Grunion*. That was the last correspondence the family ever received from the Navy.

Paul Edward Banes, Chief Motor Machinist's Mate
30 years old
Los Angeles, California
married

Paul Banes was born on January 23, 1912, in Webb City, Missouri. At nineteen, a stenotyper by trade but with a desire to travel, he enlisted in the Navy in July 1931, after his widowed mother signed a statement that she was not dependent upon him for support. Banes served at various times on submarines and joined the *Grunion* on April 11, 1942.

The "missing-in-action" Western Union telegram sent to his wife, Arvella, proved undeliverable on September 29, 1942, but the American Red Cross located her in Los Angeles. In 1943, Banes's mother, Nellie Waddell, wrote to Kay Abele: "I still haven't given up hope. I sit up late thinking every time the door bell rings it might be my son coming home."

Leo Joseph Isaie Bedard, Chief Motor Machinist's Mate

34 years old

Taftville, Connecticut

married with a son and a daughter

Born of French Canadian parents in Fitchburg, Massachusetts, on December 23, 1907, Leo Bedard lived together with two siblings in an orphanage in his early years. He enlisted in the Navy for four years on October 2, 1928, and made it his career. Bedard served on various subs from 1936 until 1941, was honorably discharged in December 1941, reenlisted after Pearl Harbor, and was assigned to the *Grunion* as Chief Motor Machinist's Mate on January 24, 1942. He and his wife Lillian had two children—Ronald was eight years old and his sister Therese was five when the *Grunion* left for war.

For the next sixty-four years they believed that the *Grunion* had been sunk by "friendly fire." Not until 2007, with the discovery of the sub, did they learn their father's fate. Ron recalls that "when the sub first disappeared, my mother kept hoping that he had been taken prisoner of war and that they might find him on some desert island…but she finally gave up hope of ever finding him….

"After having spent his young years in an orphanage, he wanted to provide a home for his young family. It was tough on us, as it was tough on everybody back then."

Wesley Hope Blinston, Radioman Third Class

23 years old

Billings, Montana

single

Wesley Blinston was born on August 14, 1918, in Ryegate, Montana, and became an avid ham-radio operator as a youth. He enlisted in the U.S. Naval Reserve on January 8, 1941, and was assigned to the *Grunion* in early 1942 during her fitting-out period.

As news of the *Grunion*'s discovery began to break, Lorna Thackeray, a reporter for the *Billings Gazette* (Montana), tracked down information about the forgotten submariners. She learned that Blinston was a quiet man and devoted to his mother, Sophie. When the missing-in-action telegram was handed to Sophie Blinston on September 29, 1942, according to Thackeray, "Sophie curled up in a great big chair for two weeks. She wouldn't eat. She just sat in that chair and grieved and grieved."

In a letter to Kay Abele in 1943, Sophie wrote, "Thank you for writing me, as it makes me feel somehow you are a link between my son and myself."

Nicholas Richard Bonadies, Fireman Second Class

21 years old
Hartford, Connecticut
single

Nicholas Bonadies, born in Hartford, Connecticut, enlisted in the Navy in March 1940 for a six-year hitch; completed training at the submarine base in New London, Connecticut; and served aboard the submarine USS *O-2* from January to April 1942, when he was assigned to the *Grunion* at her commissioning.

His sister Jan recalls that she was twelve when her mother, who worked two jobs to support seven children, answered the phone in late September 1942, "cried out, threw the phone, and fainted." The dreadful news about Nick spurred their brother Richard to punch his fist through a door. The next day, Richard enlisted in the Army and brother Franny in the Navy. Both survived the war, and to this day, Jan says, "We are all very proud of him—he was a good boy."

Robert Francis Boo, Electrician's Mate Third Class

25 years old

Des Moines, Iowa

single

Robert Boo was born on January 29, 1917, in Des Moines, Iowa, and joined the Navy for a six-year enlistment in September 1940, looking to make the Navy his career. He attended the submarine school at New London from June 1941 to March 1942, was transferred to the *Grunion* for her fitting-out, and joined the crew officially at the commissioning on April 11, 1942.

He wrote his last letter home on July 3, 1942.

In a letter to Kay Abele in October 1942, Robert's father inquired as to whether or not she had heard news that "Japs" had sunk an American sub and taken the crew prisoners. Kay received a similar letter in late January 1943 from Robert's mother, who said she had heard the same thing broadcast on the local news. His parents, brothers, and girlfriend eventually accepted the grim realization that he was gone.

Sixty-eight years later, November 12, 2010, at Iowa Veterans Cemetery, a memorial marker was placed and a ceremony with full military honors was held for Robert by his niece, Carole Boo Harrington, who said, "My dad always told me he looked up to Robert."

Chester Lewis Bouvia, Machinist's Mate First Class

39 years old

Savanna, Illinois

married with a daughter

Chester Bouvia, born on October 3, 1902, was one of the oldest crewmen aboard the *Grunion*, and an eighteen-year veteran of the

Navy. After sixteen years of active service, including time on the submarine *R-10*, he was discharged and transferred to Fleet Reserve for inactive duty. Bouvia was recalled to active duty in June 1940 and assigned to the submarine *R-6*; in October 1940 he requested shore duty, but was denied. He was transferred in December 1941 to the Electric Boat Company in New London for duty in fitting out the *Grunion*, and assigned to her crew on April 4, 1942.

Owing to his family situation, Bouvia continued to request shore duty—when he had been recalled to active duty in 1940, his wife was forced to give up their home and was left with a very difficult teenage daughter. The couple's hope was that mother and daughter could transfer somewhere closer to him because the family desperately needed him. Instead, despite even a congressman's support for his request for shore duty, Bouvia was sent out to war with the *Grunion*.

George Earl Caldwell, Chief Electrician's Mate, Warrant Officer
40 years old
Columbus, Ohio
married with a son

George Caldwell was born on August 19, 1901, in Columbus, Ohio. One of the oldest men on the *Grunion*, he had enlisted in the Navy on April 15, 1920, and made it his career.

His glamorous wife Melba enjoyed being a Navy wife and traveling with her husband from coast to coast. "She was a 'showgirl'," said her grandson, Don Caldwell, and sang for servicemen on USO tours. In 1941, when George Caldwell was about to reenlist for the fourth time, she said, "Don't join. I'm afraid you'll never come back."

Caldwell saw duty on a number of submarines from 1928 to 1942 and was an instructor at the submarine school in New London from November 1933 to November 1935. Melba was in Hawaii when her husband, assigned to help fit out the *Grunion*, requested that he be allowed to remain on board to help mentor and train the young submariners after the sub was commissioned in April 1942. His request was granted, and he was appointed the boat's Warrant Officer.

When the *Grunion* reached Pearl Harbor in June 1942, Melba got to see George and watched as the sub slipped from its berth on June 30, 1942, on course first to Midway and then to the Aleutians. After the *Grunion*'s loss, the gregarious singer, according to relatives, lost her zest for life, never remarried, and rarely socialized. She died in 1968.

Caldwell had told his sister Ruth, "If you hear that my sub is blown up, don't cry. If I have to die, that's how I want to go."

 ### Richard Harry Carroll, Seaman Second Class
18 years old
Springfield, Ohio
single

Richard "Dick" Carroll was born on February 28, 1924, in Springfield, Ohio. He enlisted shortly after Pearl Harbor, just before he turned eighteen, and after his training he was eventually sent to Pearl Harbor, where he first served on the submarine USS *Gato*. Then, on June 27, 1942, he was transferred from the *Gato* to the *Grunion*, joining nine other men to fill out Jim Abele's crew.

In letters home, Carroll reassured his family, "Everyone seems very nice here. I am enjoying the Navy and the food isn't so bad, but I still would rather be back home in Ohio.... I am getting to like the Navy more all the time, especially when we are at sea." He also alluded to the fact that he and his fellow submariners were on a war footing: "I was out in a sub for about 8 days and all the time we were out, I didn't see daylight. . . ." That was the last letter he wrote.

According to Sondra Buck, Carroll's niece, "My dad joined the Navy after USS *Grunion* went missing and all were presumed dead. He wanted to go after the people who killed his brother."

John Stewart Clift, Torpedoman's Mate Second Class
22 years old
Wichita, Kansas
married

On January 29, 1920, John Henry Stewart, the youngest of ten children, was born in Bluff City, Kansas. His mother died a few days later. The infant John and his three-year-old sister Lorraine were both given up for adoption, and John was raised by John and Flossie Clift of Bluff City. At some point John moved to Wichita, Kansas, and withdrew from high school in 1937 to join the Navy, intending to make it his career. He was transferred to the submarine *S-23* at Pearl Harbor in July 1939 and honorably discharged. But he reenlisted in January of 1942 and was soon assigned to the *Grunion*.

In February 1941, John married Agnes Lorine Boswell. In February 1942 they lived in New London. After the USS *Grunion* left New London, Agnes moved back to Wichita and was living with John's adoptive mother at the time of the submarine's loss. She moved to her own apartment seven months later and eventually remarried. Through the years, Clift's Stewart siblings and other relatives and friends sought details about the sub's loss and his life. Six members from the Stewart family attended the 2008 memorial service in Cleveland, Ohio.

Michael Francis Collins, Fireman Second Class

23 years old

Washington, D.C.

single

Born on September 3, 1918, in Cottage City, Maryland, Michael "Moe" Collins enlisted in the U.S. Naval Reserve on April 9, 1940, and went on active duty on May 7. After his training at the submarine school in New London, he was transferred to the *Grunion* fitting-out detail in March 1942 and officially assigned to the sub at its commissioning on April 11, 1942. Moe's older brother, Douglas, in the Merchant Marine, was at Pearl Harbor when the *Grunion* came in. There Moe and Douglas saw each other for the last time.

"When [Moe] was killed, it was for his mother as if her whole world closed up—she was never the same," said his niece Mary Anne Marino. Moe's sister Rosemary Lewis added, "I was fifteen years old when our family received news that USS *Grunion* was missing. I remember that my mother suffered a mild stroke when the news came...."

Lee Dale Cooksey, Motor Machinist's Mate First Class

31 years old

Greenville, South Carolina

married

Dale Cooksey was born on June 20, 1911, in Harville, Missouri. He left school in 1925 to work on the family farm, but the income from the farm could not support the family. In March 1933, Cooksey enlisted in the Navy. He served aboard battleships until 1937, when he completed submarine training in New London and served on three subs before his final assignment, to the *Grunion*. In one of his last letters he wrote, "I cannot tell you where we are going, but I hope to hear our torpedoes exploding in some enemy vessel."

Cooksey's wife Olive, in a 1942 letter to Kay Abele, wrote, "My last letter was June 29 [1942]. This knowing nothing is pretty hard, isn't it? You have your boys, though, to give you incentive to go on. We were not fortunate enough to have any children."

Daniel Cullinane, Chief Motor Machinist's Mate
47 years old
Killingly, Connecticut
married

William Hugh Cuthbertson Jr., Ensign
27 years old
Frankenmuth, Michigan
married with a daughter

William "Red" Cuthbertson Jr. was born on April 30, 1915, in Denver, Colorado. A 1938 graduate of Albion College in Michigan, he worked several jobs in Depression-wracked Michigan. Cuthbertson enlisted in the U.S. Naval Reserve in July 1941, completed Midshipman's School at Northwestern University in Chicago, and was commissioned Ensign in the Naval Reserve in January 1942. Assigned to the submarine USS *R-19* (*SS-96*) later that same month, he was transferred to the *Grunion* in March and appointed the sub's Duty Officer. On April 18, 1942, he married Dorothy Lorna Nuechterlein at a candlelight service in New London, Connecticut. The couple's attendants included fellow *Grunion* officer Lieutenant Millener Weaver Thomas and his wife.

On May 24, 1942, when the *Grunion* left for Pearl Harbor, Cuthbertson was unaware that Dorothy was expecting. Six months after he was declared missing in action, presumed dead, his daughter, Nancy Lee, was born. Dorothy Cuthbertson, who died at age seventy-three in 1983, never remarried. When daughter Nancy, a schoolteacher, learned of the *Grunion*'s discovery, she said, "It is very sad. But it is a sense of relief because we can say that now we know."

Lawrence Dale Deaton, Seaman Second Class
22 years old
Ames, Iowa
married

Lawrence Deaton was born on February 8, 1920, in Boone, Iowa. He enlisted in the Navy in September 1941, graduated from submarine school at New London, Connecticut, in April 1942, and was assigned to the *Grunion*. He had been married to Deloris Deaton for less than a year when the *Grunion* left for war.

At the age of ninety-three, Lawrence's older sister Lenore Gearhart reflected, "We were broken-hearted when he was lost; everyone liked him." She wrote to Kay Abele in November, 1942, "Lawrence said, in one of the letters we received from him, 'the men are all great guys, and there isn't a coward among them.' So we are proud of him and the ones that were with him. He was young, just twenty-two.

"We were afraid to tell my mom because she had a bad heart. My dad never recovered. He went downhill after that."

 **Albert Edward DeStoop, Chief Torpedoman's Mate**
26 years old
Revere, Massachusetts
engaged

Albert DeStoop was born on August 31, 1916, in Chelsea, Massachusetts. Upon graduation from Revere High School, he enlisted in the Navy in November 1934 and served on a number of both surface vessels and subs before his assignment to the *Grunion* in April 1942. He and his fiancée, Mary Channell, also from Revere, planned to marry in June 1942, but the sub left before they could do so.

On September 30, 1942, her parish priest called Mary asking if she had heard from Al lately. She replied that the last letter from Al, sent to her from Pearl Harbor, had arrived on July 2. Then the priest told her that a telegram from the Navy announcing that the *Grunion* was missing in action had been received at the DeStoop home on the previous day.

She wrote a heartbreaking letter to Kay Abele in May 1943: "Please, please tell me just what does it mean? Do they know something? Mrs. Abele, you know how I feel. I am not as 'brave and strong' as American women are supposed to be. Yes, I go along. There is nothing else to do. But, I love Al. I am lost without him.... A year has gone by. I have counted the days. I won't give up hope."

Mary eventually married and had a son. Her brother William said, "My sister never stopped loving Al." There is a park named after Albert DeStoop in Revere, Massachusetts.

William Patrick Devaney Jr., Seaman Second Class

20 years old

Ozone Park, New York

single

Born on July 3, 1922, in Ozone Park, New York, William "Billy" Devaney Jr. was the eldest of eight children. He enlisted in the Navy in September 1940, transferred to the submarine school at New London, Connecticut, in November 1941, and was assigned to the *Grunion*. Close to his family, he wrote them often and planned to become a New York City policeman after the Navy.

When the family received the telegram that Billy was missing in action, his mother collapsed. Both of his parents refused to stop hoping that Devaney and his crewmates were still alive. After Japan surrendered and prisoners of war were freed, his father would pore through the newspaper photographs with a magnifying glass in hopes of finding his son among them.

Samuel Reed Dighton Jr., Lieutenant Junior Grade

24 years old

Sanford, Florida

engaged

Sam Dighton was born on December 13, 1917, in Savannah, Georgia. He came from a prominent military family; his father, a Yale Law graduate, was a veteran of the Army in France in World War I and served as Provost Marshall of Alaska during World War II. Dighton, a popular young man, graduated from the University of Alabama in 1939 and then earned a law degree from the University of Michigan.

In September 1940 he enlisted in the U.S. Naval Reserve and went on active duty in November 1940. Commissioned an ensign in 1941, he first saw submarine service aboard the USS *Mackerel*. Dighton was assigned to the *Grunion* in December 1941. Dighton was engaged to Jean Wallace, daughter of Vice President Henry A. Wallace.

In an October 2, 1942, letter to Kay Abele, Dighton's mother Florence wrote, "You have no doubt received the same telegram I have from the Navy Department in Washington. I have heard nothing since the 23rd of June and I heard that through Jean Wallace, who talked to Sam on long distance...."

Later in October Florence wrote again to Kay, "There is such an absolute confidence in my heart that the *Grunion* and crew are still safe—that I want to pass it on. I can't explain why I feel this way, but it is such a comfort."

Eventually she accepted that her son was not coming back. In 1945 she wrote to Vice Admiral Louis Denfield, "To say I am proud beyond words to have been his Mother is too trite—it goes deeper and beyond any human words to convey."

Louis Henry Doell Jr., Radioman Second Class
20 years old
Cincinnati, Ohio
married

Louis "Red" Doell Jr., born on August 15, 1921, in Mentor, Kentucky, was originally named Louis Fossett. His father died when Louis was three years old; after his mother remarried, his last name was changed to Doell. He enlisted in the Navy Reserve in February

1939 and after serving on a destroyer transferred to the submarine school at New London, Connecticut.

In October 1941 Doell married his childhood sweetheart, Evelyn ("Eve") Daniels, and she went with him to New London when he reported to the submarine base for radio and sound training. He was assigned to the *Grunion* in February 1942.

From Pearl Harbor in late June 1942, Doell mailed his last letter to his wife: "I don't know how often I will write because everything is so very importantly uncertain.... This silly damn war can't last forever and your old man will positively try to last forever for you, if that little thing is humanly possible."

Doell's mother, Gladys, wrote to Kay Abele in early November, 1942: "My son Louis has a very high regard for your husband, both personally and as an officer, and I am sure that he must be a fine man to merit such fierce loyalty from the members of his crew.... In no other country would the wife of a ship's captain bother about families of enlisted men.... Thank you very much, Mrs. Abele."

Eve Doell would remarry but remained very close to her first husband's parents. Eve's second marriage ended in divorce, and her daughter Nancy Springer Hagan would say, "The day my father left, Red's picture came back on my mother's bedside table and stayed there until she died in 2002."

Leon Henry Franck,
Seaman First Class
19 years old
Flushing, New York
single

Leon H. Franck was born on April 4, 1923, in New York City. He enlisted in the Navy in December 1940 and after basic training was assigned to the U.S. Naval Air Station, Pensacola. When his father fell grievously ill in August 1941, he requested a transfer to be closer to his ailing parent, but was denied. His request to enroll in the submarine school in New London, however, was granted. In March 1942 he was assigned to the *Grunion*.

Long after the *Grunion* went down—in fact, after the sub's discovery—Joe Franck, one of Leon's cousins, reflected that when Leon came home on leave, he would always hand Joe a Lucky Strike cigarette and say, "'When I come back, I'll smoke it.' I still have one of his cigarettes. The image of red-haired Leon has remained frozen in my mind."

Merritt Dayton Graham, Chief Torpedoman's Mate, Chief of the Boat
42 years old
Circleville, Ohio
married

Born on May 15, 1900, in Leistville, Ohio, Merritt Graham was the third oldest man on the *Grunion*, a career Navy man who first joined in June 1918 and served on a tugboat, destroyers, and seven submarines before the *Grunion*. For a time he was an instructor at the New London Submarine Base escape training-tank.

In 1938 he married and became father to Anna Catherine Graham's two sons. The next year he retired from the Navy as a chief torpedoman's mate to take a job at the Electric Boat Company in New London, where he helped build the *Grunion*. After the Japanese attacked Pearl Harbor, Graham requested a return to active duty—aboard the *Grunion*. His request was granted, and he was appointed chief of the boat. According to grandson Bill Graham, Jim Abele "knew of Merritt's qualifications and asked him to sail with USS *Grunion*."

Graham's wife wrote to a nephew in December 1942, "I'm very sad, as Merritt is believed lost, *Grunion* overdue since September. I just cannot believe it. These are such awful days for me, and only time will help....."

Kenneth Edward Hall, Seaman Second Class
21 years old
San Francisco, California
single

Kenneth E. Hall, born on November 10, 1920, in Hollister, California, worked with the Civilian Conservation Corps as a mechanic and later became a Greyhound bus driver before enlisting in the Navy Reserve and being called to active duty on January 28, 1942. On April 16, 1942, he was transferred to the submarine tender USS *Fulton* at Pearl Harbor and then assigned to the *Grunion* on June 27, 1942, three days before it departed Pearl Harbor for the Aleutians.

He wrote his last letter home June 28, 1942, to his parents: "Don't worry about me. I will be alright...."

Ernest Glenn Hellensmith, Electrician's Mate Third Class
22 years old
Moberly, Missouri
single

Glenn Hellensmith was born on June 4, 1920. He enlisted in the Navy in April 1941 to make it his career. His first assignment was the submarine tender *Fulton*, and on June 28, 1942, he was transferred to the submarine USS *Gato* at Pearl Harbor. The next day, he was ordered to join the crew of the *Grunion*.

In the fall of 1942, Glenn's mother responded to Kay Abele's letter of sympathy, "I'm writing in regards to know when my boy went aboard *Grunion*. The last word I got from him was June 12, 1942, and his address was USS *Fulton* which is a submarine tender. I received a telegram on the 29th of September reporting him being missing while on duty to his country. So will you please let me know if you can, when he was transferred to *Grunion*."

Hollice Beauford Henderson, Motor Machinist's Mate Second Class
27 years old
Tichnor, Arkansas
single

Hollice Henderson was born on March 31, 1915, in Tichnor, Arkansas. In 1940, at age twenty-five, he enlisted in the Navy for six years and after basic training was assigned to the Submarine School at New London. His first sub was the USS *S-1* (*SS-105*) at the Navy Yard in Philadelphia. On April 11, 1942, he was transferred to the *Grunion*.

His mother, Viola, wrote about her four sons, all in the Navy, to Kay Abele: "Hollice was on the *Grunion*.... I have heard from all except Hollice in the past week. Sometimes it looks like more than I can stand.... May we all have courage to carry on as our boys would wish us."

His niece, Sandra Woodson, writes, "Of course, I am so excited about the discovery of the USS *Grunion*. I just wish my grandmother, daddy, and uncles could have been able to experience this great event. This would have given them a sense of closure to Uncle Hollice's life."

Charles Roy Hutchinson, Torpedoman's Mate Third Class
25 years old
Sheldon, Illinois
single

Charles R. "Charlie" Hutchinson was born on April 18, 1917, in Sheldon, Illinois, and went on to enlist in the Navy in September 1940, intending to make it his career. Upon graduation from the submarine school at New London on January 27, 1941, he served aboard the submarine *O-3* and was then transferred to the *Grunion* during its fitting out. He became a permanent crew member on April 11, 1942.

His sister, Mona Kime, only four years old when the *Grunion* disappeared, has a memory of the day the missing-in-action news arrived: "They came to the house. Of course they had their uniforms on." Her parents never talked about it in front of her. In a letter to Kay Abele in November 1942, Hutchinson's mother wrote, "He has…a sister who looks and waits for him…. She asks for him most every day." On June 7, 1944, another brother, Bernard, on the minesweeper USS *Tide*, was killed in action off the Normandy beachheads.

Sylvester Joseph Kennedy Jr., Motor Machinist's Mate Second Class
25 years old
Flushing, New York
engaged

While Kennedy's story is told above, the impact of his loss upon his fiancée, Evelyn Switzer, is one of the most poignant episodes in the *Grunion*'s saga. Kennedy's family had not informed Evelyn of his death, and even when she realized that he was never coming back, she could never love another man.

In 1996 when a retired sailor from her church heard Evelyn's story, he offered to help her. He learned that the *Grunion* had been lost in the Aleutians, its fate was unknown, and that it had disappeared without a distress call. At least knowing where Sy had been gave Evelyn some comfort.

She traveled with friends to Dutch Harbor, Alaska, in 1999. According to Evelyn's friend Kitty Fleischman, "We found the old submarine dock, which would have been the last place Ken set foot on land. She had one of her cherished possessions, a little pair of wooden shoes he had purchased for her in happier times, and a poem she'd written about him. She placed them in a tiny box and dropped it in the Bering Sea."

The next morning she told Kitty that, for the first time in nearly sixty years, she felt closure and peace. On December 27, 2005, Evelyn died of heart failure at the home of her great-niece Victoria in Boise, Idaho. Evelyn was a month short of her eighty-sixth birthday. She never married.

Edward Earl Knowles Jr., Seaman Second Class
18 years old
Greenville, Mississippi
single

Earl Knowles was born on November 18, 1923, in Greenville, Mississippi, and enlisted in the Navy in January 1942. He was soon sent to serve on the submarine tender USS *Fulton* at Pearl Harbor. He was transferred first to the sub USS *Gato*, on April 29, 1942, and then, on June 27, to the *Grunion*.

Writing from Pearl Harbor to his grandmother on June 17, 1942, he worried, "Grandmother[,] if you can't get all the medicine that you need just let me know and I will try to send you the money."

The day after Knowles's family received the missing-in-action telegram on September 29, 1942, his grandmother wrote to the Navy: "We have received a telegram my Grandson is missing in action. We do not know what ship he was stationed on. We haven't had a word from him in three months. We would appreciate any information you can send us about him, if there is any hope at all that he is alive please let us know."

One of his aunts beseeched the Navy to "please tell us where he was and how he died? I know he must be gone so won't you please give us some consolation concerning him...."

Lawrence Richard Kockler, Torpedoman's Mate First Class
25 years old
New Haven, Connecticut
married

Lawrence "Larry" R. Kockler was born on January 16, 1917, in New Haven, Connecticut. A good athlete, he joined the Navy at the Naval Recruiting Station in New Haven, Connecticut, on October 10, 1935, at only seventeen and a half because he wanted to travel. His first posting was aboard the battleship USS *Tennessee*, and he transferred two years later to the submarine school at New London and served aboard three subs before his honorable discharge in November 1941.

On December 8, 1941, the day after the Pearl Harbor attack, Kockler requested reenlistment for submarine duty, was accepted, and was assigned briefly to the sub *S-20*. Then on January 9, 1942, he was assigned to the *Grunion* for its fitting-out and became a permanent member of the crew in April. He married Vera Sherry on May 16, just eight days before the sub set out for Pearl Harbor.

On October 14, 1942, Kockler's father wrote to the Navy, "Will you please advise me if there is any hope of my son returning? My wife and his wife are very ill over the telegram and I can't seem to ease their hearts in any way."

Vera, Kockler's wife, sent Kay Abele a letter in October 1943 to let her know that she [Vera] had written the Red Cross and that they had notified her that word had been received from Washington that Lawrence was not on any casualty list and was presumed to be a prisoner, and that they were still investigating in hopes of finding definite proof. Vera added, "Little as it is, it gives a bit more hope to the possibility that they may be alive somewhere."

Sixty-five years later, Kockler's sister Betty was visiting their brother Bill when they saw on television that the *Grunion* had been discovered. She says, "We never really thought it would be found."

William Gregory Kornahrens, Lieutenant, Communications Officer
26 years old
Lewiston, Maine
married

Kornahrens' daughter, Nancy Kornahrens Stark, born after the USS *Grunion* disappeared, tried to identify with her father by learning to sail. "When I'm on the water, I feel close to my dad," she said.

Sixty-five years later, when she saw the pictures of the *Grunion*, she said, "I realized that my dad was really gone." Her mother, who never remarried, passed away before the submarine was found. "In a way," she says, "I'm glad my mother didn't see the pictures of the wreckage."

Nancy adds, "I went from being an only child to having an extended family in the descendants of the *Grunion* crew. This tragedy brought seventy families together, and I can reach out to them at any time."

Moore Julius Ledford, Chief Yeoman
36 years old
Asheville, North Carolina
married

Moore Julius Ledford was born on February 23, 1906, in Asheville, North Carolina. He enlisted in the Navy in March 1924, began his career in the surface Navy aboard the destroyer USS *Parrott*, and later served on the Panama Canal steel tug USS *Bagaduce*. In September 1928 Ledford was transferred to the submarine base at Coco Solo, Canal Zone, and in November he boarded his first submarine, the *S-16*.

From 1930 to 1940, he served on a number of vessels, on shore, and even in the rigid airship (dirigible) USS *Macon*. Ledford was transferred to the submarine base in New London, Connecticut, in 1940 and was assigned to the submarine *R-6*. On December 8, 1941, he was transferred to Groton, Connecticut, for the fitting-out of the *Grunion* and became a permanent member of the crew at her commissioning on April 11, 1942. Lieutenant Commander Abele appointed him Chief Yeoman on June 16, 1942.

When the missing-in-action telegram came, it was delivered not to Ledford's wife Anna but to one of his sisters. According to nieces, Ledford married Anna Schneider in 1939 but his family knew little about the marriage. A friend of Anna's in Torrance, California, remarks that Anna talked about Ledford and always loved him.

Woodrow Wilson Lehman, Electrician's Mate First Class
28 years old
Mercer, Pennsylvania
married with a son

Born in Elgin, Texas, on June 29, 1914, Woodrow Wilson "Woodie" Lehman enlisted in the Navy in November 1933. Eventually assigned to the battleship USS *New York*, he served on her for seven years, until April of 1941. Lehman volunteered for submarine duty because he wanted more money (submariners received a higher rate of pay) to help his parents, his wife Polly, and their new baby, and he was transferred to the *Grunion* during her preparation for war in the spring of 1942.

His parents, according to his sister Lily, "until the day they died, thought the crew was going to be found on an island in the Pacific."

In a November 7, 1942, letter to Kay Abele, Polly Lehman wrote, "I just received your letter today. I have been thinking about the other wives too. You and I are luckier than some, you have your three sons and I have my little boy of 3 years. Woodie was the first man assigned to the *Grunion*. He spoke to me of your husband real often. Here's praying that our men will all get back safe from somewhere."

Lehman's son Gary and his wife Mary attended the USS *Grunion* memorial service in Cleveland in 2008. Gary said, "My dad helped build the *Grunion* and I was told that he always said, 'I'm building my own coffin.'"

Sidney Arthur Loe,
Motor Machinist's Mate Second Class
25 years old
Mountrail, North Dakota
single

Sidney A. Loe, born on August 15, 1916, in Sanish, North Dakota, was placed in a foster home at age eleven. After his mother's death, his father simply could not both work and raise nine children. Loe enlisted in the Navy in 1939 at the age of twenty-three, having decided to make it his career. Following a stint aboard the battleship USS *Oklahoma*, he transferred to the submarine school in New London in July, 1940. His first sub was the *S-1*, and he was permanently assigned to the *Grunion* in April 1942.

As was true of a number of *Grunion* families, the Loes did not even know in what theater of action Sidney Loe was serving. According to an October 3, 1942, letter from Sidney's oldest sister Maude to the Navy, the Loe family knew neither where their brother was serving nor the date he was reported missing. And Maude wrote to Kay Abele, "My sisters and I were deeply touched by your letter.... Your husband, Captain Abele, has reason to be proud of you. God bless you for your courage. No matter what happens, God grant us courage to go on bravely, as I know they would have us do. I am sure that every man aboard did his very best for his country and not just Captain Abele. I am happy that my brother had the privilege of working under Captain Abele."

Samuel Elisha Lunsford Jr., Electrician's Mate Second Class
22 years old
Dorchester, Virginia
single

Samuel E. Lunsford Jr. was born on December 12, 1919, in Dorchester, Virginia, the youngest of six boys, three of whom served in World War II. He joined the Navy in September 1938 and served on a battleship and a destroyer before transferring to the submarine *S-22*. After additional training in June 1941 at the submarine base in New London, he was assigned first to the submarine *O-3* and then to the *O-8*, commanded by Lieutenant John S. McCain Jr.

In March 1942 Lunsford was placed aboard the *Grunion* and became a permanent crew member on April 11, 1942. After the news of the *Grunion*'s disappearance, his parents responded to Kay Abele's letter, "We know that the *Grunion* must have made a wonderful record if she is lost, but we must always believe that they will return.... It has helped me [Mrs. Lunsford] so much to hear from you and the boys [Bruce, Brad, and John]. And with your help and God's we can only hope that someday they will return to us. But we must be brave and keep fighting until our son and your husband and your sons' father is avenged and the enemy is wiped out. Again, thank you and your boys for the fine letter and encouragement."

In March 1943, Ledford's sweetheart Millie implored the Navy, "Will you please help me get in touch with Samuel Lunsford, EM3/C. I haven't heard from him since March 1942...."

The Navy responded, "It is with deepest regret you are informed that Samuel Lunsford has been reported 'missing' following action in the performance of his duty and in the service of his country, USS *Grunion* being long overdue and presumed lost as of August 1, 1942."

Millie suffered a nervous breakdown, never married, and died knowing only that Lunsford was "lost at sea."

James Wallace Lyon, Fireman First Class
24 years old
Mt. Rainier, Maryland
single

James Wallace "Wally" Lyon, born February 11, 1919, in Washington, D.C., enlisted in the Navy in October 1939, served on the USS *Roe*, and then transferred in July 1941 to the Submarine School at New London. After completion of his training, he was permanently assigned in April 1942 to the *Grunion*.

The news that the *Grunion* was missing hit the Lyons family hard. Wally's father died suddenly a month after the telegram arrived, and his distraught mother, a niece remembers, never spoke of her son, nor were there any photographs of him displayed in the home.

Carson Raymond Martin, Chief Motor Machinist's Mate
32 years old
Bedford, Virginia
married

Carson Martin was born on September 3, 1909, in Baltimore, Maryland, and grew up in Bedford, Virginia. He enlisted in the Navy in November 1927 and served on the destroyer USS *Breckinridge* until February 1932, when his transfer request to submarine school was granted. Before permanent assignment to the *Grunion* in April 1942, he saw duty aboard the submarines *S-24* and *R-14*.

The September 29, 1942, telegram was sent to the Martins' last listed address in Groton, Connecticut, but the family had moved in with relatives in New York City, so Martin's wife did not learn of the *Grunion*'s disappearance until she heard the news on a radio broadcast. She also received a letter from Catherine Abele and responded, "I could hardly believe my ears [on hearing the radio broadcast].... I have two children, one six the other ten. They keep asking for him all the time.... I haven't received my allotment. I'm wondering if you got yours. One day I feel as though they are living and the next day not...." She never remarried.

Thomas Edward Martin, Electrician's Mate First Class
31 years old
Lenoir, North Carolina
single

Thomas Martin, born on June 26, 1911, in Lenoir, North Carolina, joined the Navy in January 1931 and served aboard an array of surface vessels until his assignment to the submarine base in the Panama Canal Zone from March 1935 to February 1941. During this time he saw duty on the submarines *S-46* and USS *Sargo*. His next assignments were a pair of subs at the New London, Connecticut, base; in December 1941 he transferred to the *Grunion*.

In a February 4, 1943, letter to Catherine Abele, Martin's father wrote, "I would be glad to know if you have learned any little scrap of information regarding the loss of the USS *Grunion*.... I of course presume that you and your sons have become reconciled to your loss, as I have and again I want to extend my heartfelt sympathy. Respectfully, B. Frank Martin."

Ryder Mathison, Electrician's Mate First Class

36 years old

Sioux City, Iowa

married with two daughters

Ryder Mathison was born on March 15, 1906, in Sioux City, Iowa, to Norwegian immigrants who had eight other children, and enlisted in the Navy in September 1926. From then until 1941 he served on numerous vessels including at least five submarines. While serving on the *S-27* he was commended "for display of exceptional energy, willingness and interest in accomplishing ship's force overhaul work during regular Navy Yard overhaul." On the submarine *R-7*, his commanding officer lauded Mathison's "initiative, ingenuity, workmanship and industry in connection with the recommissioning overhaul of the USS *R-7*."

In January 1942 he transferred to the Electric Boat Company, in Groton, Connecticut, to help finish the construction of the *Grunion*, and he became a member of the crew on April 11, 1942. Ryder's wife Violet Nunes Mathison and their six-year-old daughter Betty Ann were living in Chula Vista, California, when the *Grunion* was declared missing. The following month his second daughter, Pearl Ryder "Bobbi" Mathison, was born.

The discovery of the *Grunion* in 2007 left Mathison's daughter Bobbi with conflicted emotions: "It's really kind of hard because I never really knew my father. No one ever really talked about what happened."

Richard George McCutcheon, Torpedoman's Mate Third Class
19 years old
Detroit, Michigan
single

Richard G. McCutcheon was born on December 27, 1923, in Detroit, Michigan. He joined the Navy in January 1941 and after basic training transferred to the submarine base in New London. On June 9, 1941, he was assigned to the submarine *O-2*. He became a member of Jim Abele's crew on April 11, 1942.

In an October 31, 1942, letter to Catherine Abele, McCutcheon's mother Margaret wrote, "The news of Richard being missing was about the last straw, as our older son Donald was reported missing in the Philippines Area, May 13. To lose two of the finest sons in the whole world in less than five months is surely trying our souls to the breaking point.... Richard worshipped his commander and wanted to follow in his footsteps. With men like ours aboard the *Grunion*, she couldn't help but make a record hard to beat. I try not to grieve as my sons wouldn't want me to, but oh how I want them back. I say that you and your sons are very brave, and pray we have more Americans like you."

John Merton McMahon, Lieutenant, Engineering and Diving Officer
30 years old
Belfast, New York
married with two sons

John Merton McMahon was born on July 15, 1912, in Rochester, New York, attended Canisius College in Buffalo, New York, for one year, and then was appointed to the U.S. Naval Academy in 1930.

While at the Naval Academy, he was a member of the Navy Crew for four years and played a year of football. He was assigned first to the battleship USS *California* but in January 1936 requested submarine training. His request was granted and he transferred to the submarine base at New London. In July 1937 he reported for duty aboard the submarine USS *Permit* in San Diego.

McMahon married Francis "Fran" Wiley, of Glen Ridge, New Jersey, in June 1938 and served on the *Permit* at San Diego and then in Manila until ordered back to the United States in the summer of 1940.

Promoted to full lieutenant in July 1941, he received orders to leave the *Permit* on November 12 and report to the Electric Boat Co. for duty in fitting out the *Grunion*, on which he became Engineering and Diving Officer. Fran McMahon and Kay Abele soon became good friends. In fact, they kept up a lifelong friendship through phone calls and letters, and Bruce and John Abele have many fond memories of Fran.

In a letter to the Abele brothers after Kay's death in 1976, Fran wrote, "I keep remembering all the difficult things Kay was called on to do as the skipper's wife in 1942 when *Grunion* was lost—all the letters she wrote to every single next-of-kin of the crew. I will certainly miss your mother though we saw each other seldom over the years; we shared an enduring and sustaining friendship. Thus in some small measure we all share our great loss. All of you have a lot to be proud of—and a lot to live up to—raised by a sterling mother. It was certainly my pleasure and privilege to be a friend of your mother and I send my deepest sympathy to you all in your loss.... Fran."

Fran McMahon had two sons, Michael and James. "I wish my mother had been alive to learn that the *Grunion* had been found," says son Michael.

Ernest Carl Miller,
Fireman Second Class
26 years old
West McHenry, Illinois
single

Ernest Carl Miller was born Ernest Carl Pace on August 27, 1915, in Elburn, Illinois, one of three children to Signa Marie and Lewis Pace. But after his parents divorced and his mother married Ben J. Miller, all three children adopted the last name of Miller. A trained aluminum welder, Miller enlisted in the Navy in June 1941 and was assigned to the submarine base at New London in October 1941. He was transferred to the *Grunion* and made a permanent member of the crew on April 11, 1942.

On December 1, 1942, Ernest's mother wrote to Kay Abele, "I don't feel they are gone for good and I hope and pray they are all together, they will be a comfort for each other. They were so close to each other perhaps because of what they were doing. My son wrote, 'Mom the fellows are swell and our Commander is tops....' I find myself wondering how big your boys are and I feel so sorry for them."

David Oliver Myers,
Fireman First Class
25 years old
Jacksonville, Illinois
single

David Myers and his twin sister Dorothy were born on the family farm in Winchester, Illinois, on July 3, 1917. After one year at Illinois College, he enrolled at a diesel engineering school in Chicago and enlisted in the Naval Reserve. He was called up in August 1940 and transferred to the submarine base at New London, Connecticut, later that year. On February 14, 1942, Myers transferred to the *Grunion* fitting-out detail; and he became a permanent crew member on April 11, 1942.

Despite the passage of sixty-five years, David's sister-in-law Cecile Myers, married to David's brother Donald, vividly recalls the terrible day that the news about the *Grunion* arrived: "We were at his parents' home when the telegram came. Donald went into a bedroom, and I soon heard a noise. I went in, and he was sitting on the side of a bed bawling. It was the first time I saw him cry like that. Donald and David were very close."

In February 1942, Myers wrote home, "Mom, the Skipper's orders are to tell you not to pay any attention to any rumors you hear about ships being sunk or anything else along that line. Propaganda spreads fast and that is the best way they have to do it. If something happens the Bureau of Navigation will let you know. Just because I told you this there is no need to become alarmed. I will be safer where I am than I would be if I stayed here at the base. You don't know what minute a bomb might fall in these barracks.... I'll be able to send you about two or three dollars a day around a month from now.... Dave."

In a letter dated September 31, 1942, David's twin sister Dorothy wrote to the U.S. submarine base in San Francisco, "We received a telegram last night about David reported missing. We called Washington, D.C., last night, but the answer did not satisfy us, sir. Can't you please tell us more? If you could see the condition my mother is in today, you would have some sympathy on us. Any information you could give us will be kept absolutely a secret.... We must know something, or we will all go crazy. Can't you even tell us where he was and on what ship, just tell us something, please. Please send us a telegram telling us just something, just something...."

Frank Thomas Nave,
Motor Machinist's Mate Second Class
26 years old
Arlington, Virginia
single

Frank T. Nave, born on November 1, 1915, enlisted in the Navy in May 1937 and served on two destroyers before he transferred in August 1940 to the submarine *S-25* at New London, Connecticut. He transferred again, to the *S-22*, on November 10, 1941, and to his final sub, the *Grunion*, on March 17, 1942.

Some years ago in a shopping center parking lot a passer-by saw a Purple Heart in a dumpster, realized what it was, picked it up, and held on to it. After reading in the newspaper or seeing on television that the *Grunion* had been located, the anonymous finder of the Purple Heart researched the name on the medal. It had been awarded to Motor Machinist's Mate Second Class Frank Thomas Nave, and so the medal was returned to the Nave family.

Arthur G. Newcomb,
Radioman First Class
23 years old
Los Angeles, California
single

Arthur "Ginger" Newcomb was born on August 20, 1918, in Benson, Arizona, as Arthur Young, son of Arthur Young and Bertha Theodora Hague. His parents divorced and when his mother remarried he assumed the last name of his stepfather, Major Erwin Barrett Newcomb. He lived with his family on the grounds of the National Military Home in Los Angeles, where his stepfather was employed as the chief engineer of the facility, which later became the Veterans Administration. Major Newcomb had fought in the trenches of France in World War I and been awarded the Silver Star.

Newcomb entered the Navy in February 1938 and graduated from Communication School with high marks. He transferred to the submarine *S-29* at Pearl Harbor and went on to serve on the submarines *R-2* and *S-30*. In September 1941 he transferred to the submarine base in New London for instruction in the Sound Operator's Course and returned briefly to the *S-30* before assignment to the *Grunion* in January 1942.

His mother wrote to Kay Abele about her son and the *Grunion*: "He took such pride in helping to fit out such a fine boat; his letters home were so enthusiastic about her, that I have somehow felt that she could get through and would someday be safely back in port. I always carry the thought that my son is missing for awhile [*sic*], but I have never given up hope."

Many years later, Ginger's brother Fred said that their family finally lost hope when the war ended and "he didn't come home."

"Now," he adds, "when I visit [Ginger's memorial marker at the Los Angeles National Cemetery] I know the true fate of my brother. It gives me peace of mind. The ship probably sank in a hurry and bingo, it was over."

John Wesley Nobles, Motor Machinist's Mate First Class
25 years old
Jeffersonville, Georgia
married with a son and daughter

John W. Nobles was born on February 1, 1917, in Jeffersonville, Georgia. John's mother died when he was three years old, but his father kept the family together. With his older brother a submariner on the *S-9*, John enlisted in the Navy in March 1938 to follow in his brother's footsteps. He served aboard four submarines in the years before World War II, and on January 20, 1942, he transferred to the *Grunion*.

Married to Charlotte "Sally" Laura Brostek in 1938, Nobles fathered a son and a daughter. Like Bruce and John Abele, John Nobles Jr. recalls being taken onboard *Grunion* in New London. He also remembers the day his mother received the Western Union telegram saying that *Grunion* was missing in action—he remembers telling her not to cry.

Even though John Jr. and his sister do not remember their father very well, their mother kept his memory alive. John recalls Memorial Days from his youth when he and his sister would go with their mother to the ocean and throw flowers in memory of their dad. Charlotte never remarried.

Friends and fellow sailors remembered John Nobles as a legendary poker player who probably made more money at the poker table than he did from the Navy. Before leaving on patrol he bought his family a new Packard sedan with his poker winnings.

A memorial marker for John was placed near his parents' graves in Jeffersonville Cemetery, Jeffersonville, Georgia.

John Edwin Pancoast, Motor Machinist's Mate Second Class
23 years old
West Homestead, Pennsylvania
married with a son

Some time after Julia Pancoast traveled from the Philippines to the U.S. with her son, John Jr., she married a man named Ray Wells. They lived for a short while in Mt. Holly, New Jersey, but they later divorced. Julia enrolled in St. Francis School of Nursing in Trenton, New Jersey, in 1950; graduated in 1952; and went on to earn a degree in Nursing from the University of Miami. Her third marriage, to Charles Genter, lasted thirty years.

Julia died in 1988 and her son, Jack Jr., and her husband Charles honored her final wish—to be buried at sea with a scarf that Jack Pancoast had given her before he was ordered to ship out from the Philippines in 1941. On May 5, 2011, Jack Jr. passed away, having lived long enough to see his father's missing submarine found. His final wish, too, was to be buried at sea.

Carmine Anthony Parziale, Torpedoman's Mate Third Class
21 years old
Weedville, Pennsylvania
single

In 2009 Carmine's nieces Janet Mehall and "Sub Lady" Mary Bentz placed a memorial marker with full military honors for their uncle at the foot of his mother's grave at St. Joseph's Cemetery in Force, Pennsylvania.

Cornelius Paul Jr., Mess Attendant Second Class
No Photo Available
24 years old
from Birmingham, Alabama
single

Very little is known of Jim Abele's steward, who had joined the Navy to escape Jim Crow Alabama. On October 5, 2007, *The Birmingham News* reported, "A hunt is on for the relatives of a Birmingham sailor lost with the rest of his crew when his submarine was sunk off the Aleutian Islands during World War II."

According to his cousin Margaret Moore, Paul's family had nicknamed him "Little Cornelius." Soon after his enlistment his parents separated, and both wanted the Navy to release him so that he could return home to provide for their support. Paul's father died in 1950 and is buried in an unmarked grave in Cleveland, Ohio. His mother died in 1955 in Birmingham, Alabama.

Even though a few current members of the Paul family knew of him, nobody recalls ever having met him. There are no known photographs of Cornelius Paul.

Bernard Joseph Pickel, Seaman First Class
18 years old
Clayton, Missouri
single

Born on March 20, 1924, in St. Louis, Missouri, Bernard Joseph "Ben" Pickel was the son of unwed, abandoned mother Clara Pickel. Although there was a stigma attached to being an illegitimate child in that era, Clara's German-Catholic family—which included an uncle who was a priest and an aunt who was a nun—loved and accepted him utterly. He enlisted in the Navy in September 1941 and was transferred to the submarine base in New London on January 8, 1942, for submarine and torpedo training. After his training, Pickel was assigned first to the submarine tender USS *Fulton* at Pearl Harbor, then to the submarine USS *Gato*, and finally to the *Grunion* on June 29, 1942—the last crewman to board the sub before she left for the Aleutians the next day.

The telegram reporting him missing in action devastated his mother. In a reply to Kay Abele's letter, Clara Pickel wrote, "Your letter really helped me a lot toward looking on the brighter side of the situation. I have felt all along that I will hear from my little sailor boy again." But as time went on, Ben's mother lost hope.

Arnold Charles Post,
Seaman Second Class
19 years old
Midland, Michigan
single

Arnold Charles Post was born on April 30, 1923, in Midland, Michigan. He joined the Navy in December 1941, and his first assignment was to the submarine tender USS *Fulton* at Pearl Harbor. Shortly afterward he was transferred to the submarine *Gato* and then on June 27, 1942, to the *Grunion*. In a letter to his sister he wrote, "By the way I want to tell you something. I want you to keep it a secret until I come home.... Well...if anything ever happens to me, I want Bruce [their brother] to have my drums. Don't for God's sake show this to Mom. I'd only worry her. Not that I don't plan on coming home, but this is just in case...."

In January 1943, his mother Doris wrote to Kay Abele, "In almost his [Arnold's] last letter he said, 'I hope you are not crying as hard as when I left. It isn't good for you.'" And in another letter to Kay, "It has been a year last Tuesday, January 5 since I saw him. I have never seen Arnold in uniform. I will never give up looking for him."

William Howard Randall,
Radioman Second Class
22 years old
Pekin, Illinois
single

William H. "Billy" Randall was born on October 8, 1920, in Peoria, Illinois. When he was twelve he and his brother moved with their mother to San Diego. She died there in 1939, and one of her friends, Mrs. Blanche Miller, became Randall's legal guardian. He enlisted in the Navy in October 1939, began his service on a light cruiser, and transferred to the submarine *S-42* in December 1940. On January 30, 1942, Randall transferred to the New London Submarine Base to attend Sound Operator School and was assigned to the *Grunion* on April 11, 1942.

Because Mrs. Blanche Miller was Randall's guardian, she received the telegram and also a letter from Catherine Abele. In her reply to Kay, Miller wrote, "I have no doubt but that the officers and crew of the USS *Grunion* gave a good account of themselves and their ship for they were United States Navy Men.... Billy was almost like my own son.... The last letter I received from him...he expressed his pride in his new ship...."

Loyal Ryan Jr., Seaman Second Class

17 years old

Lansing, Michigan

single

Loyal Ryan Jr. was born on December 20, 1924, in Bannister, Michigan. He enlisted in the Navy at seventeen years old on January 5, 1942, and was transferred on February 6, 1942, to New London, Connecticut, for submarine training and then to the Submarine Base at Coco Solo, in the Panama Canal Zone, for assignment. That assignment came on June 5, 1942, when he joined the *Grunion* to replace ailing Seaman Second Class Henry W. Jameson.

Loyal Ryan had a sister, Doris Woodbury, who was given up for adoption by their parents. Years later, Doris received a letter from her biological mother, Edith May Ryan, saying that she wanted to meet her. It was in that meeting that Doris was told she had a brother who had died on the *Grunion* in 1942. Doris and her family met Edith two or three more times before Edith's death in 1960.

As the Abele family's search in the Aleutians was underway in August 2007, there still had been no family contact found for Loyal Ryan. A friend of Doris Woodbury happened to see a television news segment about the ongoing search for the *Grunion* and mentioned it to Doris. The friend was stunned when Doris replied, "My brother was on the *Grunion*." Doris soon contacted Bruce Abele.

Howard Alfred Sanders, Motor Machinist's Mate First Class
23 years old
Bemidji, Minnesota
married

Howard Alfred Sanders was born on August 22, 1918, in Rhinelander, Wisconsin. He joined the Navy in February 1937 to make it his career. First assigned to the battleship USS *California*, Sanders requested and was granted a transfer in October 1938 to the New London Submarine Base. His first sub was the *S-29*. That same year he met Lucy Casserino at a dance, soon fell in love, and married her.

Sanders served briefly on a second sub, the *O-2*, and then transferred to the *Grunion*. On May 19, 1942, after Sanders brought Lucy to stay with her family in Middletown, Connecticut, her brother gave the submariner a lift back to the *Grunion*. Sanders said, "I won't be back." In what was probably his last letter home, he wrote, "I guess you know my new home goes into commission Saturday morning. Then the work really starts. We have to make 150 dives in five weeks and then off to the races. These new boats are certainly swell."

Elmer Taylor Schumann, Chief Quartermaster
42 years old
Tripoli, Wisconsin
married with children

Schumann was the second oldest man on the *Grunion*. Born on November 16, 1899, in Underwood, Iowa, Elmer Schumann, a farmer, enlisted in the Navy in January 1919 and went on to serve on surface vessels and submarines until his honorable discharge on December 29, 1926. He reenlisted on January 10, 1927, and served until March 13, 1935, when he joined the Fleet Naval Reserve. Chief Quartermaster Schumann returned to active duty on October 6, 1936, but with thirteen years, ten months, and eleven days previous duty and now a family man with several children, he requested shore duty, which was granted. After the attack on Pearl Harbor, he told his wife Teckla that he was transferring to the *Grunion*. She objected in vain.

When the news of the *Grunion*'s disappearance came, Teckla was devastated. Her son Jim recalled that his mother awoke him one night and handed him his father's Purple Heart. "Take good care of this," she said. "Give it to your son someday."

Paul Patrick Sullivan, Pharmacist's Mate First Class
27 years old
Akron, Ohio
married

Paul P. Sullivan, born in Marietta, Ohio, on January 25, 1915, enlisted in the Navy in November 1933 and after a stint on the battleship USS *Idaho* was recommended for training at the Hospital Corps School in Portsmouth, Virginia. By March 1, 1937, he had advanced to Pharmacist's Mate Third Class. He transferred in May 1940 to the Fifth Medical Company, First Marine Brigade, in

Quantico, Virginia; that same year, he married his boyhood sweetheart, Norma Wolff.

As a Pharmacist's Mate First Class he transferred in January 1942 to New London and was assigned to the *Grunion* on April 11, 1942. When the *Grunion* rescued sixteen survivors of the transport ship USAT *Jack*, which had been torpedoed by a German U-Boat, survivor George Drew wrote to Kay Abele, "I am sure had it not been for the care Captain Abele and his Pharmacist Mate Paul Sullivan gave us, quite a few of us would not have survived. Paul treated our severe sunburns, salt water poison, and bruises that had become infected. He couldn't possibly have done more for us while we were on board the *Grunion*."

Paul's brother Stanley, fifteen years old when the *Grunion* was lost, recalls "the very loud long knock on the door the day the Navy representatives came to give them the bad news." Their mother was never the same.

Steven Surofchek,
Ship's Cook First Class
32 years old
Cottageville, South Carolina
married with a daughter

Steven Surofchek was born on July 15, 1908, and in 1927 enlisted in the Navy with his father's signed consent at the age of sixteen. In the following eight years he served aboard two battleships, becoming a ship's cook in 1932. After six years at sea, Surofchek requested a transfer to shore duty but was denied. He was assigned to a number of surface ships, and in August 1937 he requested a transfer to the heavy cruiser USS *Wichita*, then under construction, so that he could bring his wife Caroline to Norfolk, Virginia; but he was denied again, this time because of a clerical error.

Surofchek's wife Caroline and daughter Patsy were living in New London, Connecticut, while he was assigned to the submarine base for duty on several subs and gaining a reputation as a terrific cook. On November 9, 1941, he was assigned to the sub *Gato* and was soon en route to Pearl Harbor. There he transferred to the *Grunion* on June 26, 1942.

Caroline Surofchek Colson, one of three surviving *Grunion* widows, attended the *Grunion* family gathering in Newton, Massachusetts, in 2007 with her daughter, granddaughter, and great granddaughter—four generations of Surofchek women. When she received her vial of Kiska water from the Abeles, she held it and said, "Patsy, this is real—this is where your daddy is."

David Nathaniel Swartwood, Seaman Second Class
19 years old
Flint, Michigan
single

On March 17, 1923, David N. Swartwood was born in Greensburg, Pennsylvania; he was one of ten children in the family. After the deaths of both parents, his sister Millie became his legal guardian. At seventeen, he enlisted in the Navy in January 1942, was soon sent to Pearl Harbor to serve on the submarine tender *Fulton*, and was assigned on April 24, 1942, to the submarine *Gato*—and then to the *Grunion* on June 27, 1942. His sister Millie never got over his loss.

Samuel Artist Templeton, Gunner's Mate First Class
22 years old
Goodlettsville, Tennessee
single

Samuel Templeton was born on April 5, 1920, in Greenbrier, Tennessee, and joined the Navy in June 1927 to make it his career. After serving aboard a battleship and a destroyer, he was granted a transfer to the submarine school at New London in December 1941. His commanding officer aboard the destroyer USS *Ellis* lauded his performance: "During the period 7/1/41 to 12/1/41 this ship was employed on convoy duties in the North Atlantic under rigorous operating conditions and in face of potential enemy action. Templeton's performance of duty during this period has been commendable and a credit to the traditional high standards of the U.S. Navy."

In late February of 1942 Templeton was assigned to the *Grunion*. After the sub's loss, his distraught parents wrote to the Navy numerous times and also corresponded with Kay Abele. As time went on, Sam's mother continued to write to the Navy, yearning for "some personal effects of my boy. We remain yours, the parents of a good boy, Mr. & Mrs. Artist Templeton."

Millener Weaver Thomas, Lieutenant, Executive Officer
31 years old
Philadelphia, Pennsylvania
married

Millener W. "Tommy" Thomas, an only child, was born on May 18, 1911, in Philadelphia. He entered the U.S. Naval Academy on June 24, 1929, lettered in football and track, and was commissioned an ensign in the U.S. Navy on June 1, 1933. He began his career on the Pensacola-class heavy cruiser USS *Salt Lake City* from June 1933 to June 1935.

On June 1, 1935, Thomas married debutante Laura Elizabeth Kennedy in Philadelphia and was then transferred to VS (aircraft) Squadron 9 for flying duty in the cruiser's float aircraft, serving as Aircraft Gunnery Observer aboard the USS *Salt Lake City* from June 1935 to April 1936. Thomas next attended submarine school at New London from June to December 1936 and was assigned to the submarine *R-14* and then to the sub USS *Cuttlefish*. On April 11, 1942, having helped fit out the *Grunion*, he remained aboard the sub as Jim Abele's executive officer. In a letter dated June 15, 1942, Thomas wrote to his wife, "Did I tell you that I think Jim Abele is one of the most remarkable people I have ever known. I think any experience I gain from him will be of great help later. He has let me take charge at times with full confidence."

Byron Allen Traviss, Seaman Second Class
17 years old
Detroit, Michigan
single

Byron Allen "Buck" Traviss, born on August 5, 1924, in Rose City, Michigan, enlisted in the Navy in December of 1941, his father and stepmother signing the consent papers for the seventeen-year-old. His first assignment was to the submarine tender USS *Fulton* at Pearl Harbor. He next joined the submarine *Gato* on April 20, 1942, and was transferred to the *Grunion* on June 27.

To Kay Abele, Traviss's parents wrote, "We have no words capable of expressing our thanks and it is hard to tell you how proud we are."

Traviss's father continued to be wracked by guilt for signing the enlistment papers for his son, who died five days short of his eighteenth birthday.

On the morning after the *Grunion* was located, Traviss's cousin Barbara Larish of Dearborn, Michigan, heard on local radio that families of the *Grunion* crew were being sought. She immediately telephoned the radio station and said, "I have his [Traviss's] Purple Heart hanging on my dining room wall." That phone call completed the Sub Ladies' search for *Grunion* crewmen's families.

Albert Ullmann,
Seaman First Class
20 years old

Philadelphia, Pennsylvania

single

Albert Ullmann was born on August 12, 1922, in Philadelphia. Wishing to make the Navy his career, he enlisted in September 1940. He transferred from the surface Navy to the New London Submarine School in November 1941 and was assigned to the *Grunion* in January 1942.

Ullman's older brother Joseph died seven months before the *Grunion* was found, and a granddaughter says, "My grandfather [Joseph] spent the past sixty-five years wondering what happened to his baby brother. They saw each other for the last time when they were in Hawaii."

Marshall Frelinghuysen Van Woggelum,
Fireman Third Class
22 years old

New Brunswick, New Jersey

single

Marshall Frelinghuysen Van Woggelum and his twin brother Herbert were born on April 27, 1920, in Perth Amboy, New Jersey. Herbert died at age two. In March 1941, Marshall enlisted in the Navy and was assigned to the *Grunion* on March 9, 1942.

A story in the *Daily News* of New Brunswick, New Jersey, in October 1942 reported that he was missing in action, and noted that five of his ancestors had served in the American Revolution and that his family's roots in America could be traced back to the 1600s.

In her response to Kay Abele's letter, his mother Ella wrote on October 12, 1942, "Words cannot express my gratitude for your loving and explicit letter.... One thing I would appreciate is, if you receive ONE encouraging word would you let me know. All I ask is one ONE word, 'SAFE.' Signed: A Mother and Oh where is my boy tonight! —Sincerely, Herbert D. and Ella Van Woggelum."

Marshall's mother corresponded with the Navy through 1946. Numerous letters were sent to Randall Jacobs, Rear Admiral Chief of Naval Personnel, one of which said, "PLEASE help us find him!" This flood of letters, sent also to Senator Howard Alexander Smith of New Jersey and Presidents Roosevelt and Truman, begging them for information on her son, inspired an interoffice memo that read, "There is nothing we can do to console this mother."

Melvin Hillary Walter, Fireman Third Class
22 years old
Perryville, Missouri
single

Melvin Walter was born on October 21, 1920, in Sereno, Missouri. Smart but too poor to consider college, he enlisted in the Navy in August 1941 to further his education. On November 15, 1941, he was transferred to the submarine base in New London and assigned to the *Grunion* in March 1942.

The American Legion hall in his hometown bears his name, as does the local VFW post. Cousins Ed Walter and Roger Lueckenhoff remember that "Melvin was very popular, a bit of an actor, and all the girls had a crush on him. It is remembered how incredibly sad the whole town was when they knew he was gone. Everyone loved him."

Raymond Eugene Webster, Electrician's Mate Second Class

24 years old

Philadelphia, Pennsylvania

single

Born on September 14, 1917, in Sanford, Maine, Raymond E. Webster enlisted in the Navy in September 1935 and spent over three years on the aircraft carrier USS *Lexington*. He reenlisted in August 1940 and was assigned to the attack transport USS *McCawley*; he transferred to the New London Submarine Base in December 1941 for submarine and battery/gyroscope training and was permanently assigned to the *Grunion* on April 11, 1942.

Donald Francis Welch, Fire Controlman Second Class

22 years old

Springfield, Massachusetts

married with a child

Donald Welch was born on September 17, 1919, in Springfield, Massachusetts. He joined the Navy in May 1938, was assigned to the light cruiser USS *Nashville*, and transferred to the *Grunion* in February 1942. That same month, on Valentine's Day, he married Doris Terrell; when the *Grunion* departed New London, she saw the sub leaving, expectant with their first and only child.

In late June 1942 he wrote to her, "When does the doctor say you will have the baby? I got to stay up all night that night. Boy Dot, if anything happens to you I think that I would go out of my head...."

He reassured his parents in a June 24, 1942, letter: "You needn't worry about me Ma. I am much safer here than if I were still on the cruiser. You see, every day I get more respect for these submarines.

I guess that the nicest place to be during an air attack is at the bottom of the ocean."

After receiving the missing-in-action telegram on September 29, 1942, Welch's mother wrote a letter to the Navy on October 2, 1942: "Is it possible that there has been a mistake. I would appreciate it if you could be more helpful than the telegram was."

Don's last letter to his wife was dated June 27, 1942: "I received your letters, but you didn't tell me how you were feeling. I don't want anything to happen to you!! I was figuring baby. This war ought to be over in a year or two. (At least I hope so.) And then we will just grab us a spot in California's sunshine and raise a slew of kids. (One anyway)."

In 1994, Dot Welch, Don's wife, wrote a letter to the U.S. Submarine Veterans in Groton, Connecticut, regarding the memorial for World War II submariners who lost their lives: "My husband Donald Francis Welch was one of those men. He departed the submarine base in Groton in May 1942. Little did I know as I watched his boat go down the river that I would never see him again. . . ." She had written to Don's parents, "I became a widow and mother before the year was out at the age of 19."

John Harrison Wells, Torpedoman's Mate Second Class
22 years old
Gales Ferry, Connecticut
married

Born on March 23, 1920, in Marion, Ohio, John H. "Jude" Wells enlisted in the Navy in January 1939, and after serving aboard the destroyer USS *Wasmuth* was transferred in August 1939 to the New London Submarine Base. His first sub was the *R-2*, and then he served on the *O-7*. On March 13, 1942, he transferred to the *Grunion*; he also got married that month to Elizabeth May Wells in Gales Ferry, Connecticut. His siblings never met his wife, soon to be widow.

John Edgar Wilson Jr., Ship's Cook Third Class

20 years old

Canandaigua, New York

single

John E. "Jack" Wilson Jr., was born on April 16, 1922, in Brock-port, New York. He enlisted in the Naval Reserve in April 1940 and went on active duty in June. After attending the submarine school at New London from August 1940 to January 1941, his first assignment was aboard the submarine *S-20*. After serving aboard the *S-20* from February 1941 to March 1942, he helped fit out the *Grunion* and then remained aboard as a crewman.

Wilson wrote to an aunt, "I like the Navy very much and plan to stay in 20 years and retire with a pension, not bad is it?"

In probably the last letter to his father, on June 23, 1942, Wilson wrote, "If sometime you don't hear from me for three months don't worry as I'll be all right, but not able to write.... Can't say where I am, but I'm happy and enjoying myself. —Love, Jack."

On September 29, 1942, his father sent his eldest son Dick, who was in the Army, a nine-word telegram: "WIRE FROM NAVY THIS MORNING, JACK IS GONE. DAD."

Ralph Junior Youngman, Fireman Second Class

22 years old

Cleveland, Ohio

single

Ralph Junior Youngman, the oldest of nine children, was born on July 22, 1920, in Cleveland, Ohio. On March 21, 1941, before his twenty-first birthday and with his father's signed consent, he joined the Navy for travel and excitement. After basic training, Youngman transferred to the New London Submarine Base in June 1941, graduated from submarine school on February 16, 1942, and was assigned to the *Grunion*.

His younger sister Betty Krueger was expecting a child when the news that the sub was missing arrived. When her son was born, she named him Ralph after her brother. She attended the memorial service in Cleveland in 2008 and said, "I know that my brother is at peace."

Crew Photo Credits

Mannert Lincoln Abele photo courtesy of the Abele family.

Frank Elgin Alexander photo courtesy of Robert Berrington.

Daniel Emery Allen photo courtesy of sister Pat Allen Pare.

Paul Edward Banes photo courtesy of Lorraine Butler and Rhonda Raye.

Leo Joseph Isaie Bedard photo courtesy of son Ron Bedard and daughter Therese Bedard Marsh.

Wesley Hope Blinston photo courtesy of Shelby M. Starling.

Nicoholas Richard Bonadies photo courtesy of sister Janice Bonadies.

Robert Francis Boo photo courtesy of niece Carole Boo-Harrington.

Chester Lewis Bouvia photo courtesy of cousin Tom Greenwald.

George Earl Caldwell photo courtesy of great-niece Kimberly Payne and Mary Bentz.

Richard Harry Carroll photo courtesy of Vickie Rodgers.

John Stewart Clift photo courtesy of niece Lois Rehn.

Michael Francis Collins photo courtesy of niece Mary Anne Marino.

Lee Dale Cooksey photo courtesy of Cleo and Lavena Burton.

Daniel Cullinane photo courtesy of Stephen Finnigan.

William Hugh Cuthbertson Jr. photo courtesy of daughter Nancy Lee Wilson and Bruce Abele.

Lawrence Dale Deaton photo courtesy of niece Pat Kyle.

Albert Edward DeStoop photo courtesy of brother Hank DeStoop and Bruce Abele.

William Patrick Devaney Jr. photo courtesy of Mary Bentz.

Samuel Reed Dighton Jr. photo courtesy of Sam Dighton.

Louis Henry Doell Jr. photo courtesy of Russell Dieselberg.

Leon Henry Franck photo courtesy of Paul W. Wittmer.

Merritt Dayton Graham photo courtesy of great-niece Vickie Rodgers.

Kenneth Edward Hall photo courtesy of niece Susan Ann Hall Strobel.

Ernest Glenn Hellensmith photo courtesty of niece Becky Franke.

Hollice Beauford Henderson photo courtesy of Sandra Woodson.

Charles Roy Hutchinson photo courtesy of sister Mona Hutchinson Kime.

Sylvester Joseph Kennedy Jr. photo courtesy of cousin Barbara Kennedy Burke.

Edward Earl Knowles Jr. photo courtesy of Mary Bentz.

Lawrence Richard Kockler photo courtesy of Vickie Rodgers.

William Gregory Kornahrens photo courtesy of daughter Nancy Kornahrens Stark.

Moore Julius Ledford photo courtesy of nieces Haven Miller Teague and Betty Jo Kiser Edwards.

Woodrow Wilson Lehman photo courtesy of Gary R. Lehman and Stuart D. Wade.

Sidney Arther Loe photo courtesy of niece Diane Loe.

Samuel Elisha Lunsford Jr. photo courtesy of Vickie Rodgers and Rhonda Robertson.

James Wallace Lyon photo courtesy of great-niece Tara Curtin.

Carson Raymond Martin photo courtesy of daughter Meryl Kretschmann.

Thomas Edward Martin photo courtesy of Captain USN (retired) James Hickerson, Martin's nephew.

Ryder Mathison photo courtesy of daughter Bobbi Mathison Heims, grandson Stephen Kamei, and nieces Lynne Blinco Earle and Bev Douwstra.

Richard George McCutcheon photo courtesy of Paul W. Wittmer.

John Merton McMahon photo courtesy of son James McMahon.

Ernest Carl photo courtesy of nephew William Petersen.

David Oliver Myers photo courtesy of sister-in-law Cecile Myers and niece Shirley Gregory.

Frank Thomas Nave photo courtesy of niece Sue Mills.

Arthur G. Newcomb photo courtesy of sister Barbara Hart.

John Wesley Nobles photo courtesy of Bruce Abele.

Jack Edwin Pancoast photo courtesy of sister Lila Beardsley.

Carmine Anthony Parziale photo courtesy of brother-in-law Francis Gerber and niece Mary Parziale Bentz.

Bernard Joseph Pickel photo courtesy of Bruce Abele.

Arnold Charles Post photo courtesy of Mary Bentz and Sheila Anderson.

William Howard Randall photo courtesy of Mary Bentz and Nancy Hansen.

Loyal Ryan Jr. photo courtesy of sister Doris Woodbury.

Howard Alfred Sanders photo courtesy of son Howard A. Sanders Jr.

Elmer Taylor Schumann photo courtesy of Ralph and Jacqueline (Schumann) Tramm.

Paul Patrick Sullivan photo courtesy of niece Linda Sullivan.

Steven Surofchek photo courtesy of widow Caroline F. Surofchek Colson, daughter Patricia Surofchek Stokes, and granddaughter Teresa Stokes Baker.

David Nathaniel Swartwood photo courtesy of niece Patricia Swartwood Shooltz.

Samuel Artist Templeton photo courtesy of Bruce Abele.

Millener Weaver Thomas photo courtesy of Peter Thomas Stephens.

Byron Allen Traviss photo courtesy of Barbara Larish.

Albert Ullmann photo courtesy of Theresa Ullman Flury.

Marshall Frelinghuysen Van Woggelum photo courtesy of Bruce Abele.

Melvin Hillary Walter photo courtesy of cousin Robert Walter.

Raymond Eugene Webster photo courtesy of Paul W. Wittmer.

Donald Francis Welch photo courtesy of granddaughter Laura Conley.

John Harrison Wells photo courtesy of Paul W. Wittmer.

John Edgar Wilson Jr. photo courtesy of nephew John Edgar Wilson III.

Ralph Junior Youngman photo courtesy of sister Betty Krueger.

ACKNOWLEDGEMENTS

———◆◆◆———

This project unfolded in an unconventional manner long before any book began to take shape. People all over the world were drawn to the saga of the Abeles, the USS *Grunion*, and the mystery of her whereabouts and final moments; a legion of men and women, the "Grunion community," have contributed their skills, knowledge, and effort. As Brad and John Abele have so often pointed out, the story illuminates the value of collaboration—how it can make possible incredible things in all facets of life.

First and foremost, this book would not have been possible without the Abele family. The late Brad Abele, with the steadfast support of his wife Robbie, began digging for any scrap of information about the *Grunion* on the 1990s, putting it all in a family manuscript entitled *Jim*, which was both a jumping-off point and an invaluable reference for this book. Bruce and John Abele joined

Brad to gather even more information, and their efforts, as well as the phenomenal archival research of Yutaka, provided a solid foundation for my account of the *Grunion*'s story. John and Bruce provided not only a wealth of personal memories but also the nuts and bolts of how the search for *the Grunion* unfolded, from start to finish. That search would never have been undertaken without the knowledge and advice of Dr. Robert Ballard, discoverer of the *Titanic* and the expert who educated the Abeles on how to find a submarine. The Abeles, in turn, educated the author of this book.

Bruce drew on his countless discussions with sonar and ROV experts and his own engineering and technical background to educate me in a way that would make both technologies comprehensible. Whenever I needed to refer to the voluminous correspondence of Jim and Kay Abele, all I had to do was turn to Susan Abele's deftly organized cataloguing of every letter, as well as her careful organization of Kay's correspondence with the next of kin of the sixty-nine men under her husband's command. Bruce Abele and Richard Bentz supplied a vast and essential array of archival material—the *Grunion*'s logbooks, Submarine Task Force Eight War Diaries, documents detailing every step and stop along the way of Jim Abele's naval career, submarine records, and countless other official sources.

When it came to Jim Abele's sixty-nine officers and crew, Mary Bentz, with Richard, was the go-to source; she has compiled a meticulous file of every crewman's records and life, as well as photographs of all but two men. Other essential sources for writing the book included John Carcioppolo, base commander of the United Submarine Veterans, Inc., Groton, Connecticut; John Crouse, the late director of St. Mary's Submarine Museum, Georgia; Michael Mohl, who runs the invaluable Navsource website; and the videography and photography of Peter Lowney, who chronicled both the 2006 and 2007 expeditions to the Bering Sea; and Charles Hinman of the On Eternal Patrol website.

Shinoda Kazuo, Chiyo, and Isamu's oldest son, graciously fur-
nished a treasure trove of material that included family letters,
Japanese naval records, and photographs that have made it possible
for this book to present the literal faces of a Japanese family so
similar in many ways to the Abeles and tied into the *Grunion* saga
every bit as deeply as their American counterparts.

Special gratitude goes out to Commander Charlie Tate (USN,
ret.), "discovered" by Bruce Abele and serving as a font of information and insights—all born of his vast World War II submarine
experience in the Aleutians and other theaters. Thanks also to Tuck
Weaver, Executive Officer on the World War II submarine USS *Barb*,
who experienced a circular run and lived to tell of it.

Without the technical insights of Jim Christley and Dr. John
Fakan and their analysis of the wreck of the USS *Grunion*, it would
have been impossible to give readers any sense of what the sunken
submarine 3,000 feet beneath the Bering Sea revealed.

Fred Milford, one of the foremost experts on World War II torpedoes, detailed for the book how the MK 14 debacle, which he aptly
branded "The Great Torpedo Scandal," was handled, or rather mis-
handled. Another invaluable source on the MK 14 was Tony Newpower, the author of *Iron Men and Tin Fish*.

Kale Garcia, skipper of the *Aquila*, and his wife Anji provided
accounts of both the 2006 and 2007 expeditions that captured all
the dangers of the venture as only those who sail and fish the waters
of "the Deadliest Catch" can do. Dave Gallo of the famed Woods
Hole Oceanographic Institute provided his fascinating take on the
2007 expedition, on which he accompanied his friend John Abele.

Key to my understanding of the ROV expedition was a visit to
Deep Sea Systems International (division of Oceaneering, Inc.),
Falmouth, Massachusetts, with the Abeles and the Bentzes. Chris
Nicholson, president of DSSI and an ROV expert who helped plan
the 2007 expedition, and Toshinobu Mikagawa, the ROV operations

manager aboard the *Aquila* on that trip, talked at length about the entire process and showed me the Max Rover, the very vehicle that captured the first view of the *Grunion* since July 30, 1942.

To my literary agent and friend, Frank Weimann, president of The Literary Group International, who represented me as well as the Abeles and the Bentzes on this project, my deep thanks as always. Thanks, too, to Elyse Tanzillo, of The Literary Group; Regnery publisher Alex Novak and editor Elizabeth Kantor for their boundless skills; and Sarah Haera Tocco for her uncanny sense of syntax and grammar and her patience with my queries about Japanese symbols.

I wish it were possible to mention all the many people who gave their time and knowledge to the research and writing of this book.

NOTES

Chapter One: "We've Got a Target"

1. Interviews of Kale and Anj Garcia by the author, March 2011. All other quotations in this chapter are from interviews with John and Bruce Abele and with the members of the search team, and from materials supplied by them, including videos of the August 2007 expedition.

Chapter Two: An Unconventional Course

1. Quotations in this chapter are from Abele family letters, documents, and memorabilia, and from the Naval records of the career of Arthur Abele in the National Archives, Washington, DC.

Chapter Three: The Submariner

1. U.S. Navy Investigation and Report, Submarine Division, of Electrical Accident aboard Submarine *R-13* on August 26, 1938, and Mannert L.

Abele's Performance, September 1938, National Archives, Naval Records Branch.

2. Letter from Jim Abele to Kay Abele, December 21, 1940.
3. Letter from Jim Abele to Kay Abele, December 23, 1940.
4. Letter from Jim Abele to Kay Abele, December 25, 1940.
5. Letter from Jim Abele to Kay Abele, January 7, 1941.
6. Letter from Jim Abele to Kay Abele, January 28, 1941.
7. Letter from Jim Abele to Kay Abele, January 30, 1941.
8. Material throughout this chapter is from Brad Abele, *Jim* (hereinafter "Brad Abele manuscript"). This meticulously researched manuscript about Jim Abele, the family, and the first and final voyage of the *Grunion* was the catalyst for the Abele brothers' search for their father and his submarine. Brad Abele interviewed dozens of submarine officers, naval historians, naval architects, scientists, and numerous other experts in compiling this work. It can be read in its entirety at ussgrunion.com.

Chapter Four: "Into the Thick of Things"

1. Brad Abele manuscript.
2. Clay Blair, *Silent Victory* (Annapolis, MD: Naval Institute Press, 2001), p. 169.
3. Common expression among submariners of the era.
4. "Dayville Hero of Two Wars Is Lost at Sea—Danny Cullinane Believed Dead in Submarine Grunion," Windham [Connecticut] County Transcript, February 11, 1943, p. 1.
5. Ibid.
6. Brad Abele manuscript.
7. "Dayville Hero," p. 3.
8. Information on Carmine Parziale provided by his niece Mary Bentz, including letters and interviews with relatives.
9. Mary Bentz interview of Andy Juettner, 2007.
10. Transfer Request of Cornelius Paul, January 1942, National Archives, Naval Records Branch.
11. Brad Abele manuscript.

Chapter Five: Battle Stations

1. Brad Abele manuscript.
2. Note from Jim Abele to Kay Abele, May 24, 1942.
3. USS *Grunion* logbook, May 23, 1942, National Archives, Naval Records Branch.
4. USS *Grunion* logbook, May 31, 1942.
5. Ibid.
6. William R. Manchester, *Goodbye, Darkness: A Memoir of the Pacific War* (Boston: Little, Brown, 1980), pp. 51–52.
7. USS *Grunion* logbook, June 22, 1942.
8. Letter from George Drew to Kay Abele, June 27, 1942.
9. Blair, *Silent Victory*, p. 226.
10. Anthony Newpower, *Iron Men and Tin Fish: The Race to Build a Better Torpedo during World War II* (Annapolis, MD: Naval Institute Press, 2010), p.65.
11. Brad Abele manuscript.
12. Newpower, *Iron Men*, p. 67.
13. Blair, *Silent Victory*, p. 229.
14. USS *Grunion* logbook, June 29, 1942.
15. Task Force Eight, Submarine Division, War Diary, June 1942, National Archives, Naval Records Branch.

Chapter Six: The Enemy Awaiting Them

1. Seiichi Aiura, Navy Superintendent of the *Kano Maru*, "We Have Sunk U.S. Submarine," *Maru* (magazine), March 1963, p. 71. This article includes a reprint of Seiichi's original battle report of the engagement between the *Kano Maru* and the *Grunion*, Imperial Japanese Naval Records, Aleutian Campaign, Japan Center for Asian Historical Records (JACAR).
2. Letter of Commander Shinoda Isamu to his wife, Chiyo, June 30, 1942.
3. Shinoda Kazuo, "My Father's Memory," an account of the Shinoda family and Shinoda Isamu's World War II service and death from the Shinoda Family Collection.
4. Ibid.

5. Ibid.
6. Battle account of Commander Matsushima Minoru, *CH-26*, July 15, 1942, Imperial Japanese War Archives and Records, Tokyo, Japan.

Chapter Seven: A Mysterious Message

1. U.S. Navy, Task Force Eight War Diary, Submarine Division, July 30, 1942, National Archives, Naval Records Branch.
2. Edward L. Beach, *Submarine!* (Annapolis, MD: Bluejacket Books, 2003), p. 10.
3. Commander (retired) Charles Tate interviews by Peter Stevens and Bruce Abele, 2010–2011.
4. U.S. Navy, Task Force Eight War Diary, Submarine Division, July 30, 1942, National Archives, Naval Records Branch.
5. Letters from Kay, Bruce, and Brad Abele to Jim Abele, July 30, 1942.

Chapter Eight: "As We Waited for the End"

1. A common expression in the U.S. Submarine Fleet in World War II. See Alex Kershaw, *Escape from the Deep: A True Story of Courage and Survival during World War II* (Philadelphia: Da Capo Press, 2008), p. 4.
2. Quotations throughout this account are from Seiichi, "We Have Sunk U.S. Submarine," including the reprint of Seiichi's original battle report, and from personal letters by Japanese sailors.

Chapter Nine: "Missing and Presumed Lost"

1. Letter from Kay Abele to Jim Abele, August 5, 1942.
2. War Department Telegram to Kay Abele, September 30, 1942.
3. Brad Abele manuscript.
4. "American Sub Captured Somewhere Off Aleutians," *New York Times*, October 4, 1942, p. 2.
5. Brad Abele manuscript.
6. War Department Telegram to Kay Abele, October 1, 1942.
7. Eugene B. Fluckey, *Thunder Below* (Urbana, IL: University of Illinois Press, 1992), p. 111.
8. Letter from Fran McMahon to Kay Abele, October 1942.
9. Brad Abele manuscript.

10. Bureau of Naval Personnel, Letter to Kay Abele, March 11, 1943.
11. Letter from the mother of Signalman Daniel E. Allen to Kay Abele, February 10, 1943.
12. Letter from the mother of Cornelius Paul to Naval Bureau of Personnel, December 1, 1943.
13. Naval Bureau of Personnel, Letter to Kay Abele, October 9, 1943.
14. Letter from Shinoda Isamu to his wife, Chiyo, July 7, 1942.

Chapter Ten: Making Do with Less

1. John Abele to the author.
2. John and Bruce Abele to the author.
3. John Abele to the author.
4. Interview of Nancy Kornahrens Stark by Mary and Richard Bentz, 2007.
5. Mary and Richard Bentz interviews with Daniel Cullinane family members, 2006–2007.
6. Bruce Abele to the author.
7. Brad Abele manuscript.
8. Ibid.
9. Brad would go on to add to the *Jim* manuscript later, as the search for the *Grunion* unfolded.

Chapter Eleven: A Chart, a Clue, and a Chance Meeting

1. The date given by Seiichi was actually July 31, 1942, because Japanese records were dated according to Tokyo time and thus always a day ahead of the actual date, as the Aleutians are east of the International Date Line.
2. Seiichi, "We Have Sunk U.S. Submarine," including the reprint of Seiichi's original battle report.
3. Ibid.
4. Email from Yutaka Iwasaki to John Abele, March 7, 2002.
5. Brad Abele manuscript.
6. Interviews with John and Brad Abele by the author.
7. Bruce Abele to the author.
8. John Abele to the author.
9. Interview of Kale and Anj Garcia by the author, August 2011.

10. John and Bruce Abele to the author.

Chapter Twelve: Logistics of a Long Shot

1. Interviews of Kale and Anj Garcia by the author, July 2010.
2. Ibid.
3. Ibid.

Chapter Thirteen: "We Haven't Seen the Worst of It Yet"

1. All quoted dialogue in this chapter is from Peter Lowney's video and sound recordings of the 2006 expedition to the Aleutians.
2. Email from Kale Garcia to the Abele Brothers, August 11, 2006.
3. Email from Art Wright to the Abele Brothers, August 11, 2006.
4. Email from Peter Lowney to the Abele Brothers, August 11, 2006.

Chapter Fourteen: "That Looks Like a Sub"

1. Email from Kale Garcia to the Abele brothers, August 11, 2006.
2. All quoted dialogue in this chapter is from Peter Lowney's video and sound recordings of the 2006 expedition to the Aleutians and from interviews with members of the 2006 expedition team.
3. Email from Art Wright to the Abele brothers, August 12, 2006.
4. Email from Art Wright to the Abele brothers, August 15, 2006.
5. Email from Art Wright to the Abele brothers, August 16, 2006.
6. Bruce Abele to the author.

Chapter Fifteen: "Don't Let Your Desire for This to Be the Right Target Fool You"

1. Email from Robert Ballard to John Abele, August 19, 2006.
2. Ibid.
3. Ibid.
4. John Abele to the author.
5. Email from Robert Ballard to John Abele, August 19, 2006.

Chapter Sixteen: By Land, Sea, and Air

1. Craig Wilson, "Sub Ladies Uncover Tale of Lost Crew," *USA Today*, March 12, 2008, p. 1.
2. Email from Kale Garcia to the Abele brothers, August 18, 2007.

3. Ibid.
4. Email from Kale Garcia to John Abele, August 19, 2007.
5. Logbook of the *Aquila*, August 19, 2007.
6. Email from Kale Garcia to the Abele brothers, August 20, 2007.

Chapter Seventeen: "There She Is"

1. John Abele to the author.
2. Ibid.

Chapter Eighteen: Lost and Found—Again

1. Reported by Bruce Abele to the author.
2. Wilson, "Sub Ladies," p. 1.

Chapter Nineteen: From Bow to Stern

1. Quotations throughout this account are taken from Seiichi, "We Have Sunk U.S. Submarine," including the reprint of Seiichi's original battle report.
2. Brad Abele Manuscript.
3. Ibid.
4. Commander John Alden (ret.), "Loss of *Grunion* Possibly Explained," *Submarine Review*, April 1988, p. 50.
5. Frederick J. Milford, "U.S. Navy Torpedoes—The Great Torpedo Scandal, 1941–43," *Submarine Review*, October 1996, p. 10.
6. Ibid.
7. Ibid.

Chapter Twenty: "They Wanted to Be Found"

1. All quotations in this chapter are from the Abeles, the Bentzes, Kale Garcia, and other participants in the saga, and are presented as told to the author.

Epilogue: "There One Moment, Gone the Next"

1. From the discoveries of the search team aboard the *Aquila*, from the eyewitness accounts, charts, and diagrams of Japanese officers aboard

the *Kano Maru*, and from the expertise of submariners and scientists who have reviewed the evidence.

2. Kale Garcia's impression of the wreck of the USS *Grunion*.

3. Medical Sublieutenant Rikimaru's eyewitness addition to Seiichi Aiura's battle report, July 31, 1942 [actually July 30, 1942, but dated July 31 to accord with Tokyo time].

SELECTED BIBLIOGRAPHY

Archival

Abele Family Collection. Letters, photos, documents, diaries, and memorabilia.

Imperial Japanese War Archives and Records, Tokyo, Japan.

National Archives Records Administration, Washington, D.C.; College Park, MD; St. Louis, MO.

Shinoda Family Collection: Letters, photos, documents, and memorabilia.

U.S.S. *Grunion* Logbooks and War Diary (April 1942–July 6, 1942).

Books

Abele, Brad. *Jim* (unpublished 150-page manuscript investigating the loss and mystery of the USS *Grunion*, whose commander was Jim Abele), 2002.

Alden, John Doughty, *U.S. Submarine Attacks During World War II*. Annapolis, MD: U.S. Naval Institute, 1989.

Beach, Edward L. *Run Silent, Run Deep*. London: Cassell, 2003.

———. *Submarine!* Annapolis, MD: Bluejacket Books, 2003.

Blair, Clay. *Silent Victory*. Annapolis, MD: Naval Institute Press, 2001.

Calvert, James F. *Silent Running*. New York: John Wiley & Sons, 1995.

Chambliss, William C. *The Silent Service*. New York: New American Library. Signet Books, 1959.

Compton-Hall, Richard. *The Underwater War: 1939–1945*. Poole, Dorset, England: Blandford Press, 1982.

DeRose, James. *Unrestricted Warfare: How a New Breed of Officers Led the Submarine Force to Victory in World War II*. New York: John Wiley & Sons, 2000.

Fluckey, Eugene B. *Thunder Below!* Urbana, IL: University of Illinois Press, 1992.

Galantin, Ignatius Joseph. *Take Her Deep*. Chapel Hill, NC: Algonquin Books, 1987.

Glusman, John. *Conduct Under Fire*. New York: Viking, 2005.

Gray, Edwyn. *Few Survived: A History of Submarine Disasters*. London, Leo Cooper, 1986.

Grider, George William. *Warfish*. New York: Little, Brown, 1958.

Gugliotta, Bobette. *Pigboat 39: An American Sub Goes to War*. Lexington, KY: University Press of Kentucky, 1984.

Hara, Tameichi. *Japanese Destroyer Captain*. New York: Ballantine, 1961.

Haufler, Hervie. *Codebreakers' Victory*. New York: New American Library, 2003.

Holmes, W. J. *Double-Edged Secrets: U.S. Naval Intelligence Operations in the Pacific during World War II*. Annapolis, MD: U.S. Naval Institute, 1979.

———. *Underseas Victory: The Influence of Submarine Operations in the Pacific World War II*. New York: Doubleday, 1966.

Horton, Edward. *The Illustrated History of the Submarine*. London: Sidgwick & Jackson, 1974.

Hoyt, Edwin P. *Japan's War*. New York: McGraw-Hill Book Company, 1986.

———. *Submarines at War: The History of the American Silent Service*. New York: Stein & Day, 1983.

Keegan, John. *The Price of Admiralty*. London: Viking Penguin, 1989.

Kershaw, Alex. *Escape from the Deep: A True Story of Courage and Survival during World War II*. Philadelphia: Da Capo Press, 2008.

Kimmet, Larry, and Margaret Regis. *U.S. Submarines in World War II: An Illustrated History*. Seattle, WA: Navigator Publishing, 1996.

Lavo, Carl. *Back from the Deep*. Annapolis, MD: U.S. Naval Institute, 1994.

Lockwood, Charles A. *Down to the Sea in Subs*. New York: W. W. Norton, 1967.

———. *Sink 'Em All*. New York: Bantam Books, 1984.

———. *Through Hell and Deep Waters*. Philadelphia: Childon, 1956.

Maas, Peter. *The Rescuer*. New York: Harper & Row, 1967.

Manchester, William R. *Goodbye, Darkness: A Memoir of the Pacific War*. Boston: Little, Brown, 1980.

Mason, John T., Jr. *The Pacific War Remembered*. Annapolis, MD: U.S. Naval Institute, 1986.

McDaniel, J. T., ed. *USS Tang* (SS-306) *American Submarine War Patrol Reports*. GA: Riverdale Books, 2005.

Mendenhall, Corwin. *Submarine Diary*. Chapel Hill, NC: Algonquin Books, 1991.

Miller, David. *Submarines of the World*. New York: Salamander Books, 1991.

Miller, Nathan. *War at Sea*. Oxford, England: Oxford University Press, 1995.

Morison, Samuel Eliot. *The Two-Ocean War: A Short History of the United States Navy in the Second World War*. Boston: Little, Brown, 1963.

Navy Times editors. *They Fought Under the Sea*. Harrisburg, PA: Stackpole, 1962.

Newpower, Anthony. *Iron Men and Tin Fish: The Race to Build a Better Torpedo during World War II*. Annapolis, MD: Naval Institute Press, 2010.

O'Kane, Richard H. *Clear the Bridge! The War Patrols of the USS Tang*. New York: Ballantine Books, 1977.

———. *Wahoo: The Patrols of America's Most Famous World War II Submarines*. Novato, CA: Presidio Press, 1987.

Padfield, Peter. *War Beneath the Sea: Submarine Conflict 1939–1945*. London: John Murray, 1995.

Parrish, Thomas. *The Submarine*. New York: Viking, 2004.

Polmar, Norman. *The Naval Institute Guide to the Ships and Aircraft of the U.S. Fleet*. Annapolis, MD: U.S. Naval Institute, 1965.

Roscoe, Theodore. *U.S. Submarine Operations in World War II*. Annapolis, MD: U.S. Naval Institute, 1949.

Shelford, W. O. *Subsunk*. New York: Doubleday, 1960.

Sterling, Forest J. *Wake of the Wahoo*. Chapel Hill, NC: Professional Press, 1997.

Stern, Robert C. *U.S. Subs in Action*. Carrollton, TX: Squadron Signal Publications, 1983.

Tuohy, William. *The Bravest Man: The Story of Richard O'Kane & U.S. Submarines in the Pacific War*. Stroud, England: Sutton Publishing, 2001.

U.S. Naval History Division. *The Submarine in the United States Navy*. Washington DC, 1969.

———. *U.S. Submarine Losses in World War II*. Washington, D.C., 1963.

Van der Vat, Dan. *Stealth at Sea: The History of the Submarine*. London: Orion, 1994.

———. *The Pacific Campaign*. New York: Simon & Schuster, 1991.

Walkowiak, Thomas F. *Fleet Submarines of World War II*. Missoula, MT: Pictorial Histories Publishing Company, 1969.

Werner, Herbert A. *Iron Coffins*. New York: Henry Holt and Company, 1969.

Wheeler, Keith. *War Under the Pacific*. New York Time Life Books, 1980.

Winton, John. *Ultra in the Pacific: How Breaking Japanese Codes and Ciphers Affected Naval Operations Against Japan*. London: Leo Cooper, 1993.

Articles

Alden, John A. "Loss of Grunion Possibly Explained." In *Submarine Review*, April 1988.

Cooper, Rand. "Flowers on the Water." In *Amherst College Alumni Magazine*, Spring 2009.

Milford, Frederick J. "U.S. Navy Torpedoes—The Great Torpedo Scandal, 1941–43." In *Submarine Review*, October 1996.

Miller, Vernon J. "The Loss of the U.S.S. *Grunion* (SS-216)." In *Warships International Fleet Review*, January 1981.

Webster, Donovan. "Mystery at Sea." In *Reader's Digest*, January 2008.

Wilson, Craig. "Sub Ladies Uncover Tale of Lost Crew." In *USA Today*, March 12, 2008.

INDEX

A

Abele, Bradford ("Brad"), xiii, 2–5, 19–23, 38–39, 61–62, 73–74, 79, 86–89, 92, 98, 107, 113, 116, 129, 132, 140–41, 159, 166

Abele, Bruce, xiii, 2–5, 18, 22–23, 27, 38–39, 61, 73–74, 79, 84, 86–87, 92–101, 107, 113, 116, 125–26, 128, 130–33, 135–36, 140–41, 150–51, 166–68

Abele, Catherine ("Kay") xiii, 3, 15–23, 36–39, 44, 54, 61, 73–81, 84–86, 100, 128, 166

Abele, Clarence Arthur, 11

Abele, Francis ("Frank"), 9–10

Abele, John, 2–5, 19, 38, 61,73–74, 79, 83–106, 113, 130–35, 140–51, 159, 166–67

Abele, Karl, 87

Abele, Kurt, 87, 92

Abele, Lou, 7–9

Abele, Mannert Lincoln ("Jim")
  career of, 14–38, 40–48, 50–51, 54–56
  childhood of, 7, 10–13
  death of, 57–66, 69, 76
  as father, 21, 74, 80, 84, 87,
  marriage of, 15, 39, 73, 75
  parents of, 7–9

Abele, Mary, 3, 16

Abele, Susan ("Sue"), 100, 126

Abele, Trescott Tupper ("Tet"), 8–9

Adak, 116–17, 129–33, 137–42, 152

Adams, Abigail, 9

Adams, John, 9

Adams, John Quincy, 9

Ahiro Wakisaka, 67

Alden, John, 134, 159

Aleutian Islands, 1, 48, 54, 77, 87, 96, 151

"Aleutian roller coaster," 2

"Aleutian Turkey Shoot," 106

Alexander, Frank Elgin, 178–79

Allen, Daniel Emery, 179

American Expeditionary Force (AEF), 31

Amherst College, 86

Anchorage, Alaska, 1, 25, 129, 140–41

Annapolis, Maryland, 13–15, 35, 45, 75, 106

Aquila, 1–5, 96–104, 105–24, 127, 134, 137–52, 167

Arare, 102, 111, 113–14, 131, 152

Army, 32, 37, 40, 54, 66, 88

Arvan, Herbert Joseph, 179–80

Asheville Citizen-Times, 141

Atlantic Fleet, 13

Atlantic Ocean, 10, 23, 30, 36, 39, 133

Atlantic Squadron, 11, 13

Attu Island, 48, 53, 55, 58, 60, 63, 158

Axis powers, 23

B

Ballard, Robert ("Bob"), 3–4, 94–96, 99, 102, 122, 130–34, 136, 140, 144

Bancroft Hall, 14

Banes, Paul Edward, 128, 176, 180

Battle of Midway, 49, 54, 89

Battle of Santiago, 14

Battleship Row, 43

Beach, Edward L., 58, 89

Beck, Kevin, 109, 113, 119–20

Bedard, Leo Joseph Isaie, 181

Biesel, Douglass T., 165

Benson, William, 13

Bentz, Mary, 128, 139, 141, 150, 165–67, 179

Bentz, Richard, 165, 175

Bering Sea, 1–6, 48, 55–56, 94–97, 102, 104, 107, 109–10, 118, 122, 127, 132, 135, 137, 145, 151, 167

Birmingham, Alabama, 37

Bismarck, 1

"black-shoe" Navy, 35, 37

Blair, Clay, 29, 45, 47

Blinston, Wesley Hope, 181–82

Bonadies, Nicholas Richard, 182

Boo, Robert Francis, 183

Boston, Massachusetts, 11, 18, 31–32, 73, 86, 94

Boston Children's Hospital, 83

Boston Globe, 130

Boston Navy Yard, 10, 13

Boston Scientific Corporation, 86

Bouvia, Chester Lewis, 183–84

Brad Abele manuscript *see also* "*Jim*", 87, 92, 98

Braintree, Massachusetts, 8

Bridgewater Normal School, 8

Brookline, Massachusetts, 15, 22–23, 73

Brooklyn, New York, 35

"brown-shoe Navy," 18, 37, 86

Bureau of Naval Personnel, 77

Bureau of Navigation, 19

Burlington, Vermont, 140–41

Burma, 43

C

Caba, Joe, 4–6, 136, 140, 145, 147–50

Caldwell, George Earl, 184–85

Cape Hatteras, 23

Caribbean, 24, 39–40, 89

Carroll, Richard Harry, 185–86

Cervera, Pascual, 11

CH-25, 49, 55

CH-26, 55–56, 63

CH-27, 50–56, 80

Charlestown Naval Yard, 32

Chateau Thierry, 31

Chesapeake Bay, 13

Chevak, 103–4
Christley, Jim, 154, 157
Churchill, Winston, 52
"circular run," 29–30, 157–61
Cleveland, Ohio, 165
Clift, John Stewart, 186
Coco Solo, 42
Cold Bay, Alaska, 100, 129, 141
Cold Bay Lodge, 129
Collins, Michael Francis, 187
Colon, 11
Colored Division, 37
ComSubPac, 76, 92–93
Congress, 11, 79
Constantinople, 13
Cooksey, Lee Dale, 187
County Cork, Ireland, 31
Crider, Bob, 137
Cullinane, Daniel "Danny", 31–32,
    41, 44, 81, 86, 173, 188
Cullinane, Genevieve, 32, 86
Cullinane, John, 86
Cullinane, Lois, 32
Cullinane, Norma, 32
Cuthbertson, William Hugh, 188

D
Deaton, Lawrence Dale, 189
Deep Sea Systems International
    (DSSI), 134–38
"Deep Submergence Test," 31
"Devil Sea," 50, 67
Denver, Colorado, 89, 91, 167
DeStoop, Albert Edward, 190
Devaney, William Patrick, 191
Dighton, Samuel Reed, 191
Doell, Louis Henry, 192–93
Drew, George F., 42, 44
"drop-outs," 111
Dutch Harbor, Unalaska, 53, 57–61,
    65, 75, 97, 100–2, 107, 140, 160, 170

E
Eastman School of Music, 15
Edwards, William, 23–26
Electric Boat Company, 26, 27, 32
English, Joseph, 79
English, Robert, 44–45
Eternal Patrol, ix, 101

F
Fakan, John, 153–57, 160, 165
Faxon House, 7
Ferrall, Pete, 29
Fleet Command, 38, 40, 44, 47–48
Fluckey, Gene, 76
"Flying Squadron," 11
Fore River Shipyard, 20
Franck, Leon Henry, 193
Freedom of Information, 88

G
Gable, Clark, 37
Gallo, David ("Dave"), 3, 136, 140,
    143–44, 149
Garcia, Anj, 103–4, 107, 112–13, 124
Garcia, Kale, 2, 96–99, 103–7, 114,
    116, 120–24, 137–39, 141, 146, 151,
    167
Garcia, Kenzie, 103–4, 107, 112–15,
    124
Garcia, Tanner, 103–9, 113, 121, 124
Germany, 30, 44, 163
Gifu City, Japan, 50
Gilmore, Howard, 45, 47
*Goodbye Darkness: A Memoir of the
    Pacific War*, 43
GPS, 109, 145–46, 148
Graham, Merritt Dayton, 128, 176,
    194
Graham, Richard, 5, 100, 108, 131,
    133, 136
Great Britain, 15
Great Depression, 22, 33

"Great Torpedo Scandal of 1941-43, The," 160, 162
Gromeko, 105–6, 109–13, 118–20, 124
Groton, Connecticut, 26–28, 31
Grunion Community, 128, 158
Guadalcanal campaign, 48

H

Hall, Mrs. Frank, 7–8
Hall, Kenneth Edward, 195
Hampton Roads, Virginia, 13
Hart, John, 160
Harvard, 22–23
Hauber, G. K., 20
Hawaii, 16, 18, 47
Heath, Bill, 107–10
Hellensmith, Ernest Glenn, 195
Hemphill Diesel School, 35
Henderson, Hollice Beauford, 196
Hinman, Charles, 101
History Channel, 125
Hitler, Adolf, 23
Hong Kong, 43, 52
Honolulu, Hawaii, 19, 45
Horita Kyo, 55
Horse Brigade, 31
Hutchinson, Charles Roy, 197

I

Imperial General Staff, 53
Imperial Naval Academy, 50
Imperial Navy Gunnery School, 51
Infante Maria Theresa, 12
"iron coffin," 17
Iron Men and Tin Fish, 45
Ishizaki, 158
Isoruku Yamamoto, 49, 53–54

J

Jacobs, Tyrell Dwight, 29, 45
Japanese Navy, 50–51, 63, 67, 107
    Combined Fleet, 53

Java Sea, 43
j-crane, 103, 109–10, 121
"Jim" see also Brad Abele
    manuscript, 87, 89, 92
Jim Crow, 37
Juettner, Andy, 34–35

K

Kamehameha School, 19
Kano Maru, 49, 54, 63–71, 91–97, 101–2, 112, 117, 127, 133, 150, 153–62, 167, 169, 170–73
Katori Maru, 51
Kelly, Mike, 113, 116, 124
Kennedy, Sylvester Joseph ("Sy," "Ken"), 34, 85, 197
Key West, 23
Kinomoto National Elementary School, 52
Kirkpatrick, Chuck, 45
Kiska, Alaska, 1–4, 48, 53, 55–58, 60, 63–71, 75, 77, 78, 80, 88, 89, 92, 101–168
Knowles, Edward Earl, 198
Kobe Nautical College (Kobe University), 51
Kockler, Lawrence Richard, 199
Kornahrens, Nancy, 85
Kornahrens, Trudie Tripp, 36
Kornahrens, William Gregory ("Billie"), 35–36, 42, 58, 60, 85, 173, 200
Kure, 50, 54, 80
Kyushu, 53

L

Lake Erie, 166
Lancaster, Burt, 37
Lane, Richard, 91–92, 101, 167
Lanier, Newman, 101
Larson, Jay, 100, 106, 109–10, 118–22
League Island, 23
Ledford, Moore Julius, 139, 141, 201

Lee, Carter, 112, 119–24
Lehman, Woodrow Wilson, 202
Lisbon Harbor, Portugal, 36
Lockwood, Charles, 76
Loe, Sidney Arthur, 203
Lord of the Rings, 3
Lowell, Massachusetts, 15
Lowney, Linda, 96
Lowney, Pete, 96, 100–1, 107, 111,
    113–14, 124, 137, 140
Lunsford Jr., Samuel Elisha, 204
Lyon, James Wallace, 205

M

MacArthur, Douglas, 85
Malaya, 43
Manchester, William, 43
Manila, 36, 43, 52, 85
Martin, Carson Raymond, 205
Martin, Mary, 129
Martin, Thomas Edward, 206
Mathison, Ryder, 207
Max Rover *see also* Remotely
  Operated Vehicle (ROV), 1, 4, 5,
  136, 142–45, 147–50
McArthur Reef, 63, 115–17, 120, 121,
  126
McCann, Allan R., 45
McCutcheon, Richard George, 208
McMahon, Fran, 76, 78, 86
McMahon, John Merton, 208
Merchant Seaman School
Merry Makers, The, 33
Middleboro, Massachusetts, 15
Midway Island, 48
Milford, Frederick J., 160, 162
Miller, Ernest Carl, 210
Miller, Vernon J., 159
Minoru Matsushima, 55–56
MIT, 162
Mitsubishi F1M ("Pete"), 69–70
MK 14 torpedo, 28–30, 45, 47, 69–70,
  157, 161–63

Mohican, 135
Mohl, Michael, 101
Mount Kinka, 50
Mount Pavlov, 141
Myers, David Oliver, 210
Mystic, Connecticut, 73

N

Nagara River, 50
Nanook of the North, 3
National Geographic, 3, 95, 140
Nautilus, 94, 99
Naval Academy, 11–14, 22, 35, 58,
  106, 156
Naval Officers' Club, 3
Naval Register, 77
Naval Torpedo Station, 12, 28, 34,
  163
Nave, Frank Thomas, 212
Navy Cross, 12, 7
Navy ROTC, 22
Nazi, 30, 40, 43–44, 108, 163
Nazima Maru, 108
Newcomb, Arthur G., 212
New Guinea, 43
New London, Connecticut, 3, 18–26,
  28, 35–37, 81, 85, 87
New London Naval Hospital, 20
New London Submarine Base, 28
New York, 15, 34–35, 64
New York Times, 75
Newport, Rhode Island, 12, 28, 30,
  34–35, 47, 163
Newpower, Anthony, 45, 47
Newton Tab, 101
Newton, Massachusetts, 5, 73, 74, 77,
  79, 80, 84, 87, 125
Nichols, Peter, 86
Nicholson, Chris, 136, 138,
Nimitz, Chester, 22–26, 76
Nobles, John Wesley, 213
North Pacific Force, 48

Northwest Underwater
  Construction, 135

O

Offinger, Cathy, 95
Oregon Institute of Technology, 103

P

Pacific Fleet, 13, 16, 18, 43, 53
Panama Canal, 23, 26, 42
Pancoast, John Edwin ("Jack"), 36,
  139, 214
Pancoast, Julia Zulueta, 36, 84–85
Parziale, Carmine Anthony, 33–34,
  84, 128, 173, 176
Parziale, Faye, 34
Parziale, Louise Cimenari, 33, 84
Parziale, Ralph, 33
Paul, Cornelius, 37, 40, 78, 173, 215
Peabody, Endicott "Chub," 22
Pearl Harbor, 16–18, 30, 32, 36, 38,
  40–48, 51–53, 87
Pell, Herbert, 36
Philadelphia, 23, 26
Philippines, 36, 44, 85, 139
Pickel, Bernard Joseph, 216
"pig boats," 17
Polaroid Instant Camera, 86
Port Moeller, Alaska, 103
Portland, Oregon, 99
Portsmouth, Virginia 15, 18, 32, 34
Post, Arnold Charles, 217
Presidents' Hill, 10
Prince of Wales, 43, 52
Progressive Supernuclear Palsey
  (PSP), 98
PT-109, 94
Purple Heart, 77, 151

Q

Quincy, Massachusetts, 7, 9, 10, 15
Quincy Bay, 10
Quincy High School, 13

R

Raeder, Eric, 163
Randall, William Howard, 217
Rasawa, 69–70
Raye, Rhonda, 128, 138–39
Reader's Digest, 140
Reina Mercedes, 14
Remotely Operated Vehicle (ROV)
  see also Max Rover, 1, 4–5, 30,
  94–95, 126, 133–50, 152, 155
Repulse, 43, 52
Rikimaru Nakagawa, 66–71, 158,
  169–70
"Rising Sun" battle flag, 52
Rochester, New York, 15
Rodgers, Vickie, 128, 176–77
Roosevelt, Franklin D., 34, 52
ROV *see* Remotely Operated Vehicle
Rumsfeld, Donald, 163
Run Silent, Run Deep, 37
Ryan Jr., Loyal, 218

S

Saeki Navy Base, 53
Sakae Nakano, 54
Saki, 151
Sampson, William T., 11
Sanders, Howard Alfred, 219
San Francisco, 85
San Juan, Puerto Rico, 12
Santiago Harbor, 11
Schley, Winfield Scott, 11
Schumann, Elmer Taylor, 65, 170
Segula Island, 122
Seiichi Aiura, 49, 54, 63–71, 92–94,
  101–2, 112–15, 122–27, 133, 154,
  158–61, 170
Shinoda Chiyo, 54, 80–81, 166
Shinoda Isamu, 49–51, 54–55, 80–81,
  151, 166
Shinoda Kazuo, 52, 54, 80–81
Shumigan Islands, 141

side-scan sonar *see also* towfish, 97, 98, 102, 108–11, 127–28, 136, 142, 144
Singapore, 43, 66
Sirius Point, 57
Spain, 11
Spear Street Gang, 8, 10
SS *America*, 24
Stevens, Bill, 73
Stevens, Fran, 73
Styer, Charles W., 45
Sub Chaser Squadron 13, 49, 54, 55
Sub Fleet Naval Reserve, 32
Sub Ladies, 128, 132, 138–41, 151
Submarine Division 44, 24
Submarine Review, 159
Submersible Systems of Louisiana, 135
Sullivan, Paul Patrick, 220
Surofchek, Steven, 221
Swartwood, David Nathaniel, 222
Switzer, Evelyn, 34, 85
Sydney, Australia, 15

T

Taketoyo Maru, 51
"Taps," 166
Tash, 105–9, 113, 118–20
Task Force 8, 48, 57, 60, 75
Tate, Charles ("Charlie"), 59, 160–61
Taylor, Art, 46
telegram, 43, 74–76, 84–85
Templeton, Samuel Artist, 222
Terrass, Terry, 156–57
Thames River, 20, 23, 27, 38
Thayer Academy, 8
Thomas, Millener Weaver, 64, 177, 223
Thunder Below, 76
"tin fish," 66
Titanic, 1, 3, 94, 95, 133
Tiverton, Rhode Island, 73–74
Tokyo Bay, 53

Torpedo Data Computer (TDC), 29, 65
Torpedo School, 34
Toshi Mikagawa, 136, 140, 143, 150–51
towfish *see also* side-scan sonar, 4, 97, 99–125, 130–34
Towlekju-class destroyer, 77
Traviss, Byron Allen, 139, 141, 151, 224
Tupper, Addie, 8
Tupper, Fred, 8
Tupper, George, 8
Tupper, Laura, 8
Tupper, Russell, 8
Tupper, Trescott, 8–9
Twenty-third Marine Regiment, 31

U

U.S. Navy, 4–5, 10, 11, 14, 24, 32, 50, 92, 93, 136, 152, 158, 159, 168
U-boat, 40–42, 44, 221
Ullman, Albert, 225
Unimak Pass, 141
University of Fairbanks, Alaska, 104
USA Today, 138
USAT *Jack*, 40–41
USS *Barney*, 12
USS *Barracuda* (SS-163), 34
USS *Bowfin* Submarine Museum and Park, 101
USS *Brooklyn*, 11–12
USS *Chester*, 10
USS *Cod* Submarine Memorial, 153–54
USS *Colorado*, 15
USS *Dorado*, 89
USS *Finback*, 45, 57
USS *Gato*, 28, 45, 48, 59, 131, 154, 160–61
USS *Growler*, 37, 45, 47, 57, 102, 108, 152
USS *Grunion*

battles of, 65, 75, 92–94, 97, 153, 158–59
bell of, 177–78
commissioning of, 28, 34–35
crew of, ix–xii, 26, 29–30, 39–40, 44, 56, 58, 66, 96, 139, 158, 161, 163, 167, 169, 175–231
finding of, 2, 4, 97, 112, 122, 136, 142
sinking of, 94, 153, 158–59, 160, 169–73
ussgrunion.com, 101, 176
USS *Guardfish*, 47
USS *Haddock*, 46
USS *Mallard*, 25
USS *Massachusetts*, 12
USS *Maui*, 12
USS *0-6* (SS-67), 36
USS *R-4*, 32
USS *R-8*, 32
USS *R-11*, 19
USS *R-13*, 19–20
USS *S-22*, 24
USS *S-23*, 18–19
USS *S-31*, 23–26, 48
USS *Sargo*, 29
USS *Tattnall*, 20
USS *Texas*, 37
USS *Trenton*, 35
USS *Trigger*, 45, 57–60
USS *Triton*, 45, 60
USS *Tuna*, 45
USS *Utah*, 13

V

Vizcaya, 12
Van Woggelum, Marshall Frelinghuysen, 225

W

Walter, Melvin Hillary, 226
"War Diary," 87
Washington, D.C., 19, 44, 77, 101

Weaver, Tuck, 160
Webster, Donovan, 140
Webster, Raymond Eugene, 227
Weedville, Pennsylvania, 33–34, 84, 128
Weedville High School, 34
Welch, Donald Francis, 38, 227
Wells, John Harrison, 228
Western Union, 74
Williamson & Associates, 97–99, 105, 136
williwaw, 108, 137
Wilson, John Edgar, 139, 229
Withers, Thomas, 45
Woods Hole Oceanographic Institute, 4, 136, 143
World War I (WWI), 12, 31
World War II (WWII), 37, 44, 88, 91, 92, 94, 96, 101, 107, 160, 167
Wright, Art, 97–100, 104–36

Y

Yale, 22
Youngman, Ralph Junior, 229
Yutaka Iwasaki, 92, 93, 101, 102, 158, 167

ML   7-12